Risk, Risk Management and Regulation in the Banking Industry

This highly original book aims to broaden the discussion about risk, the management of risk and financial regulation. Peter Pelzer employs Jacques Derrida's concept of what is 'to come' to help understand the emergent quality of risk and explore those parts of risk that cannot be grasped by calculation. The assumption is that a discussion of philosophical concepts will enrich understanding of what risk is about and what is necessarily excluded in contemporary risk management.

This work provides interesting new theoretical tools from both deconstruction and aesthetics which aim to illuminate two key areas that haunt the risk management phenomenon: that of the risks engendered by attempting to manage risk, and that aspect of uncertainty that remains radically beyond capture owing to its utter lack of presence in the present and thus the imaginable future. The real strength of this book lies in the author's ability to translate between the philosophical domain, from which theoretical resources are drawn, and the specifics of actual risk management activities in the practice of banking and international finance. The discussion is enriched by considering risk and regulation as *pharmakon* – remedy and poison at the same time.

Public discussion after the global financial crisis of 2008 proves the need for a dialogue on risk beyond the circles of specialists in the industry and its regulators. Here Derrida's notion of what is 'to come' is applied to the realm of banking to better explore those parts of risk that cannot be grasped by calculation, as sophisticated as the mathematics and statistics involved may be. This perspective offers deep insight into the shortcomings of the current discussion of the topic.

This book will be of significant interest to students and professionals interested in the topics of risk, risk management and financial regulation; and the curious reader, with an interest in finance and philosophy, who is looking for a different view on risk and regulation.

Peter Pelzer is an independent consultant for banks in Germany, Luxemburg and Switzerland, and was a visiting professor at the University of Humanistic Studies, Utrecht, the Netherlands.

Routledge international studies in money and banking

1 **Private Banking in Europe**
Lynn Bicker

2 **Bank Deregulation and Monetary Order**
George Selgin

3 **Money in Islam**
A study in Islamic political economy
Masudul Alam Choudhury

4 **The Future of European Financial Centres**
Kirsten Bindemann

5 **Payment Systems in Global Perspective**
Maxwell J. Fry, Isaak Kilato, Sandra Roger, Krzysztof Senderowicz, David Sheppard, Francisco Solis and John Trundle

6 **What is Money?**
John Smithin

7 **Finance**
A characteristics approach
Edited by David Blake

8 **Organisational Change and Retail Finance**
An ethnographic perspective
Richard Harper, Dave Randall and Mark Rouncefield

9 **The History of the Bundesbank**
Lessons for the European Central Bank
Jakob de Haan

10 **The Euro**
A challenge and opportunity for financial markets
Published on behalf of Société Universitaire Européenne de Recherches Financières (SUERF)
Edited by Michael Artis, Axel Weber and Elizabeth Hennessy

11 **Central Banking in Eastern Europe**
Edited by Nigel Healey and Barry Harrison

12 **Money, Credit and Prices Stability**
Paul Dalziel

13 **Monetary Policy, Capital Flows and Exchange Rates**
Essays in memory of Maxwell Fry
Edited by William Allen and David Dickinson

14 **Adapting to Financial Globalisation**
Published on behalf of Société Universitaire Européenne de Recherches Financières (SUERF)
Edited by Morten Balling, Eduard H. Hochreiter and Elizabeth Hennessy

15 **Monetary Macroeconomics**
A new approach
Alvaro Cencini

16 **Monetary Stability in Europe**
Stefan Collignon

17 **Technology and Finance**
Challenges for financial markets, business strategies and policy makers
Published on behalf of Société Universitaire Européenne de Recherches Financières (SUERF)
Edited by Morten Balling, Frank Lierman, and Andrew Mullineux

18 **Monetary Unions**
Theory, history, public choice
Edited by Forrest H. Capie and Geoffrey E. Wood

19 **HRM and Occupational Health and Safety**
Carol Boyd

20 **Central Banking Systems Compared**
The ECB, the pre-Euro Bundesbank and the Federal Reserve System
Emmanuel Apel

21 **A History of Monetary Unions**
John Chown

22 **Dollarization**
Lessons from Europe and the Americas
Edited by Louis-Philippe Rochon and Mario Seccareccia

23 **Islamic Economics and Finance: A Glossary, 2nd Edition**
Muhammad Akram Khan

24 **Financial Market Risk**
Measurement and analysis
Cornelis A. Los

25 **Financial Geography**
A Banker's view
Risto Laulajainen

26 **Money Doctors**
The experience of international financial advising 1850–2000
Edited by Marc Flandreau

27 **Exchange Rate Dynamics**
A new open economy macroeconomics perspective
Edited by Jean-Oliver Hairault and Thepthida Sopraseuth

28 **Fixing Financial Crises in the 21st Century**
Edited by Andrew G. Haldane

29 **Monetary Policy and Unemployment**
The U.S., Euro-area and Japan
Edited by Willi Semmler

30 **Exchange Rates, Capital Flows and Policy**
Edited by Peter Sinclair, Rebecca Driver and Christoph Thoenissen

31 **Great Architects of International Finance**
The Bretton Woods era
Anthony M. Endres

32 **The Means to Prosperity**
Fiscal policy reconsidered
Edited by Per Gunnar Berglund and Matias Vernengo

33 **Competition and Profitability in European Financial Services**
Strategic, systemic and policy issues
Edited by Morten Balling, Frank Lierman and Andy Mullineux

34 **Tax Systems and Tax Reforms in South and East Asia**
Edited by Luigi Bernardi, Angela Fraschini and Parthasarathi Shome

35 **Institutional Change in the Payments System and Monetary Policy**
Edited by Stefan W. Schmitz and Geoffrey E. Wood

36 **The Lender of Last Resort**
Edited by F.H. Capie and G.E. Wood

37 The Structure of Financial Regulation
Edited by David G. Mayes and Geoffrey E. Wood

38 Monetary Policy in Central Europe
Miroslav Beblavý

39 Money and Payments in Theory and Practice
Sergio Rossi

40 Open Market Operations and Financial Markets
Edited by David G. Mayes and Jan Toporowski

41 Banking in Central and Eastern Europe 1980–2006
A comprehensive analysis of banking sector transformation in the former Soviet Union, Czechoslovakia, East Germany, Yugoslavia, Belarus, Bulgaria, Croatia, the Czech Republic, Hungary, Kazakhstan, Poland, Romania, the Russian Federation, Serbia and Montenegro, Slovakia, Ukraine and Uzbekistan.
Stephan Barisitz

42 Debt, Risk and Liquidity in Futures Markets
Edited by Barry A. Goss

43 The Future of Payment Systems
Edited by Stephen Millard, Andrew G. Haldane and Victoria Saporta

44 Credit and Collateral
Vania Sena

45 Tax Systems and Tax Reforms in Latin America
Edited by Luigi Bernardi, Alberto Barreix, Anna Marenzi and Paola Profeta

46 The Dynamics of Organizational Collapse
The case of Barings Bank
Helga Drummond

47 International Financial Co-operation
Political economics of compliance with the 1988 Basel Accord
Bryce Quillin

48 Bank Performance
A theoretical and empirical framework for the analysis of profitability, competition and efficiency
Jacob Bikker and Jaap W.B. Bos

49 Monetary Growth Theory
Money, interest, prices, capital, knowledge and economic structure over time and space
Wei-Bin Zhang

50 Money, Uncertainty and Time
Giuseppe Fontana

51 Central Banking, Asset Prices and Financial Fragility
Éric Tymoigne

52 Financial Markets and the Macroeconomy
Willi Semmler, Peter Flaschel, Carl Chiarella and Reiner Franke

53 Inflation Theory in Economics
Welfare, velocity, growth and business cycles
Max Gillman

54 Monetary Policy Over Fifty Years
Heinz Herrman (Deutsche Bundesbank)

55 Designing Central Banks
David Mayes and Geoffrey Wood

56 Inflation Expectations
Peter J.N. Sinclair

57 The New International Monetary System
Essays in honour of Alexander Swoboda
Edited by Charles Wyplosz

58 Taxation and Gender Equity
A comparative analysis of direct and indirect taxes in developing and developed countries
Edited by Caren Grown and Imraan Valodia

59 Developing Alternative Frameworks for Explaining Tax Compliance
Edited by James Alm, Jorge Martinez-Vazquez and Benno Torgler

60 International Tax Coordination
An Interdisciplinary Perspective on Virtues and Pitfalls
Edited by Martin Zagler

61 The Capital Needs of Central Banks
Edited by Sue Milton and Peter Sinclair

62 Monetary and Banking History
Edited by Geoffrey E. Wood, Terence Mills and Nicholas Crafts

63 New Approaches to Monetary Economics and Theory
Interdisciplinary perspectives
Edited by Heiner Ganßmann

64 Social Banks and the Future of Sustainable Finance
Edited by Olaf Weber and Sven Remer

65 Policy Makers on Policy
The Mais lectures
Edited by Forrest H. Capie and Geoffrey E. Wood

66 Prediction Markets
Theory and applications
Edited by Leighton Vaughan Williams

67 Towards a Socioanalysis of Money, Finance and Capitalism
Beneath the surface of the financial industry
Edited by Susan Long and Burkard Sievers

68 Doing Money
Heiner Ganßmann

69 Banking Regulation and the Financial Crisis
Jin Cao

70 Banking Crises, Liquidity and Credit Lines
A macroeconomic perspective
Gurbachan Singh

71 New Paradigms in Financial Economics
How would Keynes reconstruct economics?
Kazem Falahati

72 Risk, Risk Management and Regulation in the Banking Industry
The risk to come
Peter Pelzer

Risk, Risk Management and Regulation in the Banking Industry

The risk to come

Peter Pelzer

Routledge
Taylor & Francis Group
LONDON AND NEW YORK

First published 2013
by Routledge
2 Park Square, Milton Park, Abingdon, Oxon OX14 4RN

Simultaneously published in the USA and Canada
by Routledge
711 Third Avenue, New York, NY 10017

Routledge is an imprint of the Taylor & Francis Group, an informa business

British Library Cataloguing in Publication Data
A catalogue record for this book is available from the British Library

Library of Congress Cataloging in Publication Data
Pelzer, Peter.
Risk, risk management and regulation in the banking industry: the risk to come/by Peter Pelzer.
p. cm.
Includes bibliographical references and index.
1. Risk management. 2. Risk. 3. Financial risk. 4. Banks and banking – risk management. 5. Banks and banking. I. Title.
HD61.P46 2012
332.1068′1–dc23

2012010872

ISBN: 978-0-415-50850-6 (hbk)
ISBN: 978-0-203-10072-1 (ebk)

Typeset in Times New Roman
by Wearset Ltd, Boldon, Tyne and Wear

Contents

Acknowledgements

The coming into existence of a book is never the merit of a single person, the author. Of course this book is no exception. Over the past years I have had numerous opportunities to present the topics developed here at conferences, workshops and lectures, or discussed them with friends and colleagues during projects in banks. I would like to thank all of you for your encouragement to publish my thoughts in this form and your supportive belief in the general thrust of argument, for the constructive reviews, suggestions for improvement and generous help in the fine details of the differences of the native language of the author and the language in which this book is written.

The author wishes to thank the editors of the following journals and books for permission to use material from my articles or chapters in books:

Philosophy of Management from 'The Im-possible – towards a different way of thinking risk'.
Society and Business Review from 'The displaced world of risk: risk management as alienated risk (perception?)'.
Culture and Organization from 'The futility of excess, or: the displaced world of rules and regulations'.
From 'Risk as present futures – an elaboration on risk and fear', chapter published in: Long, S. and Sievers, B.: *Towards a Socioanalysis of Money, Finance and Capitalism: Beneath the Surface of the Financial Industry*, Routledge.

The material was used to a different extent. It has always been reworked and updates made where necessary.

Abbreviations

ABS	Asset Backed Securities
AIG	American International Group
BIS	Bank for International Settlement
BSM	Black-Scholes-Merton
CDO	Collaterized Debt Obligations
CDS	Credit Default Swaps
CRA	Credit Rating Agencies
CRO	Chief Risk Officer
ECB	European Central Bank
ERM	Enterprise Risk Management
FSA	Financial Services Authority
GATS	General Agreement on Trade in Services
GATT	General Agreement on Trade and Tariffs
LSE	London School of Economics and Political Science
LTCM	Long-Term Capital Management
MBS	Mortgage-Backed Security
OTC	Over the Counter
ROI	Return on Investment
SCOS	Standing Conference on Organisational Symbolism
SEC	Securities and Exchange Commission
SIMEX	Singapore International Monetary Exchange
SPV	Special Purpose Vehicle
VaR	Value at Risk
WTO	World Trade Organization
UBS	Union Bank of Switzerland

1 What is to come?

> We have no future because our present is too volatile. We have only risk management. The spinning of the given moment's scenarios. Pattern recognition.
>
> William Gibson (2003: 57)

Risk is a central topic in the financial industry, more than in the rest of the economy. There are not just the risks of the normal business as any other company has to face, but also the taking over of the risks of financial aspects from other businesses. Banks turn them into products and trade them, adding to the usual spectrum of risks. A central assumption underlying risk management and regulation is that these risks can be calculated and the consequences of losses dealt with by thorough management and controlling. The assumption of this book is that this is correct in many cases. Recent history of the financial markets, however, proves that crises not only occur, but that they also have a destructive potential for whole economies. Obviously there are aspects of risk which are not sufficiently managed, to put it mildly. It is exactly there, where my interest of crossing the borders into other fields of knowledge started.

This book is the result of an existence between two worlds, or, the life in both with a clear division between them. Many of the topics I wrote about in the academic part of my life are directly motivated and fed by my professional life in the banking industry. Most of the projects I'm involved in are about the introduction of new, or the replacement of existing, IT systems where my role is usually on the border between business and IT. It needs a look from both sides: understanding business requirements and translating them into IT concepts and understanding the needs of IT to realize, together with the business, what is possible and economical. This alone is an exciting perspective as such and would provide enough material for a variety of researches. In many cases, however, it is the content of the change which provides exciting theoretical discussions and sometimes, for me, challenges beyond the scope of the project in question. It is one of these situations which served as a starting point to what has now become this book. Several years ago I had the chance to work on the topic of risk and regulation from a perspective, which until then, was unfamiliar to me. An important industrial company ran a large subsidiary especially founded for trading in their volatile supply and sales markets. Buying and selling as such is a normal activity, of course. What made it so special in this case was that this kind of trading actually represented what can be seen as the origin of investment banking, a reminder, so to speak, that all the trading in the financial markets once were based in the real economy.

Due to changes in EU regulations and the resulting national legislation, as well as the introduction of Basel II as the international banking regulation standard, our client wanted to know what these changes meant for the business of their subsidiary and if they needed to acquire a banking permit. The project team had the task to investigate the current operations, the organization and the risk management to see how much of it was already sufficient to operate as a bank, and what was needed if the subsidiary would be run under a banking licence. My colleagues and I had a solid background in the kind of trading investment banks do and banking operations. Despite our general familiarity with the products and the fact that many of the employees of the trading house started their career in a bank, so that a common language was guaranteed, we had the feeling of diving into a different world.

We soon learned the crucial difference between this subsidiary and an investment bank. While the latter either acts as an intermediary for others to the financial markets and helps to arrange investments, transfer risks, to finance growth of the company or carry out proprietary trading, i.e. trading on own account without a link to the goods traded, the former exclusively traded commodities needed for, or resulting from, the production process of the mother company. This is a crucial difference which disappeared from the discussion after the global financial crisis of 2008 and the following years. A globalized organization of production and consumption needs a more sophisticated way to manage capital and cash flows. Derivatives in many forms were developed to meet these requirements. It turned out that the derivative as a trade also worked very well with just a reference to the underlying good or asset. No physical delivery is necessary, just a payment for the result of the deal. Trades which incorporated physical deliveries were marginalized. Nowadays they form only a small fraction of the market of derivative trading, the majority of trades are exclusively financial deals, based on the material world of commodities, currencies, securities etc., but as a so-called underlying. The underlying does not have to be part of the trade. A delivery is not intended. It is just a reference for calculation and differing estimations of their price development: speculation. In 2008 the world learned that the virtual world of financial markets was still connected to the world we live in: the so-called systemic risks materialized.

Perceiving this part as the normal business in a bank, it was extremely interesting to see that these kinds of trades could also have a strategic significance for a company. Yes, of course, the trading house must be profitable, but for them it was also a significant mechanism to fix prices for a future beyond the normal delivery contracts in very volatile markets. The difference between the investment horizon of production lines of about thirty years in their case, and the certainty for prices of products of a maximum of eighteen months in contracts for only parts of the production, left the company with severe calculation and planning problems. They intended to achieve more stability with their trading house by trading derivatives. Futures and options are mechanisms to fix prices with a counterpart. The difference to financial trades is the delivery of the good at the maturity of the deal.

The trading gave hints about future price developments. The enormous knowledge of the market in terms of regional and temporal price discrepancies could be used to stabilize the own expectations and the development of the actual prices. Therefore it could be claimed that the trading house represents a sophisticated form of risk management in a globalized world.

Inspired by a conference on *Excess and Organization*[1] I wrote my first academic paper on risk, risk management and regulation (Pelzer 2007). Analysing practical issues of risk management and the calculations required by banking regulation I wondered about a strange consequence. The excesses of the financial markets, always prone to boom and bust, representing the majority of deals detached from the real economy, result in a risk management which deals with an excess of data to calculate the required risk measures. The amount of data to be processed by the IT systems of the trading house, according to Basel II and the German regulation of this time, could only just be processed during night time after the day-end routines and before the start of business the next day. There was always the danger of violating the rule that the figures must be ready at the start of trading the next morning for consideration by the board of managing directors. The suspicion that it has become impossible to rule the markets, that the uncontrollability of excesses has to be hidden by excesses of risk management ever more intensified after each burst of a bubble, but incapable of preventing the next, motivated this research to make use of a different vocabulary to get an idea of what might be missing here.

Risk is a fascinating topic to which the financial industry adds at least two crucial dimensions: risk became a product, and with this move risk became the means to manage risk. This sounds paradoxical, at least dangerous for the 'normal' economy. The global financial crisis of 2008 has proven the danger of this system. My special interest in risk, risk management and regulation is the confrontation of the management of risk in the banking industry with the philosophical thinking of Jacques Derrida. A contribution to the discussion about safety and risk from the perspective of engineering asked for the significance of Derrida's arguments (Armstrong 2003; Armstrong and Paynter 2004). The deconstruction of binary distinctions is a starting point to demonstrate the dependence of any text, also in engineering, on context, and how the context varies with changes in the use of terms, and vice versa. This has already been done in the discussion of the safety/danger distinction without the help of a philosopher. No term exists for itself, it influences the understanding of the other term; even more – they constitute each other (Derrida 1983). Above that their meaning is constantly supplemented, as will be argued in Chapter 8 during the introduction of risk as *pharmakon*. Thinking through the effects of dissemination and supplementarity leads to a fruitful re-evaluation of many terms. Likelihood, or probability, and severity, Armstrong and Paynter (2004) explain, are usually accepted as independent variables in judging the risk of accidents. A calculation of the likelihood compared with the severity of the accident, leads to a level of risk acceptance, so is the expectation. The problem is the underlying assumption that a measured probability is objective. The measured probability of an accident cannot be determined until the lifetime of the system has passed. So any accident happening immediately influences the risk acceptance. The fact of the accident as well as a potentially different severity will probably [*sic*!] lead to a re-judgement of the risk acceptance. The leading question in the following will be what Derridean terms, elaborations of paradoxes, and especially his thinking of what is 'to come', can add to the discussion of risk. A lot, I would claim: it adds a dimension necessarily neglected in the calculative mode of risk management today.

Using philosophy to reflect on issues in organizational theory is rare – but not completely uncommon – and very stimulating as several readers (e.g. Jones and Munroe 2005; Linstead 2003) or the work of authors like Robert Cooper prove.[2] After the initial article on the futility of excess regarding risk management and the interpretation of rule following in regulation (Pelzer 2007), where I used arguments of Jacques Derrida to introduce the inevitable paradoxes when reflecting on rules and their use and the derivative character of risk management, I looked more systematically for other terms in Derrida's work which could be used to shatter the all too self-evident use of the term 'risk' itself. Given the background in banks where I experience the work with risk, I concentrated on risk in the financial industry and the effect of regulation in framing risk management. It turned out that the confrontation of Derrida's writings with these terms can be very fruitful and that it provides stimulating insight and reasoning beyond the common discussion of these topics. This book is the present result of my exploration. Present – this already indicates two constant themes influencing each other permanently: on the one hand, to shatter the arrow of time as the image of a clear sequence of past over present to the future. Risk is an exemplary term which confuses the progression of times in favour of the consciousness that they constantly influence, destruct, reconstruct and deconstruct each other. On the other hand, the insistence on the 'present' shall raise the consciousness of the tentativeness of any result, as final as it may have been announced.

For me it was very instructive to learn about the different layers of risk management during the project, or, to be more precise, I realized that there are different layers apart from the management of the risk involved in the production and delivery of goods. Risk management in the banking business is additionally about the risk management of products designed for risk management which have come to lead a life of their own. To formulate it is apparently paradoxical: risk becomes a means for the management of risk. Encouraged by my first attempt to make use of the work of Derrida, I started to consider a variety of terms he used, or deconstructed, and became increasingly convinced that they are able to serve a valuable task to enrich a discussion about risk.

The heading used for this introduction therefore contains a double meaning and certain ambivalence. At first it is, of course, the question of what can be expected of this book. The reader expects an overview of the topics presented; an explanation of the red thread. Using the words 'to come', however, is also the announcement of what Derrida intends to express with the term 'to come': the denial of fixed meanings, the dependency on context and time, the crucial dynamic of moving targets. The examples he chooses – democracy to come (Derrida 2006), or justice to come (Derrida 1992) – show that the understanding of what democracy or justice is, changes on the way to its realization. The more we know about it, the more the moves of the target become unpredictable, because it changes as a consequence of what is tried to be realized, and what is learned on the way. It is the denial of an ideal, not just the impossibility of achieving the ideal, but the idea that that which is aimed at is also developed with the attempts to realize. It is an expression of the dynamics of human society and as such very appropriate for a topic with such a dynamic as risk.

Looking at the literature reveals that risk is certainly not a topic which does not get enough attention. On the contrary, the amount of valuable literature was almost overwhelming before the global financial crises of 2008 and even more so since. Risk is a topic which covers almost all areas of our private and professional lives. Being so extensively covered, I thought, it would be easy to find definitions to start reflecting on what we are actually talking about when we talk about risk, risk assessment, risk control or risk management. To my surprise attempts to define the phenomenon risk, as such, are scarce. Generalizations are as rare as deductions from a broader concept. Most of the texts rely on a common understanding and shape the notion specifically for the topic addressed. It is not easy to see what credit risk, as defined in the financial industry as the risk of the loss of the credit sum, has in common with the risk of sharps in a hospital for HIV patients or the risk a gambler takes. Niklas Luhmann was quite explicit about this observation. Looking for a definition of risk, he wrote, one feels like being in dense fog and unable to look beyond the own buffer-bar. He claimed that not even the literature explicitly dealing with defining risk covers the problem adequately (Luhmann 1991: 15).

Thus risk, which can be described as a vague everyday understanding, is a consequence of a decision, an action, the processes of an industrial plant, etc. Different views developed from different areas like disaster research (Perrow 1984), banking (BIS 2004), insurance (Skipper and Kwon 2007), health care (Carroll 2009) and others arrive at special understandings of risk and the necessary action to be taken. On the theoretical level it makes a huge difference if looking at risk from an economical (Knight 1921/1940), psychological (Kahneman and Tversky 1984; Slovic 1987), sociological (Beck 1986, 2008), cultural (Douglas 2003a, 2003b), mathematical (MacKenzie 2003a), statistical (Hacking 1975), postmodern (Miller 2009), or philosophical (Sloterdijk 2006) point of view. Ulrich Beck had a huge effect beyond an academic audience with coining the risk society (1986, updated as the 'world risk society' in 2008), publishing his book in the midst of a public debate about the risks inherent in modern life after reports about the *Waldsterben* and Chernobyl. Researching the global financial crisis with socio-analytic methods (Long and Sievers 2011; Sievers 2010, 2011) is another way to achieve an understanding beyond the obvious facts and figures. The conclusions partly overlap, partly they contradict each other. A good discussion about a complex, controversial topic so to speak. Hansson (2005) called the conviction that risk must have a single, well-defined meaning a myth. In the past years the decisive role of ignorance as impossibility to know for certain has increasingly found attention (Wehling 2001).[3] The variety of approaches on risk clearly demonstrates that it is a relevant and fascinating topic which can and should be researched from very different angles. However, even if these theoretical and empirical contributions to the research on risk are quite diverse, they share a common understanding about the content of the notion of risk. In these works risk is usually accompanied by terms like uncertainty, probability, danger. There is a threat of potential harm, a hazard to life or property. Risk, one could say, represents a hazard, and therefore it is to be prevented.

Writing on risk started for me before the global financial crisis, but of course was very much influenced by the changes of the world as a result. The following is not an exploration into the immediate causes of the 2008 financial crisis. Others have already done this in very different and competent ways (e.g. a special issue of the Journal Critical Perspectives on International Business 2009; ECB 2008; Hellwig 2008; Sinn 2009).[4] What I want to achieve here is a double move. On the one hand I want to demonstrate that the use of philosophical insights can be of help to explain or interpret events on the financial markets. On the other, I want to use these insights to open up the discussion on risk and regulation for a dimension other than for just the immediate practical use for changes of details in banking regulation like the Basel accords, to explore the effects of thinking the 'im-possible'[5] beyond calculation and pricing. The term 'essay' in the subtitle of this book is very consciously chosen. The chapters are by no means meant to be exhaustive of an elaboration of risk or the use of Derridean thinking for risk. The book is not a complete introduction into a new way of thinking risk and regulation. Rather, it is the curious confrontation of two worlds of thinking to see if that can be made productive for a more sophisticated view of considering the topics. The insights presented are preliminary in many ways. The most fundamental is a consequence of the expression 'to come' itself. What is 'to come' remains to come, whatever has been achieved to realize it. The crucial point is that the expectations develop with the concrete steps in direction of realizing, of making it arrive, as a result of understanding better what can be the content of what is to come. Important aspects are discussed, always linked to the situation on the financial markets, the flow of the arguments influenced by the rapid changes of the context. Perhaps, so is my hope, the arguments presented here help to develop an additional language to understand the inevitability of these kinds of crises if risk is exclusively conceptualized as calculation as it is in the banking industry and its regulation. To prevent disappointment on the part of the readers, this book restricts itself to forming an idea of what is missing and *not* on developing new ways, new methods. This must be left for future research.

Carter and Jackson (1997) used the term 'riscomancy' to indicate their discontent about the clear tendencies in risk research and risk management. What at first appeared to be a seemingly inappropriate term for the situation where risk in disaster research is part of the rationalistic, scientific tradition, turned out to be an adequate description for their purposes. The characteristics of risk management that creates structure from apparently unstructured data; the work at a distance, both in time and in space, from the site of the risk; the image of a value-free commentator on risk and a non-participant, are all ingredients which will be identified in risk management in the banking industry, as well and as part of an ongoing problem. '-mancy' refers to divination and prophecy, as they found out when looking for the etymology. The connection is closer than they might have had in mind, when seeing risk as the successor of fate, as will be argued in Chapter 2.

Beck draws our attention to the fact that risk is an expression about a component of the future. Risk is about foresight, about something which has not happened yet, but which becomes real in exactly this context. By imagining what can go wrong, the images become a part of the decision. Risks are a future which should be prevented (Beck 1986: 44). While this is already a reduction, as Douglas (2003a) notes, exclusively emphasizing the potential negative aspects and not that the deviation can also be a positive, there is also another reduction of risk's complexity in Beck's argument. The centre of the risk consciousness, he explains, is not in the present, but in the future. In this way, the past looses its determining power for the present. Instead of the past the future is placed as something not existent, constructed, fictive as a cause for present experience and acting (Beck 1986: 44). While this already takes a huge step in the direction of the necessary change to thinking about a risk society, it falls short of the necessary complexity whenever calculation is a prerequisite for risk management. Risk calculation relies on data from the past and tries to extrapolate the path identified of the past over the present into the future.

Calculation is at the centre of risk management. Much of the Basel accord banking regulations heavily rely on mathematical models and statistical methods to identify an overall level of risk to which a bank is exposed. While it has its merits, there are also serious shortcomings. Calculated risk, so it will be argued in the following, is order, and suffers from this restricted view. It denies a basic feature, as Mansfield put it from his interpretation of Derrida's considerations of absolute risk: 'Calculation is a dream of the erasure of contingency, and thus of history, of accident, of the possibility of open-ness' (Mansfield 2006: 480). As will be shown, neither contingency, nor the event has the slightest tendency of being erased, or just controlled by calculation. Chapter 2 provides an introduction to the theoretical foundation on which the following chapters build their argument. It comprises three parts. The first, *Perhaps – and other ingredients of risk* introduces several terms Derrida used in different contexts which together provide a powerful vocabulary for a dimension of risk not covered by the statistical endeavours of risk management. Expressions such as perhaps, the impossible, the event, the invention, the horizon, competence, the paradoxes involved in decision making or justice, Derrida's understanding of responsibility and his, at first impression, strange term of what is 'to come' offer valuable insight for a dimension that is almost completely absent from the current understanding of risk. His brief dealing with the absolute risk can very well be included in a discussion about the role of the market as the absolute other. The second part describes, or re-constructs, the way from a dangerous profession like going to sea to the introduction of the concept of risk as globalized calculations of return. Chapter 3 interprets risk as the attempt to order future. The process of risk's detachment from life to an independent calculation and further abstraction will lead to the conclusion that risk turns out to be order.

Chapter 3 in some way represents an exception of the flow of arguments used otherwise in the book. The crisis on the global financial markets is taken as an opportunity to reflect on these markets as being in the state of exception with the help of an author who extensively wrote about it. Giorgio Agamben's terms 'sovereign exception' and 'state of exception' are transferred from politics to the level of actors in the markets and the banks' environment.[6] To illustrate the importance of the terms 'exclusion' and 'inclusion' for these concepts – especially in the form of the included excluded – E.A. Poe's arabesque *The Masque of the Red Death* is used as an example of failed risk management. As with multiple sovereign exceptions made possible by the state of exception on international financial markets, so is the thesis here; risk was excluded from the individual bank, hedged away, but demonstrated its remained inclusion by materializing and damaging the banks' balance sheets. Regulation carried out in the same way as before the crisis will be unable to deal with this development.

The behaviour of international investors was in the public's focus for some time before the current financial crisis. A good example was the 'locust-debate' during an election campaign in Germany. The metaphor of locusts characterizing investors ravenously falling upon the country, not wasting any thought on the people whose jobs they destroy, has become part of the political debate since then. A closer look at the content of the metaphor in Chapter 4 shows a confusion in terms that were discussed during the theodicy as the natural and the moral evil. The time in which this discussion took place also saw globalization start and develop. This was the time when the concept of risk was invented and developed into a basic notion for the voyages of discovery and economical activity. Today it looks as if the original outward movement of discovery and risk is returning to where it started – fully developed, still in the mood of the conquerors – but threatening the successors with the basic drive of their predecessors in a new guise. The postsocial world of traders and fund managers is described as a transformation of risk which faces the addressees of the election campaign as evil. Chapter 4 takes the public verbalizing of this 'locust plague' threat as the opportunity to combine several lines of thought, which usually held apart, to provide a background on which the impression of alienation of everyday risk perception at the 'interface' of the world, as financial markets and the world of production markets becomes better understandable. Developments of the international financial markets over the past three decades undermine the common understanding from at least two directions. The methods used represent a level of abstraction that only specialists can deal with them. And – more important for everyday experience – certain forms of investment and risk management have developed in a way which is threatening to many people in companies producing goods or providing services.

Risk and responsibility are two terms which are closely linked. Anyone who takes a risk accepts responsibility for the consequences: be it the positive outcome; the profit, if everything goes according to the assumptions of the risky action; or taking the losses, respectively paying for the damage. At least this would be the layperson's assumption. Considering the global financial crises of 2008, or other implosions of bubbles before, this seemingly self-evident connection appears questionable. Where are those held responsible for the massive losses created in the market to be taken by the public? What has become different, where can changes be identified that can provide explanations for a disturbed relationship between risk and responsibility? In Chapter 5 I highlight a subtle change in the relationship between these two terms: from risk *and* responsibility to the risk *of* responsibility. The basis of the discussion is the confrontation of Jacques Derrida's and Anthony Giddens' (who provided the title *Risk and Responsibility* in a 1999 paper) elaborations on responsibility. The contributions of two other authors are used to develop the point further. Ulrich Beck's term 'organized irresponsibility' presented as part of the whole argument on risk society (1986, 1988) will be further developed for the banking industry with the term of 'structured irresponsibility' which was introduced by Honegger *et al.* (2010) as a book title, but not discussed in the necessary depth. A short quote by a manager of a public organization, who took responsibility in a very special way, makes the new dimension stunningly clear: he admitted to be responsible, but not culpable ('*responsable, mais non coupable*', Boltanski 2010: 213). The similarities to organized irresponsibility are striking, yet there is a crucial difference, or the explanation is taken a crucial step further. Luc Boltanski's work on the bearer of responsibility (2008, 2010) combined with Derrida's combination of responsibility with the absolute other is used to give an image of the situation of the financial industry in a state of structured irresponsibility. That the relationship between risk and responsibility is disturbed is my starting assumption, and this is not just a temporary imbalance which can be restored, but indicates the need for a fundamental reconsideration.

Risk is fascinating. At least a certain kind of person is drawn into risky behaviour. The assumption is that risk has an aesthetic value, that parts of its fascination can be interpreted by the aesthetical concept of the sublime. Chapter 6 intends to look at the scene from an aesthetic perspective. The assumption is that risk has an aesthetic value, that parts of its fascination can be interpreted by the aesthetical concept of the sublime. Is there something sublime in investment banking, and if yes, what can that be? The research on the sublime aspects of risk is not very well developed. There are a few articles to be found in the realm of sports, and an elaboration of edgework (Lyng 1990) can be fruitfully linked to risk taking in the financial industry. With the use of ethnographic material from different sources collected on trading floors, it can be demonstrated that the sublime goes beyond any rational risk management. At the same time, the different structure of risk taking on the trading floor implies a decisive difference to the philosophical concept of the sublime (Burke 1998/1757; Kant 1974/1790; Lyotard 1984) which makes it ever more attractive for those who have the opportunity to take the risk. It is adequate to speak of risk in this sphere as a sublime simulacrum. Looking on the sublime aspects of risk, the assumption here is, therefore, a necessary contribution to the discussion on risk and risk management to critically evaluate chances of risk management and regulation in the financial industry.

Chapter 7 develops the central argument of this book, placing the title into focus: the risk to come. Derrida's concept 'to come' is so important, because it acknowledges the contingency of the future on several layers. Future as such is not completely unpredictable, but as a result of an im-possible event it might look completely different from what we assume today. It highlights that risk always contains what we do not know, what cannot be calculated, in other words that which takes us by absolute surprise. This is a point that can easily be accepted. However, Derrida's argument is more complex. It is not only that the outcome of present decisions are contingent, even unknown, he also insists that the understanding of the future state, aimed at with the decision, changes along with the execution of the decision. Any attempt to achieve more democracy adds to the experience of democracy and changes the idea of democracy due to the changed circumstances while realizing the idea. It remains a moving target. This kind of dynamics is extremely demanding to think about, let alone to predict the consequences. But it acknowledges the performativity of decisions and refuses a central assumption of risk management: that risk management as such does not influence the environment in which it takes place. Enlarging the view of taking the unavoidable complexity of human action into consideration and accepting that any aim is preliminary, changing by aiming at it is a fundamental challenge for risk management.

Chapter 8 accompanies Derrida on his visit in Plato's pharmacy for a further exploration of the risk to come. Risk and regulation disseminate, so is the lesson of 'Dissemination', Derrida's (2004c) attempt to demonstrate his concepts of *différance*, trace and supplement at work. It is mind blowing, as he admits: 'To lose one's head, no longer to know where one's head is, such is perhaps the effect of dissemination' (Derrida 2004c: 17). Dissemination is another of Derrida's terms rendering all attempts to fix meanings impossible. The effect is that any term is changing with its context, with its use and its users, the time passing and the space over which it is moving. When talking about a term like risk, with its obvious inherent ambiguity denoting chance and potential failure at the same time, an elaboration of the term with the help of a Derridean thinking adds the necessary complexity to the notoriously blurred meaning of the term risk. Showing how risk disseminated, disseminates while talking (writing) about it, and will inevitably go on disseminating is a valuable exercise when delving into topics of the international financial markets. A closer look on the family of expressions connected to *pharmakon* – *pharmakeia*, *pharmakeus* and *pharmakos* – and an interpretation of their role in a discussion on risk and regulation adds to an understanding of how the fundamental ambiguities of these terms influence the understanding of risk and regulation. The *pharmakon,* one should never forget, is both at the same time, remedy and poison. Risk and regulation are interpreted as *pharmakon.*

The name of the city of Basel, added with Roman numbers I, II and III has become a synonym for the international framework of banking regulation. In the first part of Chapter 9 the framework is taken as an opportunity to reflect on the possibilities of regulating excess in hyperreal markets from two perspectives. Basel II represents both, the attempt to tame the excesses of markets by excessive controlling, and an attempt to shift the regulation to an understanding of risk management beyond pure quantification. Against this background, the insights of a leading supervisor are confronted with a Derridean interpretation of rules and rule following to support a view of setting rules and regulations which cannot fix the intended result beforehand. A rule's meaning is (re-)constructed when it is applied. The second part of this chapter aims at developing the potential of Derrida's concept of 'to come' as outlined in the previous chapters to an idea that can be called a regulation to come. If risk is something which is 'to come', the regulation dealing with risk must be as open to future developments as risk is. If financial risk is becoming an integral part of life planning for every individual, financialization, as some authors call it (Martin 2002), a regulation must consider the consequences of risk as *pharmakon* beyond the soundness of banks. It must decide how to deal with 'socially useless transactions', as Adair Turner, chair of the Financial Services Authority (FSA) in the UK, called large parts of financial transactions (Turner 2010b: 33). Most of all regulation must have an idea of how to manage the future. If risk as order with its linear thinking of the arrow of time is a dangerously incomplete way to consider the complexity of past, present and future, mutually influencing each other with ever changing perspectives, then regulation must enforce a thinking of risk and regulation to come. If the task of financial markets is to stabilize economic expectations about the future, part of the responsibility of the actors on both sides, risk traders and regulators, is to avoid transforming risk into second-order dangers; that the management of risk itself becomes the source of an im-possible event.

The discussion about the underlying [*sic*!] understanding of time will be taken up at several points, but especially in a final Derridean move in the last chapter, which, to a certain extent, will not have been a conclusion. When reflecting about spectres in his discussion of the contemporaneity of Marx, Derrida (1994) draws on one of Hamlet's famous remarks: time is out of joint. The present is haunted by the past and the future is the surprising, but for a consideration of risk, very adequate insight. The arrow of time loses its linear force. Risk as a very special consideration of the relation of times cannot remain detached when time is haunted, when the present faces its own non-contemporaneity with itself: risk, introduced as order, is profoundly out of joint.

When coming to the end of this book, trying to wrap up the thoughts in a conclusion, I remembered my first lectures at university. Ekkehard Kappler showed a strong refusal of conclusions. This was not the arrogance of a lecturer, implicating that students of the first semester have still so much to learn that they should refrain from any conclusion. It was borne out of the conviction that any statement can only be preliminary, always challenged by many forces: better argument, learning, changes of the context, the time lag between writing and publication, etc. Derrida was still then not very well translated and most of his *oeuvre* unwritten, but after my attempts to dive into the world of his thinking, I think I get the point much better now than at that time. So the end of this book in the form of Chapter 10 insists that it will not have been a conclusion. It uses a paper by Heinrich von Kleist, a German romantic of the beginning of the nineteenth century, to demonstrate that the gradual development of thoughts while proceeding, while stepping into the future – always conscious of the *perhaps* – has always been around, ready to be remembered. I leave the reader with a transformation of Kleist's title – on the gradual development of risk in the process of taking and managing it: against competent bearers of responsibility.

I tried to write the chapters so that they can be read independently. The topics offered the opportunity to dig a bit deeper into aspects which seem unusual in the current discussion, such as asking for the role of aesthetics or the state of exception. That leads to certain redundancies in the argument, especially in the opening passages of the chapters where the starting point of the argument shows some recurrence/replication. The diversity of the views on the topic of risk and regulation mirror Gibson's observation quoted at the beginning, that our present is too volatile. The diversity of perspectives used in this book aims at some kind of pattern recognition, but with the clear conviction that the volatility implied results in a constant change of the patterns.

2 Thinking about the im-possible risk in the financial industry

Perhaps – and other ingredients of risk

Perhaps[1] it makes sense to shatter the familiar by insisting on the gentle explosive force of the *perhaps*, to render all these so self-evident certainties uncertain again. All the so-called self-evident terms should be brushed the other way to remind the thought patterns running in such contentedly familiar lanes, that these self-evidences do contain contradictions upon which the thinking ought to stumble, but all too often simply ignores these contradictions. Perhaps – or: hopefully? – the wallowing in all the paradoxes and aporias, which might be discovered by looking closer, reveals insight. To omit these reflections – such is the implicit thesis here, elaborated on the term risk – may lead to distortions like the global financial crisis in 2008.

But the first impression is that the *perhaps* is so familiar itself that there seems to be no sting triggering the chance of change, of infusing a situation with an uncertainty challenging the foundation of decisions to be made. On the contrary *perhaps* is used whenever an unanswered question shall be left open, vague, when a decision shall be avoided: 'perhaps we should...' to denote a doubt if this should really be done, to implicate that things would better be left as they are. There are several assumptions on what has happened; several possibilities of remedy, a decision should be taken. However, a decision always means to rule out all other possibilities than the chosen. 'Perhaps' avoids the decision denying the other possibilities, the decision is postponed for a vague amount of time. It keeps the uncertainty, paradoxically because of the uncertainties involved in the decision, but at the same time it offers the potential of reaction once the situation becomes clearer. But perhaps the situation remains unclear. While this attitude draws on the uncertainty and the risk involved, another perspective addresses the potential differences to a given situation in the present. Perhaps we can see it the other way round, or another solution is possible for the present situation; for betterment, development, or just change for changes sake. This view is directed to the chances, a necessity to act in order to achieve the change; to realize the chances expected, instead of a hesitation or an avoidance to decide or act.

The etymology confirms the dynamics of the term. 'Perhaps' replaced the Middle English '*by hap(s)*'. Happ is Old Norse for chance, good luck and is related to the Old English *gehæp(lic)* which means fitting, convenient, orderly (Oxford 1989). The German word '*vielleicht*' goes back to Middle High German and is a combination of *vil* and *lîthe*. According to Grimm (1854/1960) the term was not only used to express 'very easy, without difficulty', but already in a broader context to denote a certain expectation, assumption or fear. The French *peut être* is combined by two verbs and sounds more concrete: may be, with an almost ontological undertone: things may be completely different.

Chance and good luck – expectation of future events – but also assuming, less certain and therefore combined with negative anticipation: fear. It is a description of the opposite reactions to the uncertainty of future events, outcomes of actions or decisions. We cannot know for sure and this is either a source for pessimism – the assumption then is that things turn out to develop negatively and worsen the present state; or it is a source for hope – things may turn out to develop into the intended direction, to improve the present situation. While the relation to fitting, convenient in the Old English use is similar to the German, the mention of the orderly is surprising, as if a need for control, an early longing for a reduction of uncertainties was expressed; as if to speak a quest for risk management *avant la lettre*.

Starting a book about risk and risk management with *perhaps* sets the scene for a basic consideration of the imponderability of a world which is inherently uncertain. Something may occur, or not, or differently than anticipated. Probably it will be a deviation inside the normal distribution. But perhaps the deviation goes beyond the normal measure, even creates something new, a situation which was not expected at all. A dimension of the new which can only be recognized when it has taken place, when the possibility is realized. Perhaps? Or: Perhaps! We are used to the exclamation mark as a traffic sign, a warning of a danger: narrow streets with blind bends, a rock fall or men at work. It makes clear that something potentially damaging may happen, but we are warned and can act accordingly by driving slowly, being prepared for stones on the street or heavy vehicles crossing. This *perhaps* is a warning which works. It is a warning within the expectable, i.e. something within the possible and already experienced.

Nietzsche's superior game with punctuation, which I have attempted to use here, is of course not directed to the behaviour on the roads – he would have regarded these examples as trivial at least – he draws the attention to a much more basic context:

> It might even be possible that WHAT constitutes the value of those good and respected things, consists precisely in their being insidiously related, knotted, and crocheted to these evil and apparently opposed things – perhaps even in being essentially identical with them. Perhaps! But who wishes to concern himself with such dangerous 'perhapses'!
>
> (Nietzsche 1993: 17)[2]

Nietzsche explores the area *Beyond Good and Evil* as that of the dangerous '*perhaps*'. Hesitation, even animosities have to be accepted as part of the exploration. It is the risk of those who intend to look behind the horizon, who refuse to see the coming as the continuation of the always already to be expected. Thinking the coming requires a new type of philosophers, philosophers who have a reversed taste and character than the ones so far. Who has the nerves to withstand new insights which shatter the fundaments of the hitherto certain knowledge? Derrida, referring to Nietzsche, writes:

> Between day and night, between noon and midnight, the conspiracy concocts, not without the risk of the *perhaps* and therefore already in the incalculable anticipation of that risk which will distinguish the new philosophy. The *already* of the *perhaps* is an active one, it brings about effect.
>
> (Derrida 2002b: 75, emphasis original, author's translation)

The *perhaps* is a risk, even if it is just a provisional one. It takes place before the risk in question and points to the event which will be the new philosophy. This *perhaps* is not constative, it is performative. It undermines the normal subversively, opens the consciousness for the possibility of the impossible, that what is possible to think beyond the boundaries of the existing dogmas of the ruling philosophy, that which can be made observable, ascertainable, thinkable additionally or differently. Although it is not the world of the philosopher, we can (re-)introduce the term risk here. A new world may unfold when moving beyond the horizon, enriching the existing reality. New dimensions may be added which enable problems to be solved on a level not yet achieved so far. It may become possible to identify mistakes that couldn't be identified as mistakes with the methods in use. Or a completely new dimension of risk unfolds with the chances of the move forward. This is not Nietzsche's intention. It would still be too trivial for him. However, the direction is the same. It is about the will to engage with the dangerous *perhaps* which sets oneself into conflict with the ruling opinions and convictions and easily leads into isolation. The enemy of the philosopher of the new type has always been the ideal of today, Nietzsche concludes (1993: 145).

The experience of the *perhaps* is essential: 'Without the experience of the *perhaps* there is no future and there is no relation to the event to come' (Derrida 2001: 74, author's translation). Three central terms are named in this short quote: future, event and the coming. Derrida has developed these terms alongside other topics to which they form a foundation. *Perhaps* it is necessary to make use of the gentle explosive force of Derrida's thinking beyond the topics he explored in favour of more profane topics. A discussion of the terms horizon, event, perhaps and the exploration of what is 'to come' – in Derrida's case the democracy to come (Derrida 2006), justice to come (Derrida 1992), in his book about friendship (Derrida 2002b) and other texts – is also illuminating for the contents of the term risk and especially for the restrictions of the present conception of risk management. Especially illuminating is a reflection of the relationship of the family of terms around the *pharmakon* and risk, risk management and regulation. To an extent the use of Derrida's terms in the context of risk turns the argument from a positive, desirable content in Derrida's case to something negative, better to be avoided. This book is written out of the conviction that this risk should be taken to prove that any move taken into the future as Derrida understands it, is closely linked with risk. Risk adds to the argument, as is already indicated in the quote above. The *perhaps* names an openness of the future, which cannot be closed. This unavoidable openness will haunt the term risk and its management. Risk management aims at the exclusion of the *perhaps*. A thinking about risk, informed by Derrida's thinking of the *perhaps* and its inherent risk, the future and the event, will be enriched by a dimension, which at least nowadays, risk management completely lacks. Risk is a *pharmakon*.[3]

The im-possible event

Derrida's understanding of the event is a somehow disturbing description, upsetting the everyday understanding of the event. It is narrower, more concrete, but also more paradoxical. When we speak of an event we are looking for, we think of the concert, the football game of the local team against the leading team in the league next weekend, or the event as an incident, or the realization of a risk. These are all examples of a planned or foreseeable nature, something where the possible outcomes can be clearly seen in advance. The concert and the football match are announced, planned exactly, it is clear where it will take place and the time it starts is fixed; the incident and the realization of the risk are not planned and the time of occurrence, when it will occur or if it will occur at all is not fixed, but both are within the framework of the possible and the expectable. When everything takes its course experience informs about what can go wrong. Even if the incident is not expected, it can be anticipated.

Besides the expectable, the repeatable, the determinable, there are events of other form, something clearly moving beyond the predictable, beyond any regulation. The event in this sense is the radically not foreseeable. It cannot be anticipated (Derrida 1993). We know that the event will have taken place – because we have the grammatical form of future perfect which allows us to imagine the world differently, as if something radically new will have turned up – but not what that possibly could be, when it will take place and which consequences it might have. If we could answer just one of these questions, the event would not be entirely in the future, it would become imaginable, already part of the present. This is normal as long as we are within the limits of a teleological horizon. The horizon marks an ideal within which something can take place, which derives from the historicity of what has already taken place and therefore has to be seen as something existing.

An event, however, is 'un-predictable'. It interrupts the normal way things go and is of absolute singularity (Derrida 2003).[4] It did not exist before, and even talking about it is too late. Talking must necessarily come after the event, because the event was im-possible before. 'The experience of the impossible is the condition for the eventness of the event', writes Derrida (ibid.: 33, author's translation), 'what occurs as an event, can only occur, where it is impossible'.

By splitting the term impossible – im-possible – it becomes clear that possible is always present, even when it is masked by the 'im'. Whenever the mask of the impossible is taken away, the not expected, not expectable all of a sudden appears. It appears as absolute surprise and immediately interrupts the context of the existing.

> If it exists, the singular eventness of *what* happens and happens to me, or the one who unexpectedly comes and comes across *me* (what I call l'arrivant in French), *if* there is something like that, then it presupposes a break-in or an eruption which *interrupts* each performative regulation, each agreement and every context ruled by conventions. What means nothing else than that the event only occurs where it isn't tamed by an 'as if', at least not by an already readable, decipherable and *as such* articulatable 'as if'.
>
> (Derrida 2001: 72f., emphasis in original, author's translation)

From its first occurrence on, the event loses its singularity. It is included by description and at the same time becomes substituted and reusable. It has become possible. In other words, changes which point towards the future, beyond the existing can only occur by events; or, they threaten the existing from an unexpected position. An event points beyond risk. Therefore it makes so much sense to develop an understanding for this kind of framing the event, even if this consideration goes against the grain of conventional thinking. By attempting to (re-) open the, perhaps, closed thinking about risk in such a way, that it becomes possible to think of the presently unpredictable as the paradox which it is: the possible impossible – the im-possible. Right here and now the event is impossible, it doesn't exist, there is no imagination and therefore it is impossible. It occurs, it becomes possible, future presents itself, a future event impossible so far is moved into the present and the presence.

The im-possible would be the other of the possible, the possible that which was realized and placed inside a horizon. The im-possible is the included excluded of the possible. It defines the world of the possible and what will have become possible by its exclusion of the possible. The boundary which defines the difference between the possible and the impossible marks the importance of the other by the exclusion. Possible is what is not impossible. This sounds incredibly banal, but the dependency of the possible is fundamental, constitutive.

Future – horizon

The possible remains inside the horizon of what is known. The im-possible event is therefore a demanding idea as it aims beyond what is known. It is easy to see that it is not about potentiality. The potential remains inside the horizon of the possible, the already considered. It is a continuation of the already thought, the exhaustion of the possible, but not yet realized. Considering the future and the event as the source and the expression of the im-possible, attention is drawn to the boundary between now and then, between present and future beyond a temporal perspective. It is also the horizon of what is possible to think here and now. The horizon is the central expression here. It is of at least double significance. On the one hand, the horizon denotes the context within what we think. It is the mixture between the knowledge and experience acquired in the past, the consequences taken, and the expectations of what will happen in the near future based on this knowledge. The horizon marks the boundary between what is known and can be controlled, and the unknown. Control and controlling are very good keywords here. Controlling as the craft of getting information about the state an organization is in to get a basis for planning and adjusting former plans, mostly by collection and interpretation of numbers, is the preparation for a projection into the future. Controlling, planning, projecting are all actions to make future present. They draw scenarios in order to transform the unknown future into controllable items to make plans with, to project the known present into the future. They form a teleological horizon within which no future exists. The horizon is, 'as the Greek word indicates, a limit from which I pre-comprehend the future. I wait for it. I predetermine it. And thus, I annul it' (Derrida and Ferraris 2001: 20). In the attempt to control the future I annul it. Although we have to add: 'for us'. The one who makes plans, projects her estimations of the present into the future, draws a horizon up to what she can see. And with this gain of control she draws a boundary which becomes impenetrable for her; although not for the event, as we have to insist here, following the traces of Derrida. Therefore the other side consists for Derrida in trying to free the value of the future from the value of 'horizon' (ibid.). The future is that which has yet to come. The whole load of what is to come lies on the other side of the horizon. But as the horizon is not a clear boundary between the 'real' future and a projected future, because it is a boundary created in the course of a teleological action, it cannot be said that beyond the horizon future begins. There is no line on the arrow of time which would denote the beginning of the future and separate it from the time in front of us on which some kind of control can be assumed. The projection is completely artificial, invents a scenario which would fit into the existing and declares this as intended future. Future is effectively (or, in organizations perhaps even efficiently) locked out.

Decision

Derrida's notion of decision is determined by his thinking of the undecidable, the perhaps and the im-possible. A decision must have something undetermined. From that point it can be easily seen that such an understanding of decision puts a serious challenge to the understanding of decision in the everyday routine of organizations. This challenge, the infusion with the trembling caused by the 'perhaps', is needed to also make a decision hesitate and inquire in its own preconditions to understand what is locked out if someone claims 'this is my decision'.

The discussion of justice (Derrida 1992) elaborates on the undecidable as a result of the experience of multiple aporias. Derrida insists on the difference between justice and law. Law as the means to achieve justice needs both, interpretative power and authority. To achieve justice one has to go through law(s). There must be a judge using the laws to achieve justice. But using laws means following a rule which is nothing else than following a program. The judge turns into a calculating machine. By following a program justice cannot be achieved, as there is no decision about the concrete case in question. To be just, the decision must be a fresh judgement (Derrida 1992: 23). Such a decision must conform to a pre-existing law, but nevertheless it is an interpretation and as such not just consisting in conformity: 'it must conserve the law and also destroy and suspend it enough to have to reinvent it in each case, rejustify it, at least reinvent it in the reaffirmation and the new and free confirmation of its principle' (ibid.: 23). A decision to be just and responsible must at the same time follow a rule and deny the rule. But this is an impossible experience. Experience, however, is a traversal, it finds its way to a destination. In this sense it is impossible to have a full experience of the aporias. There is no way through, the passage is denied. Justice would be the experience of what we can't make an experience. Conversely, there is no chance for justice without this impossible experience. Justice is the experience of impossibility. Law is the element of calculation, justice is incalculable and requires exactly this: to calculate with the incalculable. Discerning and acknowledging aporias and the resulting undecidables are the necessary preconditions for dealing with what is to come. This is the challenge Derrida puts up.

Justice to come suffers from the contradiction between the necessity of following a law and achieving justice that is more than the execution of rules formulated in a law. For a decision to be just and responsible it must, at the same time, follow a rule and deny it, as was said above. Adding the arguments about decision making in the case of the justice to come, there is a slight tension in the conception of rule following. Considering rules from the perspective of Derrida's earlier work on *différance* and supplement a difficulty with the terms, law and rule emerges. The expression 'following a rule' seems to indicate an origin, something which exists independent of its use. One of the most radical insights of *Grammatology* (Derrida 1983) is the denial of the possibility of an origin. There is no such thing as an origin. There is only trace, always already supplemented and changed by supplementing. Thus there can be no original rule. Rules are always understood and interpreted differently by different users and even the same user may apply the same rule differently in various contexts. There are formulations in the discussion of the decision which seem to indicate a more rigid view: 'For me the "undecidable" has never been the opposite of the decision, but the condition of the decision, in all the cases where it could not be derived from a knowledge as a calculator would do' (Derrida 2004b: 63, author's translation). A calculator does not decide. It is a machine, it follows the logic of a machine, the logic implemented in the program, without tolerance, without possibility of altering the execution.[5] Rule following as execution of programmed sequences of action has nothing to do with a decision. The problem I see here is, that rule following is treated as equivalent with a machine logic when it is set as the opposite to the decision. Following the arguments of the trace and the supplement (Derrida 1983) any human behaviour changes a rule while applying it.[6] Even more radical: we don't follow rules, rules follow our actions: 'Laws, institutions, rules contain imperatives which shall orient our actions, but what they explicitly mean will in a strange way only be decided during these actions, by these actions which the rules shall guide' (Ortmann, 2004: 42, author's translation). Rules follow actors: Ortmann calls this reversal of the usual view – i.e. when actors follow rules, to the retrospective view that rules also follow actors – upsetting, almost Kafkaesque, but nevertheless an inevitable ambiguity (Pelzer 2007). Rule following cannot be the result of a calculator as long as humans are involved. This is a basic insight: *cannot*, and not *should not*. This track of thought is developed further in the context of the Basel accords, the international banking regulation in Chapter 9.

However, even if there is a slight contradiction, this is not the point Derrida wants to make. Applying a rule, interpreting it during the normal course of things remains in the realm of the possible. The rule dictates what is possible. The outcomes of a rule are predictable, calculable and reliable. Following a rule can never be a decision. But it is not just the reference to the im-possible which marks the crucial difference to the decision. The argument is more subtle. It already starts with using the rule. Using a rule implies the decision to use it. If the rule is calculation, we cannot ascribe the decision to use this calculation on to the calculation (Derrida 1992). The boundary between law and justice is marked by undecidability. Any decision has to go through the experience of the undecidable.

> The undecidable is not merely the oscillation or the tension between two decisions; it is the experience of that which, though heterogeneous, foreign to the order of the calculable and the rule, is still obliged – it is of obligation that we must speak – to give itself up to the impossible decision, while taking into account of law and rules.
>
> (Derrida 1992: 24)

Without the experience of undecidability, there is no decision, there is only programmable application. But the suspension of calculation which is the moment of the undecidable does not guarantee justice either. In going through the undecidability the rule is postponed and obeyed, it is altered and applied; more exactly – the applying of the rule means changing the rule in the moment of opening it to the future of its concrete use, inventing or reinventing it.

> There is apparently no moment in which a decision can be called presently and fully just: either it has not yet been made according to a rule, and nothing allows us to call it just, or it has already followed a rule – whether received, confirmed, conserved or reinvented – which in its turn is not guaranteed by anything; and, moreover, if it were guaranteed, the decision would be reduced to calculation and we couldn't call it just.
>
> (Ibid.)

The consequence of that will have an important impact on the discussion about risk. The ordeal of the undecidable will never be resolved in the dialectical sense, it remains caught, ready to have effects, and to haunt the future as an essential ghost. The ghostliness deconstructs from within the certitude any good feeling of having made a just decision; in fact, of any decision.

A decision must tear apart or cut open and therefore go beyond the scope of the possible (Derrida 2003: 44). It acts out the basic aporias of *perhaps*. It is the game of the two poles *perhaps* and rule, openness of the future and the closedness of the present, the im-possible and the possible, aiming at the event beyond the horizon. There is no event and no decision without the openness of an indeterminate possible, without a *perhaps* which leaves everything in the balance, where it remains undecided. But nothing ever happens or nothing is decided without a break which postpones the *perhaps* and at the same time keeps its 'living' possibility, remembers it. If there is no decision possible which would not interrupt the certainty to put itself at stake in the *perhaps*, the decision has to interrupt what is the condition of its own possibility, i.e. the *perhaps*. Without certainty, calculability and without power against the *perhaps* there would be no rule, law, contract or institution (Derrida 2002b: 104). Within this area of conflict a decision takes place, or not.

Competence

Earlier Derrida was involved in a colloquium on nuclear criticism. It was still the time of the Cold War. The strategic debate about no use, first use or no first use of nuclear weapons gained intense public interest. His contribution to the discussion (Derrida 1984) is interesting here for two reasons: the elaboration of the importance of speed, but most of all his considerations on competence and the relationship of competence to decision. Competence and incompetence, to be exact. A competent decision is a contradiction in terms, is the provocative consequence of this article. Likewise for his understanding of other common terms this also needs some explanation. Competence, so it is known from the everyday understanding of the term, means that the person knows what she is talking about, has a sound understanding of what she is doing and can therefore make the best, well-founded decision. Ingredients of competence are: long experience in the field, expertise, the knowledge of processes and how to carry them out, to exactly knowing the sequence of steps to be taken to achieve certain targets. There is no long hesitation before deciding and acting, because for the competent the situation is obvious. It needs competent experts all the more when the time frame is crucial. When there is no time for hesitation, it is good to have someone around who is able to judge, decide and act immediately. *Perhaps*. Having the arguments about decisions in mind, it becomes clear what runs counter to this understanding. Competence here is seen as ruling the possible, acting as perfectly as possible inside a horizon. Competence is reassuring, especially when time is so short that there is no time to postpone a decision for better information, discuss it with others, weighing the pros and cons. The background for the article was the discussion around the first use of nuclear weapons. The thinking pattern behind the policy of deterrence was that the one who fired a nuclear missile first would die in second place. This means that the ultimately short time between firing an intercontinental missile by one side and its reaching its target must be used to return a missile by the other side. To make it even more difficult this reaction must be taken under extreme uncertainty: is it really a missile coming, do the radar systems represent the unbelievable correctly or is it just a mirage? Is the threat real or just an error? 'At the beginning there will have been speed' (Derrida 1984: 20). And while speed has ever accelerated into the nuclear age, there is no room left for decisions, just the triggering of a program. This is what competence is about: knowledge of programs and acting according to them. But again Derrida radicalizes an argument. He insists that despite the fact that the world experienced two nuclear bombs at the end of Second World War, this was not a nuclear war. These bombs ended a conventional war. A nuclear war as discussed in the Cold War has not turned into an event yet. It is still language, text, something to talk about, and therefore something to deconstruct – what Derrida does with pleasure.

Perhaps, we may conclude, the gentle force of the *perhaps* is exactly what is needed in a competent discussion, closed and inclusive as it is, to tear down the boundaries, to broaden the perspective, and not less informed. Very politely, almost delusively modest, Derrida proposes the contribution of the humanities which were in the Kantian University situated in the inferior class of the philosophy school, far away from and foreign to any power. But of course: 'We are the specialists in discourse and texts, all sorts of texts' (Derrida 1984: 22). Seven missiles sent as a message in the form of seven missives, as the title suggests, taking up the topic in their own way, but like the missiles on a trajectory, aimed at the blind spots of the competent arguments. Nuclear war is fabulously textual. It doesn't only depend on information and communication, strategic texts and discussions, it is textual because of the fact that it has not taken place yet. It can only be written and talked about. It is not an event, as it is not yet experienced. However, nuclear war is not just a fable. Even if it had not taken place so far, it already had and still has a reality due to the fact that the forces of destruction exist in the form of nuclear weapons and that they are used as a means of politics. They represent the absolute power of absolute destruction. The 'reality' of the nuclear age is constructed by the fable of an event that has never happened, but Freud reminds us that this fantasy is not nothing at all (Derrida 1984: 23). It shows effects. It divided the world into blocks during the Cold War and nowadays helps to mark nations as rogue states (Derrida 2006). It creates power on one side and fear on other, or a longing for nuclear power out of fear of being the target of missiles.

Linking these considerations on nuclear war with the arguments about decision leads to a devastating conclusion for competence: a competent person is unable to decide. The necessary interruption of the programs' logic for breaking the fatal trajectory, the enabling of the im-possible is excluded effectively. And it needs the intervention from the outside of the closed circle of the competent to prevent the fatal logic from unfolding. Despite the severe effects of the crisis in the financial markets these days, the argument here of course does not see an equivalence to the threat of nuclear war. The arguments of speed, 'in-competence' and competence for texts, however, contribute nicely to the overall thrust followed here. Acceleration up to a point where business is only imaginable in the virtual space of electronic data processing with software programs reacting to market changes, because the distribution of information has become so fast that an analysis by humans and their decision taking are much too slow to react in an adequate time frame seems to be the ultimate materialization of what Derrida proposed with the nice phrase that speed will have been there at the beginning. The Cold War's time frame, as short as it already was, given the ultrasonic speed of intercontinental missiles, has evaporated in present days' financial markets. There is no distance to be crossed any more, trading is possible from any part of the world to any other part of the world instantly, without time lag. This has created several fields of specialists, competent only in a tiny segment, the most eminent being the separation of traders and risk managers, and the trading and general management of the bank. Risk management should have provided the link between trading and the general management, but something has obviously massively gone wrong. The interesting question arising here is, if an intervention – leaving aside the assumption that those in power in the banks would not have listened to a philosopher or even taking his arguments seriously enough to have their normal business disturbed – would have effects, or, if these kinds of arguments are not useful at all. Before answering this and moving into the realm of risk itself, a short discussion of responsibility is deemed necessary.

Responsibility

Is it to take responsibility in form of an in-competence for the topic of nuclear war because of the competence for texts and, therefore, for deconstructing the fatal logics in competent decision programs? Of course the argument sounds a bit arrogant, as if the humanities are the owners of the key to (eternal?) wisdom, if not *the* truth. But again *of course* this would run diametrically against Derrida's intention. For him any aporia identified works in any given context and therefore also in the texts produced by the specialists, the competent professionals of texts. But what can responsibility mean in such a context?

To decide is always linked to a person: who decides? If an institution decides, the actual decision can be linked to a person representing the institution. Or, framed differently: who is responsible for the decision? Or, in a broader sense, about anything what is said: who says something, or, as I do here, writes the text? In this text so far, I write about Derrida's understanding of several terms. Am I not responsible for what I wrote, as I can refer the reader to the books of another person? But, if I am not responsible for *what* I wrote, am I responsible *that* I wrote, for the *fact* that I wrote? These questions are the introduction of a discourse on responsibility in the *politics of friendship* (Derrida 2002b: 306). Up to now I might not have said anything significant in my name, but so is the argument that writing and publishing indicate I write in my name. It links what is written to a person who wrote it.

The name is crucial. Having a name, bearing it, but also being carried by the name, the relation to the name and what carries us to the name – the name even survives us. The word reputation is not mentioned here, but there is a clear connection to these characteristics of the name. A consequence is that the reader holds me responsible for my writing. 'What does it mean to speak in one's own name?' (ibid.: 309f.). A close look at the word 'responsibility' reveals that the word response is contained. The act of reading is a mutual response. I invite the reader to read the text, and her reading, the engagement with the text is the first response, on which more may follow. The reader invites me, the author, to present a text by opening the book, which is to invite the text of 'an other' and includes the responsibility for an engagement with the text, to give a response like nodding approvingly with the head, write a review, recommend to read or to avoid reading to others or smashing the book into a corner. The precondition for responsibility is a relationship to the other. With the act of responding we are included in a responsibility. As soon as we begin to say something meaningful we face an undeniable responsibility. Anything we do includes the other, so that it can be said that we have the freedom to take responsibility only insofar as it has come across us from the other. Responsibility gives us the freedom to act without leaving us unconditional freedom. We cannot take responsibility in our own name, in the space of autonomy. It is always connected to the other. Not another name, but the other as such: '*tout autre est tout autre* – every other (one) is every (bit) other' (Derrida 1995: 82).[7]

Derrida gives two introductions into his thinking of responsibility, created roughly at the same time (Derrida 1995, 2002b). Both, as to be expected, deal with the aporias which immediately turn up when digging a bit deeper, when deconstructing the meaning. In the *politics of friendship* (Derrida 2002b), he starts from the grammar of the term responding. In the French form of *répondre*, the term has three different meanings. *Répondre de*: to take responsibility, be responsible for, to be liable for, to vouch for, to guarantee something. *Répondre à*: responding, answering someone or on something (a petition, a plea). *Répondre devant*: to justify something to someone or an institution. These modalities cannot stand separated, they implicate each other. One accepts responsibility for oneself or for something by justifying to another, a community, an institution, a law. We do this by initially responding. Therefore this modality seems to be the most fundamental and therefore unconditional one. The crucial difference lies in who is addressed. To respond usually addresses an other, a concrete person, the justification happens to an institution, the law, an instance which is authorized to represent the other in an institutionalized form as a moral, legal, political community. The other term which immediately comes to mind when talking about responsibility in such a way is respect. Taking responsibility is a consequence of respecting the other or the law. However, there are two forms of respect involved in the mutual implication of respect and responsibility. To respect the other is a social relationship, may mean to offer friendship, but there is no friendship for the law. It is the difference between an example of respect for a moral law as in the case of the friend, and the cause of moral respect as with the law (Derrida 2002b: 341).

By a careful elaboration of the biblical parable of Abraham in his book *Gift of Death* (1995) Derrida presents a very clear image of the paradox involved in responsibility which, despite the fact that it is here concentrated on the absolute other, God, can be used to understand the aporias involved when using the term responsibility. Dealing with the absolute other proves in the extreme what is at stake when responsibility is linked to the duty, in this case the absolute duty, to an other. Abraham was ready to sacrifice his son Isaac as was ordered by God and did not mention this fact to his family when he left with his son. Seeing it as his duty to obey his God he was ready to accept absolute responsibility for him and follow any instruction, including killing his dearest. God, satisfied with this unquestioned loyalty, prevented him from cutting his son's throat at the very last moment. This parable describes the extreme, but it is valuable for demonstrating the basic problem of responsibility, in fact the aporias. Following the duty to an other, accepting the responsibility for it, always and undeniably means sacrificing other others. Thus holding someone responsible, taking responsibility, is not such a straightforward action as is often assumed, Derrida states with a slightly sarcastic tone:

> What the knights of good conscience don't realize, is that the sacrifice of Isaac illustrates … the most common and everyday experience of responsibility. The story is no doubt monstrous, outrageous, barely conceivable. But isn't it also the most common thing? What the most cursory examination of the concept of responsibility cannot fail to affirm? Duty or responsibility binds me to the other, to the other as other and ties me in my absolute singularity to the other as other … but of course, what binds me thus in my singularity to the absolute singularity of the other, immediately propels me into the space of risk of absolute sacrifice. There are also others, an infinite number of them, the innumerable generality of others to whom I should be bound by the same responsibility, a general and universal responsibility (what Kierkegaard calls the ethical order). I cannot respond to the call, the request, the obligation, or even the love of another without sacrificing the other other, the other others. *Every other (one) is every (bit) other (tout autre est tout autre*), every one else is completely or wholly other. The simple concepts of alterity and of singularity constitute the concept of duty as much as that of responsibility. As a result, the concepts of responsibility, of decision, or of duty, are condemned a priori to paradox, scandal, and aporias. Paradox, scandal and aporias are themselves nothing other than sacrifice, the revelation of conceptual thinking at its limit, at its death and finitude. As soon as I enter into a relation with the other, with the gaze, look, request, love, command, or call of the other, I know that I can respond only by sacrificing ethics, that is, by sacrificing whatever obliges me to also respond, in the same way, in the same instant, to all others.
>
> (Derrida 1995: 67f., emphasis in original)

The keywords here are ‘absolute’ and ‘general’, ‘singularity’ and ‘alterity’. The problem arises out of the permanent presence of both at the same time and during the same act, the decision, the taking of responsibility, the acceptance of a duty. They are in contradiction, cannot accept each other. Either one accepts absolute responsibility to the single other representing an absolute singularity herself, or one answers to a family, a community, a nation, etc. One has to sacrifice the one for the other, is Derrida’s conclusion. If I am responsible to one other, I am automatically irresponsible against other others. This can and must be generalized from the extreme of obeying the absolute other as in the case of Abraham. It is an aporia of the concept of responsibility as such.

One source for the aporia is language. Absolute duty and absolute responsibility require singularity. It is the duty to a concrete other, excluding the relationship to other others. As soon as I talk to someone, singularity is replaced by a social relation, singularity becomes impossible, alterity is the consequence. It becomes possible to respond to different others. The ethical order becomes problematic. Being responsible to a concrete other means at the same time the impossibility to be responsible to others. The extreme is the duty to the absolute other. What it means to turn away from the others to a single other, is the refusal of the ethical order, which means sacrificing ethics. And this is not just an exception in extreme cases. It is the normal, everyday experience: ‘is it not true that the spectacle of this murder, which seems intolerable in the denseness and rhythm of its theatricality, is at the same time the most common event in the world?’ (Derrida 1995: 85).

Indeed, even in the dry rational world of banking the aporias of responsibility can easily be identified. A first, rough application of Derrida’s reasoning to the organized world of banking demonstrates the relevance as well as the difficulties and potential resistances when trying to include them into daily practice of decision making in banks. To state the least, the heterogeneity of interests of actors representing internal and external roles or institutions like traders, risk management, general management, regulators, national banks, governments, the public, is as obvious as are the resulting struggles for influence. The topic of risk is the central topic in this industry. No wonder, then, that this central topic is under close observation both internally as risk management and externally in the form of regulation. However, there is not just the difference between the potential decision inside a bank and the restrictions set by external regulating bodies and legislative powers. Inside the bank there is also the difference between the business lines closing deals and risk management supervising the overall risk of the bank. Here the duties and responsibilities alter: responding to the laws and regulations will certainly prevent business opportunities – but also the risk involved, of course. The task of risk management is also to develop risk calculations which are more sophisticated than the minimum requirements of the regulations. More sophistication means more complicated calculations with ever more detailed information, but a better fine-tuning of the use of the base capital required for underlying the business. More calculation as precondition for credit decisions and trading means less room for decisions. The development moves into the direction of executing programs.

The ultimate heterogeneity of interests is an example of what Derrida refers to as normal, everyday experience. The spectacle of Abraham's almost murder is the most common event in the world (Derrida 1995: 85). All the role holders mentioned above feel responsibility to a concrete task, by whichever motivation. Following the responsibility to this task then inevitably means to sacrifice the responsibility for others. This is the motivation to have a closer look into the relationship between risk and responsibility in Chapter 5.

That events (absolute decisions?) take place or are created by a certain blindness of actors following processes, is proven by cases like the mortgage crisis of 2008 and the following difficulties in state finances and the turmoil in the markets around them, defaults on debt of Argentina in 2001, Russia in 1998, the Asian crisis in 1997, the Long-Term Capital Management (LTCM) collapse in 1998, to name just a few of the past fifteen years. Bank failures or incredibly huge losses created by individuals such as those of Herstatt Bank, Barings Bank, Societée Génerale or UBS prove that events catch individual organizations as well. These examples prove that events can also be produced as a result of the constellation of actors and structures inside the individual bank which support a too long ignorance of the potential failure. Were the deciders conscious about the consequences, did they really take a risk? Decisions do not need to be taken consciously. They can also be the consequence of keeping the status of the *perhaps*. Avoiding to stop the Dattels, Leesons, Kerviels or Adobolis,[8] whatever the reasons may be for the ignorance, turns out to be a decision, the decision not to act. It is possible to accept the absolute risk involuntarily by not deciding.

Absolute risk

Derrida did not work with the term risk as explicitly and intensively as he did with the others discussed here so far. He mentioned risk in two interviews (Derrida and Rottenberg 2002; Krapp 2000),[9] which give an impression of the depth of the term if it is thought by the somewhat annoying combination with the adjective absolute: *absolute risk*. He also mentions it at a central point of his thinking about the relation to the absolute other. The *Gift of Death* (Derrida 1995) provides a few remarks which hint into the direction which he might have taken if he had developed this term further. '...a venture into absolute risk, beyond knowledge and certainty' (Derrida 1995: 5). What can this qualification of the term risk by 'absolute' mean? On the background of the arguments on responsibility and the interpretation of the parable of Abraham the link with the other terms becomes obvious. Following the duty of the absolute other is an exclusive move: it excludes all other others, that is, it sacrifices them. The absolute cannot be had without sacrificing some other. The parable put it to the extreme. It was their own beloved family who would have had to suffer if Abraham wasn't prevented from executing what he considered as his duty. But the absolute is the norm if we take decision and responsibility as seriously as it is described here and consider the consequences of in-competence, of aiming at the im-possible, of moving beyond the horizon, of triggering the event, of accepting the *perhaps*. All these terms aim at the space beyond knowledge and certainty; a very uncomfortable place, where no experience helps and uncertainty on the way is the decisive feeling. It needs to take absolute risk to decide, to go through the ordeal of undecidability, to face the other. Not only the absolute other, God, but also the present other. But why does the reference to the absolute risk, the absolute other still makes us feel uncomfortable in secular times? Because, so we can phrase it, risk is an entirely secular concept.

The market as absolute other

Where time is money and money is time the medium in which they interact has a significant role. In a secular world, the market has become another absolute other. Money is the symbol of globalized exchangeability. The exchanges take place on the market which is globalized in a crucial double meaning. We live in a globalized world, included into the global market in a way that it has become very hard to make a difference between the two; and it is a generalized idea. Despite the fact that there are many different types of markets with many distinctions for industrial or consumer goods, for mass markets or individualized ones, and marketing intends to segment them ever further, these share a generalized idea of the market. Markets are not local any more. Competition is expected to come from everywhere and goods are produced and delivered everywhere. National peculiarities of regulations were interpreted as obstacles for international trade. National rules had to be justified against the reproach of protectionism with the intention to discriminate imports. Trade liberalization advances, because 'these "within the border" regulatory measures are increasingly seen by many liberal trade proponents as the most prominent and arguably most costly form of non-tariff barriers to trade' (Trebilcock and Howse 1995, quoted in Orford 2004: 12). The idea to globally standardize rules for trade, to prevent 'system frictions', (ibid.) is nowadays institutionalized. Markets have become the idea of a standardized exchange of goods with a specified set of rules leading to a harmonization of domestic regulatory standards. These ideas were intensively discussed and negotiated between countries and finally laid down in international rules and regulations known as, for example GATT (General Agreement on Trade and Tariffs), GATS (General Agreement on Trade in Services) or WTO (the World Trade Organization), as the institution organizing new rounds of setting rules for opening markets at a global level. Any national rule which could be interpreted as a hindrance for global trade, any protection of national markets shall be banned. Orford (2004) elaborated the foundations of these trade agreements from the perspective of the responsibility of the national law maker and the relationship to the market using Derrida's interpretation of absolute risk in the *Gift of Death* (1995). The development from GATT to the new harmonization implemented under the auspices of the WTO includes a decisive move from non-discrimination as a border measure to the control of domestic regulations. It goes beyond non-discrimination of producers to a harmonization of divergent regulatory environments which threaten to constrain commercial activity. The constraints set instead on introducing or keeping rules and regulations, procedures or decisions, are potentially extremely far reaching in that they go beyond trade agreements and become more governance agreements (Orford 2004).

Now national rules and peculiarities have to be justified. Scientific proof must be given in the form of available scientific evidence. Science provides the measure for decision in cases of different opinion. But what available scientific evidence exactly means is a highly contested area, especially if one thinks of the public debate about what food may contain or not. The WTO is now the institution which decides in cases of quarrel. But also any national regulation based on culture, tradition, religion, etc. must justify itself against the regime of trade laws. The market, so the conclusion can be drawn with different vocabulary, transformed into an absolute other. Following the market inevitably means a sacrifice. The same holds true for the Basel accords. As GATT or GATS, they represent a worldwide standard for the banking industry which intends to overrule national regulations. The intention to harmonize and raise the standard and soundness of banks to a higher level, however, may also have a flip side. Existing diversity is reduced. This represents a source for systemic risk. If any bank has to react in the same way, the disadvantages of monoculture are introduced instead of a strengthening of the system.

If money replaces God in the relationship to time and eternity,[10] it gets the status of the absolute other and the significance of the absolute risk and the sacrifice becomes obvious. The sacrifice is not just a religious feature. It can be generalized. If every engagement with the other necessarily means neglecting an other other; if every dealing with the absolute other means sacrificing a lot of others and the replacement of God by money, religion by the market means very concrete sacrifices and becomes a critical ethical issue. Absolute risk is, as Derrida insists, connected to 'religious *faith* through a form of involvement with the other that is a venture into absolute risk, beyond knowledge and certainty' (Derrida 1995: 5, emphasis in original), as he explains by the parable of Abraham. However, absolute risk cannot stand alone: 'Responsibility and faith go together, however paradoxical that might seem to some, and both should, in the same movement, exceed mastery and knowledge' (ibid.). Any involvement with the other includes the responsibility for the decisions made: responsibility is taken 'in the experience of absolute decisions made outside of knowledge or given norms, made therefore through the very ordeal of the undecidable' (ibid.). The prerequisite of absolute risk is singularity. Only the singular human can face the absolute other which is, at that time, exclusively her other. The relationship is secret, as communication immediately produces a social relation and with this also alteration. However, singularity is not negative, something to be overcome; it is the consequence of a peculiar gift. The basic and only reason for singularity is the fact that everyone must assume her own death. This is the one thing no one can give or take, it remains the individuals' very own property. This is the explanation of the strange expression 'gift of death'. It is what makes the human unique. And it is what grounds responsibility as experience of singularity. Only assuming one's own death makes freedom and responsibility possible (Derrida 1995: 43f.).

This may all sound a bit dramatical, exaggerated, but to emphasize the point made by Derrida many times: there is no routine in a responsible decision. The absolute risk is the consequence of a decision which has the ability to tear apart. Or, in other words:

> There is no 'politics', no law, no ethics without the responsibility of a decision which, to be just, cannot content itself with applying existing norms or rules but must take the absolute risk, in every singular instant, or justifying itself again, alone, as if for the first time, even if it is inscribed in a tradition.
>
> (Derrida in: Krapp 2000)

Every responsible decision must run the absolute risk. A decision is not protected by knowledge or certainty. Certainty results from the deployment of programs. To drive the argument even further, we may conclude that a decision is in-competence as responsibility. The in-competent taking the decision out of the hand of those who are ruled by executing programs, taking the right to decide to open up the horizon is a demanding outlook for what is to come in the following chapters.

From taking risk to calculation

A supplemented origin: going to sea

Nis Randers (Ernst 1907), a poem from Northern Germany, an area called Friesland, facing the North Sea, captures very well the traditional attitude towards the sea, the danger it puts on the lives of those living from it and the tragedies it puts on families. On a stormy night villagers hear a scream through the breakers and the lightning offers a view of a wreck. Nis Randers looks closely and discovers a man in the masts. He decides to rescue him. His mother intervenes and summarizes the losses the family had faced during the previous years. The father and Nils' brother died at sea, and Uwe, the dearest son, had been lost without message for three years now. Nevertheless Nis decides to go and six comrades with him. A dramatic description is given of how the sea looked, how it moved, the overwhelming power threatening to drown the little boat, a dance with the devils, the description clearly carrying all the worries and anxieties of those left on land – finally the boat can be seen coming back. And one shouts through his hands: 'Tell mother, it's Uwe!'

Nis Randers does not take a risk. It can be called a self-evident readiness to make sacrifices, or seen as fulfilling the duties of the community; no one here names it a risk. There is fear on the mother's side to lose her last son, there is clear recognition about the dangers of the fierce sea; everyone knows that this could be the last ride, but there is no calculation, no move for insurance involved. No one would carry the loss in the sense that it could be replaced by a new boat and a pension for the family who have lost their breadwinner. Using this formulation already sounds strange, completely misguided. The dangers of the sea, and the possibility of dying while fighting for the daily food, are self-evident part of the lives of the families at the coast. Everyone has lost a family member, or a close friend, or knows of losses in other families. It belongs to their life. Risk does not. Risk does not represent the situation, the meaning of the situation, although it covers a part. It covers the loss, but exclusively a special aspect of the loss. The loss had to be transformed into something measurable to be expressed as risk. Loss is reduced to value in economic terms. The risk of losing belongs to another world. In Derridean terms, we can see a *différance*. The sign is already displaced presence (Derrida 1990). If we name something 'a risk', the act of naming already imputes certain qualities to that which is so named. It is biased by the viewer; taken out of the situation. The act of naming is already a first step in the management of emotions connected with the presence. There is no chance of grasping the whole. Life world's understanding of going to sea was differed and deferred by naming it risky. To state the seemingly obvious: without a concept of risk there would be no risk. The origin – the presence – is constructed and applied to a situation so as to open up new possibilities of action.

Risk is a trace which makes the origin invisible, so it can be argued, following Derrida's terminology a step further. Derrida (1983) radicalizes the understanding of the trace in a crucial way. He develops the concept of the trace in a complex discussion on origin – an origin which does not exist, has never existed, or is always already absent. Origin as presence is strongly rejected by Derrida. For him the trace does not denote the absence of an origin; the trace is the origin, is his somehow puzzling assertion. The trace is the *différance*, in which appearance and the meaning take their beginning. Without a trace which holds on the other as the other in the same, the difference could not work and no meaning could appear. The point here is not an already constituted difference; it is, before any designation on the content level, about a movement creating difference. It is impossible to perfectly reconstruct an original presence, because it is already supplemented in the very moment of its naming. Trace is origin. The dynamics of the trace is its character as a supplement. Supplementing in contrast to the addition already changes, adds, wipes out the previously existing. The trace is the reminiscence of what has been there before. Just a trace left. Even more extreme: the trace is the result of the supplement by which the difference between what has been signified and been changed in the act of signification, differed and deferred, is already absent, or has never been there, as what has been signified is already supplemented in the act of signifying. At that moment it is not anymore what it – *an sich und für sich* – was. As we have to signify to perceive and to communicate the perception, we do not have the chance to grasp the origin. It is always already absent and, in this sense, does not exist – *für uns* – for us.

In the context of the discussion on risk there is a difference here. Derrida's arguments are very helpful in understanding why the life world's situation and understanding necessarily disappear by labelling it risk. The situation, however, does not disappear. Realizing a risk in the context of investing in a vessel, always means both: loss of ship as investment and loss of lives. We will see this logic at work in further steps of the development of risk in banking. Risk as trace, supplemented to the life at sea, becomes an origin itself, or as Derrida would express, is the origin. This difference must be understood exactly. The trace, so it was said, is that where appearance and meaning take their beginning. Although the trace started somewhere, the fact that we only see the trace and not the origin, as the trace is somewhere else and sometime later, the origin is lost from sight. It disappeared. Including later arguments, like that of dissemination with the example of the pharmakon, or haunting (Derrida 1994), Derrida seems to argue that the trace has not cut off all connections to the situation from where it was originally created, where it started from. The point is that no term, no signifier captures the reality of a presence, a situation, a signified, as it is always already later and never at exactly the same place, and each use will already have supplemented a *différance* to it. No term is stable over time, it will change meaning, even if the changes are only minimal. Nevertheless any term will always be haunted by other, older meanings. It will be influenced in unpredictable ways, because it can never be said which aspect present in the past will re-emerge in a concrete situation, remembered or re-enacted by an actor.

What this discussion in a Derridian deconstructive mood makes clear so far is that almost any concept we assume as clear, well defined, self-evident is treacherous, abyssal and with consequences often ignored or inadequately addressed. One intention of this book is to include this precariousness as necessary ingredient into the discussion on risk, risk management and regulation of financial markets.

Risk: globalized calculations of return[11]

'Risk' is a term so often used and describing such a self-evident part of our lives we tend to believe that it is in use since the beginning of human societies. It is not. It is an invention[12] in the course of modernity. Luhmann (1991) claims that ancient advanced civilizations had developed different concepts for dealing with analogous problems, and, therefore, did not need a term like 'risk'. Of course uncertainty about the future has always been a topic. Divination was the solution mainly used. According to Tedlock (2001: 189), 'divination is a way of exploring the unknown in order to elicit answers (that is, oracles) to questions beyond the range of ordinary human understanding'. Divination could not guarantee reliable knowledge and certainty, but at least it provided a decision which did not cause the anger of gods. What was able to replace divination and replace it with a completely different concept? This change is so fundamental that we have to pause here for a while to understand the significance. My assumption is that a closer look here can still inform about the necessary understanding of risk in our times.

Sloterdijk (2006) focussed the emergence of risk on one peculiar event in history: the search for the western route to India by Columbus as the starting point for what we now call globalization. The journey is set into an environment of a centuries-old tradition and experience. Every human society living near the coast went to sea and was confronted with – well, not the risk, but the fact of being overwhelmed by natural powers at any moment, as illustrated by Nis Randers. What had to happen to subsume a normal aspect of daily life under a new aspect? To see shipping as risk? Shipping had always been dangerous, the loss of lives and vessels a normal aspect of a sailor's occupation. No necessity was seen to name it differently from other aspects of life. The consideration of aspects of life as risk accompanied an increasingly complex economic environment. Angry about the public view of globalization and its coverage in the media, Peter Sloterdijk (2006) develops a view of globalization and its consequences from a philosophical point of view. His somehow provocative idea is that we can quite reliably set the beginning and the end of globalization. The beginning is marked by Columbus' discovery of America, the end can be set to the end of the Second World War.[13] Today we are living in a globalized world, i.e. completed globalization, and have to face the consequences which we, the Europeans, started with our journeys over the oceans. Globalization marks the transition of meditative spherical thinking to the practice of capturing the globe. Sloterdijk turns the lesson, that other cultures prove the conviction of an immutable local order of things to be contingent, and possibly completely different, from the own one, to the insight that this is not the loss of the middle but the loss of periphery. Nothing can be kept at a distance any more. The local is not the centre of the world – such a centre does not exist. To leave the local involves the uncertainty if one will come back, the uncertainty of return. Exactly this marks the difference: the physical return of the person also means the return of goods – the ship, and potentially what was found or traded abroad. Manning a ship is a severe investment, so the return of investment becomes a crucial factor. Taking credit, investing in equipment and setting sail for discoveries is a race for dubious opportunities on opaque distant markets. Discoveries, claims Sloterdijk (2006: 78), are just a special form of investment. Emerging capitalism required a different method of dealing with uncertainty, with the possibility of loss of goods by wreckages, i.e. the inability of returning the investment, of paying the credit rates. The new behaviour is about taking risks and at the same time about dealing with the risk, diversifying it by inviting others to share the monetary consequences of the risk and the potential profit. Ideas of risk and insurance require a completely different type of human, one who is the architect of his own future, rather than waiting to receive it from gods. This type of humans made the experience that it is good to learn from your mistakes, but it is better to learn by debt. The fierce Copernican discussion about the earth circulating around the sun hides the main fact that in modernity the situation is better described as money circulating around the globe (ibid.: 79).

Sloterdijk plays with words here: a risk culture of television (*fernsichtiges Risikohandeln*, Sloterdijk 2006: 86), with *tele* referring to distance and vision in the double meaning of view and visionary, which is more than clear view, it includes the vision of the distance which is not seen from the point of departure, but is aimed at a vision of what to find beyond the horizon. The restructuring of European action from stability to practices and mentalities of risk action explains the somehow surprising, almost mysteriously successful offensive power of the first generations of discoverers. The readiness to take risks is fuelled by the compulsion, the obligation to gain profits to pay off the credits. Going to sea always needed luck to survive, but now it became more than a fate, it introduced the die: the opportunity. It becomes possible to calculate success and failure, gains and losses. And it needed planning – in other words a turn to the future, a futurization of governmental, entrepreneurial and epistemic action. Taking risk became the central aspect of modernity. One thing has become clear: in this world there is no place for natural evil anymore. Any idea of insurance is blasphemous when the intention is to avoid or at least weaken the negative consequences of natural catastrophes. Probabilistic calculation to evaluate the chances, to make the future predictable, increasingly developed and used in the unfolding risk culture is a move *Against the Gods* (Bernstein 1996). Risk management is unthinkable when fate is the predominant conception of the future.[14]

Describing the manning of a fleet to find new routes to places of trade as a central part of globalization is a convincing argument. Risk gained significance as a method to master the special uncertainties of this future, where intentions aimed at spots beyond the horizon. Going to sea could be termed risky now, but the group taking the risk was split into those who physically went to sea, and those who sent them to sea, but remained home. Risk was the invention of those who remained inland anyway. It is their interest to calculate, to evaluate opportunities. Risk entered the scene at that moment when the structure of ownership of the vessel changed. Neither the fishermen nor a king but a group of investors manned the ship for the chances of the new route.[15] An investment has to pay interest: the safe return of the ship with the intended goods, as included in the calculation, decides if the result of the investment is worthwhile. In other words: the investment will not be made if no or insufficient return can be expected. The investment is an evaluation of future results. This future does not remain in the future. It is made present by the fact of its incorporation into the calculation. Risk is the expression of what is at stake, what can be lost if things go wrong, that is in this case, if the ship does not return. Talking about risk opens the mind for coping strategies. Sharing the risk with others, a group of investors to reduce the personal involvement and avoid immediate bankruptcy is one strategy. It also offers the potential for higher investments than single investors could cope with. The potential for insurance is another aspect, a more defensive one. If the ship is lost, and with it the potential profit, at least the losses are covered.

It became possible to calculate success and failure, gains and losses. And it needed planning, in other words a turn to the future, a futurization of governmental, entrepreneurial and epistemic action. Taking risk became the central aspect of modernity.

Future – the attempt to order future; or, risk turns out to be order

Detachment of risk from life and independent calculation

On its way from the life world to the financial markets only a first step of a longer development was taken by making this difference, by isolating the uncertainties of an investment. Risk, abstracted from something that was very different, supplemented Nis Randers' consciousness of what is at stake in the life world, which did not bear the name risk, so that the risk now having the attention while investing is just the residual trace of what was not even named before. More steps needed to be taken, and were taken in the following centuries, to develop the financial markets to the actual state.

This observation supports a central assumption of Luhmann in his *Sociology of Risk* (1991) and Baecker's (1991) analysis of risk in the banking industry. Risk is self-referential, they conclude from their central assumption. Luhmann clearly positioned himself against one of the most influential differences in risk calculation, that of Frank Knight. He insisted on separating risk and uncertainty. Although risk in everyday use is about uncertainties, there is a fundamental difference resulting from the possibility to measure uncertainty. Knight names measurable uncertainty risk, because in becoming measurable it is not uncertain at all. Uncertainty is restricted to cases of the non-quantifiable type (Knight 1921/1940). Luhmann (1991) considers Knight's definition as ossified into a dogma so that any further development of the term risk is confronted with the reproach of not having understood the term sufficiently (Luhmann 1991: 9). He claims that there is no definition of risk which would satisfy scientific demands and proposes an unusual difference instead, which nicely provides a missing link to the close connection of risk and decision. Regarding the fact that any risk presupposes a decision which has damage as a possible consequence, the contingency of the damage is clearly referred to and the double contingency of the decision comes into focus: the contingent damage is caused by a contingent decision. Taking another decision would have prevented at least this damage. Certainty as the opposite for risk is misleading. Not deciding always means preventing risk and chance. The better difference is between risk and danger. This presupposes an uncertainty on future possible damages. Either the damage can be ascribed to a decision, then it is called a risk; or the damage is caused externally, then it is a danger (Luhmann 1991: 30). Risks are the consequences of decisions, but we are exposed to dangers. Risk is a difference itself. By naming something a risk it is excluded from the environment. It is separated from what it was connected to, supplemented as an entity with own boundaries. Risk ascribed to a decision is self-referential. There is no reference outside the risk calculation. The difference is an observational category, the self-reference is an operative category (Baecker 1991).

Future is still uncertain, but instead of divination we use planning and calculation. We install trajectories into the future to provide guidance into an otherwise uncertain future. Risk is an essential, self-referential part of this process. It is a projection of what can go wrong, of potential deviations from the planned path into the future. What is the special relationship of risk to future then?

Future can be calculated, so is the conviction behind the inclusion of risk into planning. Risk is a calculation process, taking information of the past, condensing it into developments which can be prolonged into the future, which can be put on a trajectory. Risk takes the possible into consideration – into calculation. The term risk helps to draw an image of the future. It makes future present and with that known. Such a future can be calculated, it is possible to count on it. However, we can only take into calculus what is known today, or what has left traces in the past; something which has already occurred and can, therefore, be followed on the arrow of time into the future. To continue traces of the past into the future, extrapolations, forecasting, making projections, is the domain of statistics. What can be different in the future from what we expect today? How probable is a certain result of a concrete action? How often will an accident occur? How large will the losses from loans be? Such are the questions asked and answered in risk management. Problems are tamed, uncertainties are deconstructed into rationalized probabilities, Holt (2004) argues, worrying about a too narrow epistemology that refuses the insight into the complexity of organizational reality. Statistics provides impressive instruments for answering the questions. Nevertheless statistics suffers from a decisive limitation. Risk management today,[16] especially in the financial industry, consists of an 'avalanche of numbers' (Hacking 1990) which was raised, accumulated, created, calculated as the basis of scientific knowledge, transforming the nature of evidence, of knowledge and of authority. Probability theory has provided a modern way of thinking. However, *The Taming of Chance* (Hacking 1990) includes a by-product. Numbers, generated in masses and ordered to probabilities, capture at best a past development with serious shortcomings for prediction of future developments:

> probability is the expression of an assumed pre-existing order which rests on the idea of the expected and the certain, i.e. the recurrence of what is already known.... [P]robability is a form of prediction or prior awareness which defends the system against the strange and the unknown; the system is therefore incapable of dealing with information that is non-probabilistic and unpremeditated.
>
> (Cooper 1987: 397)

Taking Cooper's remark on probability seriously and holding it applicable also for the term for which probability serves as an expression, i.e. risk, then risk is an expression of an assumed pre-existence which rests on an idea of the expected though not the certain. Derrida would call that a program: 'If one were sure of the calculation, it would not be an action or a decision; it would be a programming' (Derrida, as quoted by Mansfield 2006: 479). There is no decision, it is only the continuation of what is known into the future and therefore rests inside the horizon. No warning against unfavourable outcomes can be derived beyond a failure which can be assumed from the existing numbers. No event can take place in this way of thinking, or, if an event takes place, it will take the actors by complete surprise.

In considering the future, we try to make sense of what we know. Risk is an attempt to make sense of what might happen in the future. Sensemaking is included in the thinking of risk. Weick (1995) insists on hindsight for the problem of sensemaking. Although Weick might well wince at this elaboration[17] I see his description of uncertainty containing a valuable insight for the character of risk. People try to find out if their assumptions of the present are correct by looking for new information:

> Faced with news as an outcome, people ask, what history might have generated this outcome and what should I do presuming that the history I have constructed is plausible? Uncertainty about the actual future is replaced by more certainty about the present, which itself was an actual future just a short time ago. The greater certainty about the meaning of the present news is created because the people reconstruct a history that serves as a plausible explanation how it got here.
>
> (Weick 1995: 96)

Using probability and statistics means to tell a story about the past to inform about how the past got here, into the present. This is a form of retrospective sensemaking to gain a possibility to make sense of the future assuming that we can tell how it will be if the path we identified from the past to the present will go on as identified to the present. An organization's capability for sensemaking in the face of uncertainty about the future (Weick 1995: 97) is a precondition for risk management. Making sense of the future makes decisions possible which, according to Luhmann (1991), are the sources of risk. This discussion promises to be exciting: there are obviously two different assumptions of decision at work and different understandings of future. I will return to that later.

There is a change in the perception of risk, though. The time of exploration on the seas aimed at the unknown land beyond the horizon.[18] The contradiction between the risk of total loss involved and an economic dealing with investing in these kinds of exploration beyond the adventure of discoveries was settled once the globe was explored, known. Globalized returns do not include adventure any more, at least not as the primary motivation, but concrete planning, a mapping not of the ground to conquer, but of the future. Future in organizations is a clear, linear structure developing on the arrow of time from past over present into the future. It can be seen as a trajectory. Risk is concerned with a movement across a space, something thrown from one position to another, as the Latin etymology indicates for a trajectory: *trans* = across, *jacere* = to throw. Höpfl (2000) argues as an effect of the ordinary what I would find appropriate for risk, too.

> It is the language of pro-jection, of moving forwards and of indicating a future arrival position or state, or re-jection of the throwing out of those things or people incompatible with the pro-jection, it is the language of ab-jection and the de-jection of things thrown away. So when organizations declare specific objectives, outcomes, points of arrival and so forth, they throw forward an ordering into future time.
>
> (Höpfl 2000: 21)

'To throw forward an ordering into future time' is an excellent description of the arrow of time and provides the image of an independent track reassuringly taking energy from the past to pass the present and point towards a concrete future, one which is determined, a clear, safe path on which to move forward. And if it is painted with the right swoosh, symbolizing all the positive energy by slightly pointing upwards in a seductive curve, to the northeast, the top right corner of the sheet, where in presentations always the climax of a development rests, optimism about the outcome wins over the anxiety of moving into unknown terrain. Future is an unprotected environment into which planning is directed, a decision is performed, the aim of a project is set. Anything Other is eradicated in this process. Risk is concerned with the possibility of different outcomes, that the trajectory is left and the objective failed, but in order [*sic*!] to prevent it, to eradicate the possibility of failure, variation or difference. Different outcomes are the realization of risk which is seen as a failure of risk management. Risk is an integral part of the planning process. It paints the picture of the future by describing potential differences to the intended outcome. Thinking about risk is fed by the certainty that things may turn out differently than intended. Or, in banking terms, risk is about volatility.

Risk is the form of considering possible futures, evaluate them and act accordingly. Risk, as it is seen in this context, is not just an expression of uncertainty, of what may go wrong, but the rational expression of dealing with an unknown future made known in the present as artificial, produced reality. Measurable uncertainty, so Knight (1921/1940) claimed, is risk. As it is measurable it is not uncertain. This conviction informed the thinking or risk and risk management in the banking industry. Risk is, so the somewhat unexpected and slightly disturbing insight, order. Risk orders future in making it present, in imagining the world beyond the horizon to include it into the horizon. Risk is sensemaking about the threatening future by ordering it.

Of course there is a price to pay for this achievement, as Höpfl clearly indicated with her etymological reflection on trajectory. The language of pro-jection necessarily includes connotations of other terms of the same base. Projection cannot be had without rejection of perspectives incompatible with the projection. These are excluded. By using a term with the base –jection the negative image of anything contradicting or only differing from the projection, the plan, is already included without specially emphasizing it. Dejection and abjection are close as the reproach of deviating from the golden path. Risk as order is the exclusion of the included, the active drawing of a boundary between what is expected as probable future and what is excluded from the future as not being probable. The probable becomes the desirable, the materialization of a future different from the desired probable changes into an unacceptable possibility.

Risk-ordering future presupposes two different concepts of future. The attempt to order a threatening future by calculating a trajectory of past events into the future tries to make future present. However, it has to be clearly kept in mind that risk in this case is a present future and as such may be radically different from the future presence. From Esposito's (2007) perspective – it is Luhmannian, as she draws heavily on the systems theory of this type with all the nice paradoxes created by second-order observation – there are two different types of future. She differentiates between present future and future present. We have to consider the present future to be able to act. The present future is the understanding of the observer from today's perspective, using all the information at hand to deduce an expectation about the future. But it is the view from now into an unknown and unknowable future. What will be the case in the future, once the future has become present, remains not knowable. The future presence may turn out to be as predicted, as expected, but it may also be a bit or completely different. From the moment of taking action on, the action is subject to all kinds of changes in the environment, to all kinds of reactions, explicit ones from the immediate surrounding and implicit ones emerging from the context, the organization, the organization's environment, etc. From the moment of making the mind up about the future and plan into it, it is already part of the past and, in fact, has to be realized into an already changed environment. The point of decision to act made future present, it presented an image of what is probable at that time, of what was intended, planned, but what will have been realized, what will have been the subject of sensemaking in the future when the action will have had turned into a part of the past, in other words, what will have been the future present, remains out of sight. What has been defined as risk may realize, it may realize differently from the expectation – the gains or losses higher as expected – or it may not realize. But such a pattern has a blind spot: 'pretending that the probability of risk can be transformed into certainty by stochastic calculation is equivalent to a "defuturisation of future"' (Esposito 2007: 84, author's translation). What looks like a nice play on words at first impression, reveals a serious shortcoming of risk management. The attempts to calculate future outcomes, as sophisticated as they may become, are only able to present the future which is already contained in the statistics used. It can only order the chaos we already know to make it operable right now. Relying on such a projection as the path into the future means an exclusion of anything not included in the figures forming the basis of the path. The belief in the calculation on such a fundament ignores the fundamental characteristic of future. It is always only a partial view possible. No surprise please. Only that the surprise is the essential part of the package. *The future is unwritten*, as Joe Strummer,[19] a punk musician, wonderfully put it into words.

A reflection about the future present, however, is only a preparation of an even more intricate thought. If we accept this difference, and place ourselves at the point of the future past, as language enables us at least on the basis of grammar, it becomes possible to consider the future of the future. What will have been the present future once it will have turned out into the future present is already almost vertiginous thinking. Moving beyond that point in the future, what will have been the basis of sensemaking of the future past from which to consider the present future of this future? And, what will have been the future past once the future present future will have turned into the future future present? Sounds confusing, even ridiculous? Well, that doesn't mean that it is not part of our reality. Thinking in these stages, moving forward into the future, conscious about the abysses involved by using this kind of vocabulary, might gain the capability to think future on shaky ground, on the slippery slopes (Rosa 2005) our reality actually is built on. Thinking the way through banking products, especially derivatives, the complexity involved in these products, their functioning, meaning and market and its interpretation all of a sudden opens the mind up for a speculation on their role in dealing with the future, (its actual use, its possibilities, and its performativities).

Risk as part of an investment is closely connected to the investment itself. It belongs to it and to the calculation of the ROI, the return on investment. The meaning of risk here is the expectation, the probability of failing to return the concrete investment, the manning and sending of ships in Sloterdijk's example. Any cross border trading has to face risks beyond the realm of production, the physical delivery or the quality of goods and services. They rest in payment and financing. The client may fail to pay, the exchange rates may change, so that the calculation of the price turns out to be inadequate, the interest rate for the money lent may change, so that an aspect of the financing turns out to be different than expected. Here we enter traditional banking business. In giving loans, organizing payments, changing currencies, etc. they organize the environment of other economic sectors. What others would need to organize independently in each case, and which is not their core competency to use an otherwise discussable phrase, was organized and increasingly standardized by banks. Payments flows, financing huge trades, businesses or state action, the search for investors, collection of assets able to give loans are examples. What these activities have in common, is the risk of a failure to pay. This can be seen as the core competency of banks (Baecker 1991): balancing the risks involved so that the economic system can work. The management of risk became part of the offering of banks, and during this development risk itself became a product.

Futures and options: putting future into plural and contingency[20]

Fate was in singular, something written in the book of life, fixed and not possible to influence. Risk opens the future, provides the consciousness for options. Things may be different in the future, depending on a present decision. Future is also contingent, i.e. things may turn out to be different than expected. No fate means no guaranteed outcome. We do not only not know the future, the future itself is not determined. Financial markets' products have incorporated this consideration deeply as the basic understanding of their construction. They are widely used, immensely influential in nowadays' business life, but also create anxiety and public discussion. Comparisons with locust plagues are part of reactions to a market segment which on the one hand has immediate influence on the way of making business as one aspect of the concentration on shareholder value and through this effect on employment (Pelzer 2009), and on the other is a very opaque business only intelligible to specialists. The construction and peculiarities of these markets, including the attitude and behaviour of traders are increasingly in the focus of research (e.g. Honegger *et al.* 2010; Lilley and Lightfoot 2006; Knorr Cetina and Bruegger 2002a, 2002b; MacKenzie 2003b).

Any discussion on the excesses of the market of derivatives must be reminded that these financial instruments were once introduced to manage the risks involved in volatile markets. Managing means to transfer the risk of a party not willing to accept it as part of their own business to a party who is willing to bear the risk against a premium. Banks traditionally performed this counterpart and were the agents between parties. Taking over the risk from one party immediately triggered the search for matching opposite risks. One risk involved for producing companies lies in the instability of prices on their supply as well as on their sales side. The latter also includes risks concerning currency rates in international trade. Instruments invented for transferring the risk are called futures. Futures are contracts in which one side buys and one side sells a given quantity of an asset at a set price on a given future date. The seller achieves certainty about the price of his goods on a given date in the future independent of the actual price on this day in the future. He is willing to pay a premium and to give up the chance of getting more if the price rises accordingly, but gains the certainty of not losing money if the price falls below the agreed level. An option is a contract which gives the right but not the obligation to buy or sell an asset at a given price on a given date in the future. The value of the option is dependent on the asset named in the contract: the underlying. A crucial step of abstraction was achieved once these instruments could be traded without a delivery of the underlying. Although their value is dependent on another asset, this value is their own. They are traded independently from the underlying. No delivery at the termination date is required, only cashing up.

Derivatives are about the price of underlyings in the future. Hence their name – futures. The other form is about the choice to buy (sell) or not to buy (sell), but with a fixed price – an option. Derivatives are inventions to include future into decisions today. They enable acting in volatile, global markets. Futures are products to manage future, options recognize contingency by inclusion into deciding. The remarkable fact about these instruments is how easy, self-evident future is put into a plural and how easily it is combined with the general contingency of the future and the ability to have choice, i.e. buy and sell options.

Risk copes with contingency. Future is fundamentally uncertain. If money replaces God a functional equivalent is needed for his function of acting as the reassuring instance which guarantees that what ever will be will be good, because it is in God's hands. The equivalent is the idea to have enough money at disposal to be able to react on future contingencies, i.e. future needs or threats. Risk is displaced from a product-oriented market logic to the logic of financial markets on the basis of circulation based risk (LiPuma and Lee 2004). The decentring of capital in favour of liquidity enabled money to serve the task to transform indeterminable complexity into certain complexity. Money is used to maintain options as options (Deutschmann 1999) and put future into plural.

However, a crucial difference emerges. In asking the question 'what is a risk' it is necessary to propose what can be dealt with, what can be managed as risk and what not. The discussion started in gambling (and there is good reason to assume that the topic is still dominated by this perspective (Sinn 2009; Strange 1986). By betting money on the die, the uncertain outcome can be called risk: the chance to win and the potential to lose the stake. Also described by Hacking (1975, 1990) and Bernstein (1996) gambling was a prime motivation to calculate the probability of winning. The boundary between gambling and investment is not as clear as it might be desirable. The possibilities of translation for the German expression *Einsatz* for example, can go both ways, stake and investment, depending on the context. Throwing the die and recording the results to compare them were among the first steps in statistics. Western societies became increasingly fascinated in quantification. Almost anything was measured and calculated to find out about what is normal, what can be normalized, what can be seen as deviation. This process created an avalanche of numbers with the intention of *The Taming of Chance* (Hacking 1990). The boundary is still not impervious as MacKenzie and Millo (2003) described on occasion of the legalization of the derivatives market in the USA. Up to the end of the 1960s, the initial reservations of authorities against derivative trading as gambling had to be addressed with mathematic models to get acknowledgment as a serious business to be traded at exchanges. The interesting conclusion the authors drew was the reversal of what one would expect to be the 'normal' process. There was an activity in the market not considered as approvable by authorities. In order to change authority's opinion one would expect changes in the product design, the circumstances of its use or its distribution, or the structure of the market. In the case of the derivative market a development in mathematics changed the market and the opinion of authorities: the Black–Scholes–Merton (BSM) equation of option pricing, nowadays considered as a standard in the banking industry. The development and use of this model was intensively researched by Donald MacKenzie (2003a), and together with Yuval Millo (MacKenzie and Millo 2003). His focus is not on the question of whether or not mathematical models are 'correct' but rather on the sociological aspects of the model's development and the diffusion of its use. The title of one of these papers already gives a flavour of what his interpretation is about: 'Constructing a market, performing theory' (MacKenzie and Millo 2003). Analysing the history of the Chicago Board Options Exchange and the development of the equation from forerunners into its final form, the authors describe the progress of a particular market from obscurity to becoming an accepted part of the financial markets system. The rather surprising conclusion of the research was that BSM created this market performatively. After having it developed into the final form, the creators of BSM had to accept that it had poor empirical support. For the sake of elegance and conclusiveness they included several simplistic assumptions. Despite these considerations, the model was adopted in practice, with the consequence that, rather than the simplistic assumptions being challenged or changed, 'market reality' adapted in the direction of the assumptions. As a result of this performative evolution, empirical proof for the model strengthened considerably. Part of this 'success' resulted from the removal of restricting rules by the authorities who looked favourably on the model. These authorities accepted the equation as an economic proof of the value of derivatives for handling risks and thus no longer classified derivatives as financial gambling, as they had been officially considered until that point.

This equation was the decisive market measure for almost two decades until unexpected market conditions proved that it could not accommodate the excessive possibilities of financial trading. The 1987 stock markets crash was by no means anticipated or covered by the hedging represented in the equation. No such event could be calculated due to the log-normal assumption, which prevents extreme events from being considered. The solution to this problem was the introduction of 'skews', which denote an implied volatility. The BSM equation still has, despite further developments and adaptations and its inclusion in other formulae, remained a cornerstone of financial markets risk calculation. Myron Scholes and Robert Merton received the Nobel Prize for their formula in 1997 (Fischer Black died two years before).

MacKenzie's research as outlined above also lends support to the general view that there is nothing like an objective, natural basis on which to ground risk calculation. There is no Archimedean point from which to assess risk. As a consequence, MacKenzie researches more sophisticated reactions to risk, such as those which take into account systemic pressures and multiple actors from different backgrounds (traders, mathematicians, institutions like exchanges, authorities, etc.). Standards become standard, he maintains, because they influence the structure of the market to which they are applied. As such, MacKenzie's is, so to speak, a more mature approach to the assessment of risk; mature because he explicitly accepts the inter-subjectivity of risks and the search for dealing [*sic*!] with them.

The intention of this rather cursory overview, leaving out all the exciting material already presented by Ian Hacking (1975, 1990) and Peter Bernstein (1996), is to point to a crucial development and with that a fine reformulation of the role of risk. Risk is a necessary ingredient in a globalized economy. It offers a vocabulary to represent certain aspects of business. Risk is a way to explore the unknown of the future. Trading risk can be interpreted as the rational answer to the uncertainties in a globalized economy: transforming the uncertainties into measurable units – that is risk. Risk transformed from a vocabulary to address certain aspects of economy to a commodity itself.

Risk becomes a commodity

Risk in the financial markets is the potential failure to pay, the rise or fall of prices of raw materials, changing currency rates in international trade, the volatility of exchange rates, changes in interest, etc. This summary already makes clear how difficult it is to draw a distinction between the risks of the 'normal' economic world and those of the financial markets. Banks are also companies who face risks in their business that are very similar to those also producing companies are usually exposed to. These include potential losses from the business, operational risks, reputational risks, legal risks and others. All of these directly or indirectly affect the profitability of companies. The most crucial difference between financial and commodity markets regarding risk is that the risk traded in the financial markets is not involved in the physical trade of goods, the quality of services, i.e. as a potential of their production or use. Commodities, currencies, interest rates and others serve as a reference for what is actually traded. They are underlying to what is traded; on the financial markets. It is risk itself which has become the 'good' to trade, it turned from a characteristic of a good or a service into a commodity itself. A logical step for the product portfolio of banks then was to develop instruments to make the financial result of a concrete business more reliable for the company producing goods. The name of these products, 'derivatives', makes it quite obvious that something is traded here which by construction is derived from something else. The derivative is linked to an underlying. Its value is connected to the expectations about the value of this underlying. It represents an assumption about the development of the underlying's volatility: do the prices or rates go up or down, and by how much? With derivatives the risk of changes in the value of the underlying can be traded. On globalized markets, one of the risks which a production company cannot influence is that of currency rate changes. The financial instruments invented for transferring this risk are called futures. An aspect of the commodity or the trade is isolated and traded away. One side achieves certainty, the other side a premium and the chance of profiting from the volatility of prices. A certain, clearly defined risk was taken off the company and transferred to another party. The idea is different from insuring a risk. An insurance steps in in case of a realization of a risk. It pays for the damage. The financial instrument places the buyer in the situation as if the risk doesn't exist. He cannot be affected. Whatever the currency rate will be in the example, he gets the rate agreed upon. The risk is taken over by his counterpart.[21]

Risk is commodified and this is exactly the purpose of these instruments: 'Risk analysis, the commodification of and the trade in risk are specifically designed to factor out this virtuous uncertainty that justifies profit' (Cloke 2009: 113). The uncertainty of trading these products is reduced for the producer by selling the risk. Cloke (2009) and Vaknin (2005) judge this as a mass manufacturing of moral hazard. They interpret derivatives as vehicles to buy out risk, and with that market discipline by business, failure is removed from capitalism and one of its fundaments is severely damaged. In contrast to their opinion I think that it has to be acknowledged that the present regular use of derivatives in international trade is a reaction of companies to the increased uncertainties and complexities of the global competition. They intend to reduce risk to those parts of business which they can influence and where they are not completely dependent on external market forces. The use of derivatives is not generally evil, but they have the characteristics of the 'pharmakon', as will be explained in more detail in Chapter 8.

One of the consequences of risk's commodification is its growing abstractness.[22] The realization of the risk in the life world, the wreckage, or failures in industrial plants can still be physically experienced, suffered. They are embodied. It is the difference between embodied risk and the kind of risk which can be calculated economically. The corporeal, sometimes even existential quality of a realization of risk is that what might be insured, but cannot be traded away. Financial instruments which transfer risk deal with economic, monetarized aspects of a concrete business transaction. Risk in the financial markets is cleansed of the smell of embodied risk, the dead bodies in the wreck; it is abstracted into the world of numbers to be exclusively realized as financial gains or losses. Displaced risk already solely served as a connotation of business relationships before it was abstracted more by turning it into a product. The increasing abstraction and complexity called for special treatments of risk. Derivatives were introduced of which the value depends on an expected future value of an underlying asset. Trading derivatives means a displacement of the risk. It is transferred from the underlying asset to its derivative. In this way, risk is also distilled and purified. 'This distillation of risk, from asset to future to option on future, produces an essence of risk, exorcised from assets that are now seemingly secure once more' (Lilley and Lightfoot 2006: 384). The character of risk changed. It has become an essence which can be traded independent of the underlying asset. This was the fundamental point which made financial markets of trading risk with an independence from commodity markets possible (LiPuma and Lee 2004). The supplement to life, risk, found an independent role in economic life and beyond, always ready to also dominate it. Risk haunts from the future.[23]

3 Risk – the sovereign exception

The financial industry's central topic is risk. Or, so it should be. With business models aiming at more than 25 per cent profit on base capital a basic insight of financing seems to get out of focus: the higher the income the higher the risk. And something went obviously profoundly wrong during the past years. When banks have to make use of the lender of last resort, have to accept state money despite of – at least in the eyes of the management – unacceptable conditions in the face of massive losses and the collapsing of the money markets, close scrutiny should be given to the dealing of risk and risk management. 'Dealing' can be taken in the double meaning here: it is the dealing of risks itself, and the transfer of them from one party to another which becomes problematic. Banks' normal business of accepting financial risk, transforming it, transferring it to other parties willing to accept these risks against a premium reached a new level where the process obviously ran out of control. The crisis is often presented as the result of a network of agents who have not paid enough attention to the risk involved. Everyone involved somehow made mistakes and, therefore, it could not be prevented. Therefore no one can really be blamed. That this description is too easy has not been left unnoticed (Aalbers 2009). Besides the technical questions how this could happen, there is also a more fundamental question regarding the term risk itself. Is risk, as it is understood and conceptualized in risk management, i.e. a potential of a loss which can be calculated, sufficiently understood? Is there such a thing as 'systemic risk' indicating that there is a type of risk beyond the risk in individual businesses and not directly derived from them?

In this chapter I would like to look at the term 'risk' from two other perspectives to highlight that too much is left unnoticed with a conception of calculated risks. The line of argument follows the paradoxical figures of inclusion and exclusion. Two authors shall be taken into account: Edgar Allan Poe and Giorgio Agamben. Despite its ancient setting, Poe's fable *The Masque of the Red Death* (1842) offers a clear description of the effect of an ignorance of risk, of a failed strategy of risk management. The risk of a fatal illness shall be excluded from society, but it is actually included by the same move.

Agamben's discussion of the sovereign exception and the state of exception prove to be helpful to understand a basic pattern of the emergence of the current crisis. Securitization of mortgages seen as the sovereign exception takes Agamben's argument to an area he didn't have in mind, but where it can also become fruitful for considering attempts of regulation to prevent these kinds of crises. The conclusion that global financial markets act in a permanent state of exception can be drawn from Agamben's arguments. Taken together, the authors provide us with a mutually supporting argument leaving us rather pessimistic about the current well-intended attempts to tame the financial markets.

The included excluded: a parable of risk management which went fatally wrong

Edgar Allan Poe tells the story of a horrible plague devastating Prince Prospero's country[1] (Poe 1842). No pestilence had ever been so fatal, he writes and the description includes profuse bleeding at the pores, sharp pain and the exclusion of the help of others by the sheer horror created by the view of the victims. When the plague had depopulated his land by half, Prospero decided for some kind of a reversed quarantine. He chose a thousand friends from the knights and dames of his court and retreated with them to a castellated abbey. They intended perfect seclusion, to exclude the horrible reality outside and survive:

> A long and lofty wall girdled it in. This wall had gates of iron. The courtiers, having entered, brought furnaces and massy hammers and welded the bolts. They resolved to leave means neither of ingress nor of egress to the sudden impulses of despair or of frenzy from within. The abbey was amply provisioned. The external world could take care of itself.... All these and security were within. Without was the 'Red Death'.
>
> (Ibid.)

Excluding the world to survive, leaving it to find or create a better one, or just to exclude the sight of the poor, has always been involved in utopian thinking, science fiction or in nowadays' gated communities. An intentional act of exclusion shall remove unpleasant, dangerous elements of reality, or give a clear boundary of what belongs to the order created, and what has to remain outside. Clearly, the Red Death was to be excluded. However, Poe demonstrates within the few pages of this arabesque how futile this attempt was. It was more a last celebration of wealth and voluptuousness, a succession of parties, terminating in a masked ball of the most unusual magnificence. The dancing was only interrupted by the striking of a huge ebony clock standing in the last chamber, decorated in black, lighted by fires behind red panes. There was something in the clock's chiming at the full hour which made the crowd aware of a crucial absence, the reason why they were secluded: '...there was a brief disconcert of the whole gay company,... and the more aged and sedate passed their hands over their brows as if in confused reverie or meditation'. Not just once in the evening, but at each hour came this interruption, climaxing at midnight with the twelve strokes by the bell of the clock:

> and thus it happened, perhaps, that more of thought crept, with more of time, into the meditations of the thoughtful among those who revelled. And thus, too, it happened, perhaps, that before the last echoes of the last chime had utterly sunk into silence, there were many individuals in the crowd who had found leisure to become aware of the presence of a masked figure which had arrested the attention of no single individual before.

Their unrest was justified, it was the Red Death who ended the party. 'And one by one dropped the revellers in the blood-bedewed halls of their revel, and dies each in the despairing posture of his fall.'

At first impression the Red Death is a metaphorical example of the included excluded, but not an example for the impossible. The epidemic was outside the walls of the abbey, therefore it was possible, and should have been rendered impossible by exclusion. However, the world in Poe's arabesque has a decisive lack of knowledge. Prince Prospero treats the threat as equivalent to an intruder who, adequate measures assumed, could have been locked out. But the locked out does not only return, it was never absent and, ignored, had fatal consequences. This is the point which makes the Red Death as metaphor for risk management so valuable and with this detour it becomes an expression for the event. Measures were taken to prevent the risk of infection. These measures, so we can judge today with our knowledge about the effects of viruses – easily and a bit condescendingly – were, of course, completely inadequate. They aim at an embodied enemy, attacking from the outside. That the enemy rests inside the bodies of those who deliberately lock themselves up, and perhaps just inside a single body which is part of the gay society, was not part of the risk calculation and the planning of the measures. The knowledge about viruses did not exist, an adequate reaction was impossible. The situation demanded an invention which was impossible, as the only possible invention is the invention of the impossible (Derrida 2006: 32). As the invention in form of discerning the impossible failed to materialize, the event occurred – unpredictable, unexpected, going beyond any calculation – fatally.

The abbey's inhabitants have no learning effect. The gay society passed away and no survivor could take the consequences from the bitter lesson. It becomes an example as fiction. Only fictional, narratively, the description can illustrate the failures of risk management and become the object for demonstrating the power of the impossible or the janus-faced character of exclusion. Poe showed what is at stake when the boundary between inclusion and exclusion is not considered or if the consequences of drawing the boundary where it is drawn are ignored, especially in case of a lack of knowledge.

The sovereign exception

The decisive role of the relationship of inclusion and exclusion in the form described above by Poe's arabesque, this tricky figure of the inclusion of the excluded by the act of its exclusion, is intensively dealt with by Giorgio

Agamben. For him such an act of exclusion, or the ability and the possibility to do so whenever it seems appropriate, lies at the heart of the modern state. Giorgio Agamben is well known for his discussion of the naked life, *Homo Sacer* (Agamben 2002). What at the outset appears to be a book about victims, a reasoning about the underprivileged, the losers of modern society, soon proves to be more provocative than an additional analysis of suppression. Agamben aims at the hidden intersection of the legal-institutional model and the biopolitical model of power developed by Foucault. Biopolitics is the inclusion of the natural life into the mechanisms and calculus of state power. Foucault's descriptions show humans as the object of a regulating, correcting – in short: a disciplinary power and control (Foucault 1977, 1983). The inclusion of the naked life into the sphere of the *polis* marks a radical transformation of political-philosophical categories, and enables the production of the biopolitical body as the original achievement of the sovereign power, claims Agamben (2002). As a consequence naked life in occidental politics has the unique privilege to be that on whose exclusion the polity of humans is founded (2002: 14, 17). A very double-edged privilege as the topics indicate which Agamben develops from this starting point. *Homo Sacer* (2002), *State of Exception* (2004) and *Remnants of Auschwitz* (2003) are the titles of a series of books where he immerses into the foundation of a legal thinking that has led to the camps of the twentieth century. Within this framework he spends some effort to understand the paradoxical relationship of inclusion and exclusion which, as I want to argue here, can also be used as an important point to understand the role of risk and risk management on the financial markets.

It is exemplified in the act of declaring somebody to be excluded from the community to which she belonged in a peculiar way: it is not the refusal of any relationship but a decisive redefinition of the relationship. The person is deprived of all rights and access to the polity is denied. Exiled one could claim, but with the difference that the person could be killed by everyone without consequence, although not sacrificed.[2] This is the status of *homo sacer*. Naked life, included into the *polis* as object of discipline and calculation can be excluded again by a sovereign decision. Only then it is not the way back into nature, to natural being, independent of the *polis*. The status of *homo sacer* is declared by a sovereign decision declaring an exclusion which never excludes completely. Interesting also in our consideration of the status of risk is the definition of sovereignty and exclusion, the sovereign exception.[3]

Sovereignty is essentially paradox. The sovereign is at the same time inside and outside of the legal order. If the legal order gives the right to the sovereign to proclaim the state of exception and with that to repeal, or suspend, waive the order, the sovereign stands outside this order, but at the same time belongs to that order, because she is responsible for the decision of suspension. Following Carl Schmitt in this point, Agamben insists on the close scrutiny of the topology involved to understand the boundary between inside and outside. The exception is a form of exclusion. It is a single case excluded from the general norm. This exclusion, however, does not mean that there is absolutely no relationship to the norm: it remains connected to the form of its suspension. The norm applies itself on the exception by turning its back to it. The state of exception is not the chaos preceding the order but the situation resulting from its suspension. So it might be better to say that the exception is taken out rather than just excluded (Agamben 2002: 25–27). It is an including exclusion. What is impossible to include, is included by exclusion – a paradoxical inclusion of belonging. What Agamben aims at is the radical crisis of the possibility to differentiate between belonging to the norm and inclusion, between inside and outside, norm and exception.

The state of exception is, as might be expected after the description of the sovereign exception, a tricky concept which defies an easy definition and also asks for the dealing with paradoxes. It goes beyond an understanding of exception as a clearly definable fact taken out of the norm. It is more than a single, concrete case or a clearly defined set of facts which cannot be subsumed under any law, or cannot be dealt adequately with existing norms, and therefore requires special treatment. The state of exception refers to the relationship between a sovereign, the state or its representative, a monarch, a dictator, and the state in which the normal legal order is suspended. How can this relationship be designed that the legal order, when suspended and therefore out of rule, nevertheless keeps the connection to that which replaces it? State of exception means that the norm does not take place: it is the anomy, the absence of law, lawlessness.

Agamben summarizes the arguments he found in literature in four points (Agamben 2004: 62–63). First, the state of exception is not a dictatorship but a law-free zone, a zone of anomy in which any legal rule is deactivated. It is the standstill of law, not the power of dictatorship. Here Agamben sets himself into opposition to those interpretations which see the state of exception as emergency power, or as the right of the state to defend itself, in short any theory which attempts to place it into a legal context. Second, this lawless zone seems to be of such a crucial importance for the legal order that it tries to keep a relationship with it by any means. It is as if the law needs to keep a relation to the anomy for reasons of its own grounding. Third, the main problem is the actions taking place during the suspension of law. As they are neither executive, nor legislative, nor illegal, their lawful character seems to be placed in a non-space. The fourth point deals with the character of this impossible relation. Both are connected by their boundary, they share their mutual exclusion. If the law does not want to give itself up completely and give way for its other – the anomy, the state of exception – it has to create a power which is able to control the other without direct connection. Agamben calls them '*fictio iuris par excellence*' (Agamben 2004: 71): by trying to keep the force of the force of law when suspending the law, even by constructing a juridical *mana*, set free when suspending the law. During the state of exception the legal order is replaced by human action which has lost any relationship to the law and may include civil war or revolutionary violence but also any despotic rule. The link shall be provided, the excluded remain included, especially as this link is needed to declare the end of the state of exception and return to the original legal order.

However, Agamben aims for more. Based on the summarizing remarks above he returns to the importance of understanding the biopolitics involved in the relationship between the norm and the exception. Law and life are mutually dependent. The occidental legal system presents itself as a double structure formed by two heterogeneous but coordinated elements: a legal-normative and an anomic-metalegal one. The normative element needs the anomic one to be used; and for the anomic one, the state of exception can only exist in a relationship of validation or suspension of the norm.

Agamben concentrates his reasoning on the institutions and persons representing the state, developing his examples from Roman right into the twentieth century. The connection to life is, therefore, directed to the top of a state. There is nothing wrong with this in this context. The topic is the sovereign decision about the state of exception and its replacing the legal order. The crucial point is that a norm does not exist for itself, cannot unfold its effect unless it is represented by a living person, and the state of exception also cannot exist disembodied. A person, enabled by an institution of the norm must embody the state of exception and finally be able to lead it back to the norm(al). Furthermore, the state of exception is inscribed on the social body as the removal of the distinctions between private and public, because this distinction belongs to the realm of the norm.

The possibility to make a difference between life and law, anomy and *nomos* is the consequence of the smoothly working biopolitical machine. Naked life, and here the argument comes back to the start of the other book, *Homo Sacer*, is a construct not existing independently in nature and as artificial a concept as law is. Unmasking the connection as fiction, however, does not lead back to an origin, a pure living. It solely opens up a possibility to find a new version of connecting. From the state of exception which has become the normal state of Western societies rather than the exception, so is the starting assumption of '*the state of exception*' (Agamben 2004), it is impossible to simply return to a state of law. The terms of 'state' and 'law' are themselves in question now.

Prince Prospero and the state of exception

Prince Prospero is a classical sovereign, a head of the state who owns it and therefore has full power over and responsibility for it. In the moment of crisis, a plague threatening the existence of the whole state he is capable and legally justified to declare the state of exception. Moving away from the normal living together in the space of the country he chooses a certain part of the population to retreat with him into a fortified abbey. This is a sovereign exception with a double twist: concrete people are singled out to exist outside the world they belong to, but neither as naked life, which can be killed, nor as sacrifice. The stepping outside the normal was meant to set a necessary change so that those left inside the normal were in fact excluded – from survival. The sovereign includes himself and with that act also proves symbolically his existence inside and outside the legal order at the same time. He decides about the exception and chooses where his place shall be in this case: outside, i.e. inside the abbey which was perceived as the future of further living.

The double exclusion, the separation of the 'gay society' in the abbey from the people suffering from the plague, and from the plague itself, didn't work. Considering the logic of the sovereign exception, Prospero's decision looks like a good illustration of what is at stake, though in a peculiar, ironic way. Those who are excluded from a polity represent the naked life which can be killed. The Red Death took the liberty to refuse the meaning of this exclusion which was intended as an inclusion: the polity excluded itself from the larger community of the state to include themselves into the 'true' polity, the one which should survive. An exclusion not of an other, but of the core, at least so this is their self-perception, themselves to save the polity as far as possible: an exclusion as inclusion.

The other exclusion, the intended exclusion of the risk which should have remained outside, didn't work either. Included by exclusion, it waited for its realization which inevitably came. The Red Death was implicitly invited. It serves as a metaphor for the impossibility of excluding something which is inherent in that from which it should be excluded, and this precludes that it is being removed. The Red Death can, therefore, be considered as a manifestation of the latent risk which lies at the basis of every global financial system. Those securities which during the crisis turned out to be not tradable any more and with that turned out to be of no value even if their underlying still holds a cash flow, were called toxic, an almost irritatingly synonymous image as the Red Death.

Securitization (of debt)

The securitization of debt, namely of mortgages, is at the core of the global financial crisis starting in 2008 (Mian and Sufi 2008; Sinn 2009). The following will be an attempt to interpret the realization of the risk, which was the starting point of the crisis, along the lines of the argument developed here as a form of Red Death invited by a sovereign exception.

Basic motivation of a bank to securitize credit risks is to reduce its risk position by selling a part of these contracts to another party so that these risks can be removed from its own balance sheet. Sold in this way they do not count for the base capital any more and the bank wins room for new business with a different risk balance. The limitation of the volume of credits, or to be more precise, the exposure as set by regulation, is linked to the base capital of the bank. Although this seemingly clear regulation is subject to a lot of complicated rules that interpret what base capital is and to what extent exposures have to be counted for the limit, it sets a limit for taking risks. A second motivation lies of course in the opportunities the markets offer when organizing the construction of a securitization and its trading. This sounds like the perfect world for a bank: they can solve a problem by selling it, and profit from the creation of a demand.[4]

The common way for reducing the risk position is a securitization. At its very basis, a securitization of debt is a sale of claims for payment resulting from debt.

The plural in 'claims' is essential here: it is never a single claim which is sold, it is a variety of claims which is bundled into a security. The aim is to sell the whole bundle to an investor or to create a security which is tradable. The principle sounds easy; the operation to make it work is complex.

There are at least three parties involved in the securitization: the originator, i.e. the bank selling the claims as underlying; an investment bank or a fund to organize the sales of the newly created security and with that organizing the financing; and for each securitization a company is founded, the so-called special purpose vehicle (SPV). The SPV has to coordinate the cash flows between the investors and the original debtors. In case of a true sale securitization the complete claims are transferred to the SPV. The originator transfers the risk to the SPV and the risk is transformed into a tradable security.

The initial invention of securitization and transferring the risk to other parties in order to win back opportunities for new business with a different risk structure was taken further with a logical step. The initially defensive move of getting rid of selected portfolios of loans once problems arise became a business in itself. In the case of the mortgage-backed security (MBS) mortgages are accepted not to keep them in the bank to profit from the interest paid by the homeowners, but from the beginning with the intention to securitize them and form other products with the mortgages as underlying. The mortgages were securitized to remove the complete transaction from the balance sheet, and the risk that the homeowners cannot meet their payment obligations transferred as well, so that the risks have no effect any more on the originator. The security, however, does not have the same transparency as other interest-based securities where there is one clearly identifiable issuer who guarantees the payment. Securitizations are very often constructed with several layers of assets with different creditworthiness and a hierarchy of priority payments becomes part of the security's construction. These securities were rated to achieve a minimum of transparency for investors. In fact, the rating hid the increasing complexity in the construction of these securities.

As long as everything is running normally, this represents a perfect money-making machine. The originating bank wins new room for business by accepting a *disagio*, the investors profit from a higher interest, the investment bank from fees and the trading of the security, all other participants, such as rating agencies, lawyers and others, profit from fees for their contributions in setting up the security. 'Normal' then means that the original borrowers, the homeowners, pay the interest, even if the interest rate is rising, and the redemption. As long as the losses do not rise above the calculated level, the security is still fine. If the risks are realized – when too many homeowners are not able to meet their obligations – the securities having these mortgages as underlying cannot pay their interest and lose value which immediately shows its effect on the balance sheets of those banks and other institutions which have these securities in their portfolio.

It should not be overlooked that the securitization of mortgages is by no means a new invention where the first application led to the disaster. In his book *Liar's Poker* Michael Lewis (1990) described the creation of these instruments and the negotiations about the necessary changes in legislation in the USA and gave the chapter describing the success the telling title: 'The fat men and their marvellous money machine'. In 1989 he summarized the result of the modern gold rush, which the 1980s were for traders: 'Never before have so many unskilled twenty-four-year-olds made so much money in so little time as we did this decade in New York and London' (Lewis 1990: 9). After the internet bubble at the beginning of this century the securitization of debt was a valuable means for banks to clean their balance sheets of bad credits. In the years to follow, the principle of securitization remains the same, but certainly decisive changes applied: the sheer volume traded, unimaginable US$58 trillion (Cox 2008) and with that a change in the structure of the risk takers from a few identifiable institutions to all market participants possible, including private investors.

The picture drawn here so far is already complex enough, but still a bit simplistic. Reality offered at least two more layers to complicate the situation. Of course the risk contained in the MBS was hedged as well. The instruments for that are credit default swaps (CDS). In fact this can be interpreted as an insurance against the default of payments in the original contracts, the underlyings of the MBS. There is nothing wrong with the principle, but these kinds of derivatives have nowadays reached a volume which is dramatically threatening the global economy. Originally these instruments were created to help companies deal with the risks involved in their business. The problem is that exactly the same instruments can be used for leveraged speculation, a kind of speculation which has nothing to do with any underlying business. Additionally this kind of business does not necessarily need a bank. So a lot of the speculation takes place outside the regulated banking sector in the category named 'other financial institutions' in the statistics of the Bank of International Settlements (King and Rime 2010: 28): 'smaller banks, mutual funds, money market funds, insurance companies, pension funds, hedge funds, currency funds and central banks among others', but also companies which engage in speculation with financial institutions. The result is a gigantic volume of outstanding contracts.

Additionally it was possible and took place on a large scale that the MBS were sold short, that is that there are market participants placing their bet against the stability of the system. Selling short means that these investors put their money in contracts that enable them to buy the securities, when it becomes clear that too many homeowners cannot meet their obligations and the whole construction collapses. These short sales could also be used to create new products that were completely artificial: MBS with no mortgages as underlying, in fact with no underlying at all. They were just relying on short sellers and created the opposite position for them (Lewis 2008).

What can Agamben's thinking of the exception add to an understanding of the risk involved in the global financial markets? His writing takes place in the realm of the political state and its relationship to its citizens. The structure of his argument, however, can be used to explore other relationships of inclusion and exclusion as well.

Financial markets and the state of exception

Reading the global financial crisis on the background of the Red Death and Agamben's thinking of sovereignty leads to an exciting conclusion. Risk should have been disposed of by a sovereign exception, so can the starting point be formulated here? The additional insight is: in the absence of a sovereign. The risk turned out to be an included excluded, as with the Red Death, and even as in the definition of the sovereign exception as inclusion of what belongs to the thing it should have been excluded from, which in a second step proved its belonging by realization. The similarity to a sovereign exception is intriguing, although a decisive change is involved. The sovereign exception is transferred to another level: from the polity to an individual organization – a bank. The multiple sovereign exceptions by a plethora of market participants concerning a huge part of the financial markets created a state of exception on a global level without a single sovereign decision involved. There is no Prince Prospero, no sovereign on the international financial markets.

Any law which could be applicable is on the contrary part of the state of exception in two dimensions. First it is a result of a ratification of an international agreement on regulation, as in the case of the Basel II accord. Hosted by the Bank for International Settlement (BIS), the central bank of the national central banks, the Basel Committee, consisting of representatives of ten national banks, developed this global regulation in negotiation with national associations of the banking industry, governments and other central banks. To implement this regulation internationally, it has to be transformed into national law or regulation. It is expected that any discussion which could prevent the ratification, was led before the accord was finalized by the Basel Committee. Already this can be seen as a substantial hollowing out of democracies: that more and more rules negotiated by national executives are just ratified by the legislatives instead of being initiated and developed in parliamentary discussions. As a result it can be stated that the sovereign, the legislative of democracies, is absent on international markets. Second, the absence of the sovereign at global level is replaced by individual actors at global level. Banks have their headquarters in a nation state and fall under the legislation of this state, and nation states have an interest in strong banks in their country. But the banks can establish subsidiaries anywhere in the world where a different legislation beyond the Basel II accord may hold. Even if the Basel II regulation is adequately transformed into national law in every country in the world, the combination of this regulation with other national laws offers the opportunity of finding holes.[5] In the void created by the absence of a supranational sovereign, e.g. in form of a global regulatory body for the financial markets, individual actors operate effectively as in a state of exception. There is no binding global law. It is, in fact, an anomy. Third, the complexity of the relations of market participants makes it extremely difficult to define the normal state. Homeowners looking for credit; banks granting it and transforming the resulting mortgages into an underlying for a securitization; SPVs looking for investors; investment banks selling the securities; investors out of the reach of banking regulation like hedge funds, who invest with leverages of their own capital and credits, which are again granted by banks; the state as the sovereign of national legislation and national regulating authorities form a melange in which the risk remains hidden as it is partly out of the focus of a coherent risk management.

The sovereign decision took place on another level. It has been pointed out that at the fundament of the development, which is analysed here as the state of exception, lies the neo-liberal market fundamentalism (e.g. Klimecki and Willmott 2009; Wong 2009). Regulation and the state as such prevent the markets from taking their advantage of realizing the chances of individual action, which in the end is also to the advantage of all, is the neo-liberal conviction. The absence of a sovereign is deeply implemented in the thinking of the market proponents. The market-oriented discourse has acted as a stalking horse for unrestricted and only loosely regulated financial markets (Cloke 2009). Deregulation offered financial markets the space needed for unconditional growth into any direction. The actors on the international financial markets did what is expected of them: using the space offered inventively, interpreting the rules to make them work for their own advantage. In a world where the market is seen as the instance which is alone able to solve problems of the economy in an adequate speed, the search for holes in rules is implicitly accepted, even encouraged. Adaptations to changing circumstances are possible and inventions enabled. However, there is a risk involved as well. Ironically in this case, it is the risk of dealing with risks. The neo-liberal assumption that self-regulation of the markets works best to achieve stable growth and avoiding risk which destabilizes the system has been proven wrong: 'The last six months have made it abundantly clear that voluntary regulation does not work' Christopher Cox, the chairman of the Securities and Exchange Commission said in his testimony to the US Senate (Cox 2008) and Alan Greenspan, former head of the US Central Bank admitted: 'I made a mistake in presuming that the self-interest of organizations, specifically banks and others, was such that they were best capable of protecting their own shareholders' (quoted in Jain 2009: 98). Basel II, though aiming at the right mechanisms, i.e. the capital adequacy of risk, was not able to prevent the crisis. The banking industry found the hole in regulations to exclude the risk from being covered by the regulation.

The state of exception should have been declared solely by a sovereign authority, but there is no supranational sovereign. It was not considered necessary, as the above quotes demonstrate. If it had existed, it would not have declared the state of exception for good reasons. Nevertheless, the crisis has a repercussion on the national sovereigns. It was facilitated by ignorance of effects and cross-effects of the securitization on a global scale including non-banks, i.e. non-regulated institutions as well. The fact of a sovereign exception was only realized by national states as the effects had already repercussed on the whole financial system. The sovereign in the form of the national state had to act as lender of last resort without having the authority of a global sovereign who can determine the relationship of law and exception and the adherence of the force of law in the global financial system.

The huge difference, however, is that deregulation was never thought of as an exception. It was considered as the new normalcy. This new normalcy, the absence of the sovereign and his regulation, was the basis for a state of exception no one held possible, as the representatives of the sovereign like Alan Greenspan admitted in the quote above. A state of exception emerged out of a situation without a sovereign announcing it and without reference to a sovereign who could stop it. On the contrary: it emerged from a retreat of the sovereign. Another consequence is that no sovereign can be made accountable for the result. The situation can be described as organized or structured irresponsibility: the absence of a responsible body in the presence of a damage. This will be topic of the chapter on risk and responsibility.

The sovereign decision to exclude risk can be interpreted as the separation of risk from product (Cloke 2009). Risk becomes an entity of its own, and can be traded. It became a sign just for itself. The results were completely opaque markets. Investors as locusts, as they were already called during an election campaign in Germany in 2005 (Pelzer 2009), operating in a hyperreal world: 'The hyperreal economy is an economy of signs, detached from real things, but nonetheless having the ability to affect real things' (McGoun 1997: 108). Criticized as the 'shadow banking system' (Weitzner and Darroch 2009) the global financial market entered into the state of exception where it is uncontrollable by definition.

The world today exists in a permanent state of exception, and democracy is hollowed out, as is Agamben's provoking thesis. This thesis was used to describe the sphere of the global financial markets with a crucial extension. The state of exception was intentionally created to exist in the absence of the sovereign who would be able to end it. This development led to a result which is contrary to the intentions of the Basel accord. Risks should have become more transparent and covered by base capital, but actually the regulation was seen as an incentive to devise means of moving risk from balance sheets (Klimecki and Willmott 2009).

The separation of risk from product leads to the assumption that risk can be excluded from the business completely. The state of exception, however, can be seen as the big party before the end. The risk is hedged – a remarkable term: hedged, or perhaps even castellated like Prospero's abbey? – defined out of the system, excluded, so that it was not perceived any more. It was just seen as the occasion for the pub crawl of the virtual bet. *The bank was amply provisioned. The external world could take care of itself.... All these and security were within. Without was the risk.* A few words were replaced in the preceding sentences: abbey with bank, and risk placed instead of the Red Death. The risk has not been disposed of, even if the regulation was met and the originating risk could be taken off the risk position and the balance sheet. But the exclusion of the risk from the originating bank does not mean that the risk vanishes. It remains in the same world of hyperreal finance. The link is maintained. The party, to paraphrase the situation on Prospero's abbey, went on until the Red Death decided that he has to react to the oblivion of the community. He demonstrated that he was never absent, but only needed to wait until a certain volume was reached to identify MBS as another bubble to burst. The realization of the concrete risk did not hit the originator immediately, although this bank was responsible for the original acceptance of the risk. But it hit the bank as it was part of the financial system that developed this kind of security and insofar as it was engaged in the trading and the hedging of the securities created with the mortgages whose risk should have never returned to it. Risks don't vanish, they are realized or not. They remain included in the system despite the fact that individual actors intend to take a sovereign decision to exclude them.

Agamben's take is that it is impossible to simply return to a state of law from the state of exception. The world has moved on and the new situation needs a completely new evaluation. The terms of 'state' – in the double meaning of the nation state and the state we are in – and 'law' themselves are in question now (Agamben 2004: 102). This would be the task before decisions on new institutions and regulations are taken.

4 The displaced world of risk

Risk management as alienated risk (perception?)

Locusts as a metaphor for evil behaviour

Locusts bear a distinctive image. They are always associated with their appearance in incredible masses of individual insects which fall upon an area to completely eat all plants, leaving the area devastated and the harvest gone. The insects are not directly dangerous to humans, but when appearing so massively, they destroy the basis for living. Locust plagues are not predictable in the long run. The perception is that they appear out of nowhere, with no defence possible. The expression has, as will be elaborated later, biblical connotations, making it a well-established term that can easily be used in public discussion.

Franz Müntefering, chairman of the Social Democrats in Germany, used this expression during an election campaign in 2005 to characterize the behaviour of a certain type of investor:

> Some investors do not waste any thoughts on the people whose jobs they destroy, they remain anonymous, do not have a face, pounce upon companies like swarms of locusts, do them to death and continue on their way. We are fighting against this form of capitalism.
>
> (Franz Müntefering 2005, author's translation)

When labelling hedge fund investors 'locusts', implying that they ravenously fall upon the country, Müntefering was simply giving expression to a widespread feeling of the public concerning globalized investment methods; after all, it was election time.

A brief look into the bible reveals an interesting context. Locusts are mentioned in both the Old and the New Testament. The image of the plague is given in the book of Exodus. Yahweh used it as a punishment for the Egyptians and the Pharaoh, who did not want to let Moses and his people leave the country as they had been told by Yahweh.

> Else, if thou refuse to let my people go, behold, tomorrow will I bring the locusts into thy coast: And they shall cover the face of the earth, that one cannot be able to see the earth: and they shall eat the residue of that which is

> escaped, which remaineth unto you from the hail, and shall eat every tree which groweth for you out of the field.
>
> (Bible, Exod., 10:4–6)

This is a profound threat and when carried out turned the country into devastation. In the last book of the Old Testament, the book of Joel, rules were given on how to treat a locust plague, again seen as a punishment by the Lord. A terrible plague of locusts covered Judah and destroyed the crops. Joel sees the devastation wrought by these creatures as a foretaste of the coming judgement of God, the 'day of the Lord'. Joel therefore urges the people to turn from their sin and back to God. Joel's triple call for repentance is followed and finally recognized by God who will sit to judge the surrounding nations who were Israel's enemies so that the Hebrews can live in peace.

The last book of the New Testament, the 'revelation', or the 'apocalypse', is remarkably more sinister in its description of the locusts' task. Its negative image resulting from their capability of destruction is added by a decisive ability to torture. Those people who refuse to worship God face a terrible fate. The locusts were given power like that of scorpions, but not to kill those people who did not have the seal of God on their foreheads, but to torture them for five months. During these days, says the Book of Revelation (9:3–6), men will seek death, but will not find it, death will elude them.

The dynamic of the three parts is clear. Locusts serve as a punishment by God. It is the natural evil, following its own needs to eat, or, as in the apocalypse, as a metaphor reminding of its own past effects, but combined with the terror of another animal. The effect shall be consciously endured pain, not death as may be the result of a scorpion's sting. It is a punishment for moral evil, the Pharaoh's hardened heart, an opportunity to turn from their sin and turn back to God, or as revenge for the enemies of Christianity. The close link between the moral and the natural evil, i.e. the latter being a consequence of the former, started to weaken as soon as the question was raised why God – as the good as such – can tolerate natural evil, disasters like earthquakes, floods and pestilence, and accept the misery and death of many who did no wrong or where such a punishment was seen as immensely inappropriate. Theodicy, the defence of God in juridical terms, was at the centre of intellectual debate during the late seventeenth up to the mid-eighteenth century. It climaxed after 1755, the date of the Lisbon earthquake. This incident was particularly destructive as it was followed by a huge fire and a flooding which destroyed much of the centre of Lisbon and a lot of lives and valuable property, which had been saved during the earthquake itself. It was near enough to be projected onto the own situation in other European capitals. Theodicy's dispute about the explanations of the natural evil came to a secular conclusion. Is an earthquake an intervention of God to remind humans who were all too interested in worldly affairs that there is something more important, and that the adequate reaction to this intervention is fasting and repentance as the clerics declared with the intention in mind to regain influence? Or is the adequate reaction to deal with the consequences, as the Portuguese prime minister is reported to have answered his king: 'bury the dead, and feed the living' (Neiman 2004: 364). He acted in a modern way, and with this worldly crisis management of immediately burying the dead to prevent epidemics, requisitioning grain to fight hunger, and mobilizing the military to prevent looting, he achieved a return to normal life. The more earthquakes were seen as natural incidents, the easier they could be integrated into our worldview as part of life, and the way back to normal life seen a practical problem. Since Lisbon catastrophes do not contain any moral value any more, it is possible to prevent their negative consequences. If not, it is human error. Natural evil does not have a link to moral evil any more, and because of this insight, no meaning (Neiman 2004: 76). This insight of enlightenment thinking does not prevent us from spending a lot of energy evaluating human responses to natural disaster and apportioning blame and moral responsibility, e.g. for post-disaster errors. However, this confirms the shift of emphasis from the intrinsic moral evil to the human responsibility. By emphasizing its historicity, Rousseau insisted on the contingent character of evil. Evil is fundamentally human and therefore it is possible to understand how it is created and how it proceeds (Neiman 2004: 85). From this perspective it becomes much more interesting to investigate what the evil does to us than defining its essential characteristics (Neiman 2004: 34f.).

Risk: globalized calculations of return[1]

'Risk' is a term so often used and describing such a self-evident part of our lives we tend to believe that it has been in use since the beginning of human societies. It has not. Luhmann (1991) claims that ancient advanced civilizations had developed different concepts for dealing with analogous problems and therefore did not need a term like 'risk'. Of course uncertainty about the future has always been a topic. Divination was the solution mainly used. According to Tedlock (2001: 189), 'divination is a way of exploring the unknown in order to elicit answers (that is, oracles) to questions beyond the range of ordinary human understanding'. Divination could not guarantee reliable knowledge and certainty, but at least it provided a decision which did not cause the anger of gods. For the introduction of risk a profound change must have taken place. The description is part of Peter Sloterdijk's book *Im Weltinnenraum des Kapitals* (2006), which only inadequately translates as 'inside the world-interior of capital'. This very strange formulation works much better in the German original and hints at the result of his view on globalization. Angry about the public view of globalization and its coverage in the media, he develops a view of globalization and its consequences from a philosophical point of view. His somehow provoking idea is that we can quite reliably set the beginning and the end of globalization. The beginning is marked by Columbus' discovery of America; the end can be set to the end of the Second World War. Today we are living in a globalized world, i.e. completed globalization, and have to face the consequences which we, the Europeans, started with our journeys over the oceans. Globalization marks the transition of meditative spherical thinking to the practice of capturing the globe.

Sloterdijk turns the lesson, that other cultures prove the conviction of an immutable local order of things to be contingent and possibly completely different from the own one, to the insight that this is not the loss of the middle but the loss of periphery. Nothing can be kept at a distance any more. The local is not the centre of the world – such a centre does not exist. To leave the local involves the uncertainty if one will come back, the uncertainty of return. Exactly this marks the difference: physical return of the person also means return of goods – the ship, and potentially what was found or traded abroad. Manning a ship is a severe investment, so the return of investment becomes a crucial factor. Taking credit, investing in equipment and setting sail for discoveries is a race for dubious opportunities in opaque distant markets. Discoveries, claims Sloterdijk (2006: 78) are just a special form of investment. Emerging capitalism required a different method of dealing with uncertainty, with the possibility of loss of goods by wreckage, i.e. the inability of returning the investment, of paying the credit rates. The new behaviour is about taking risks and at the same time about dealing with the risk, diversifying it by inviting others to share the monetary consequences of the risk and the potential profit. Ideas of risk and insurance require a completely different type of human, one who is the architect of his own future and does not wait to receive it from God. This type of human made the experience that it is good to learn from your mistakes but it is better to learn by debt. The fierce Copernican discussion about the earth circulating around the sun hides the main fact that in modernity the situation is better described as the money circulating around the globe (ibid.: 79).

Sloterdijk plays with words here: a risk culture of television ('*fernsichtiges Risikohandeln*', Sloterdijk 2006: 86), with *tele* referring to distance and vision in the double meaning of view and visionary, which is more than clear view, it includes the vision of the distance which is not seen from the point of departure, but is aimed at a vision of what to find beyond the horizon. The restructuring of European action from stability to practices and mentalities of risk action explains the somehow surprising, almost mysteriously successful offensive power of the first generations of discoverers. The readiness to take risks is fuelled by the compulsion, the obligation to gain profits to pay off the credits. Going to sea always needed luck to survive, but now it became more than a fate, it introduced the die: the opportunity. It becomes possible to calculate success and failure, gains and losses. And it needed planning, in other words a turn to the future, a futurization of governmental, entrepreneurial and epistemic action. Taking risk became the central aspect of modernity.

One thing has become clear: in this world there is no place for natural evil anymore. Any idea of insurance is blasphemous when the intention is to avoid, or at least weaken, the negative consequences of natural catastrophes. Probabilistic calculation to evaluate the chances, to make future predictable, increasingly developed and used in the unfolding risk culture is a move *Against the Gods* (Bernstein 1996). Risk management is unthinkable when fate is the predominant conception of the future. However, a crucial difference emerges. In asking the question 'what is a risk' it is necessary to propose what can be dealt with, what can be managed as risk and what not. The discussion started in gambling. Throwing the die and recording the results to compare them were among the first steps in statistics. Western societies became increasingly fascinated in quantification. Almost anything was measured and calculated to find out about what is normal, what can be normalized, what can be seen as deviation. This process created an avalanche of numbers with the intention of *The Taming of Chance* (Hacking 1990).

One of the most influential differences in risk calculation is that of Frank Knight. He insisted on separating risk and uncertainty. Although risk in everyday use is about uncertainties, there is a fundamental difference resulting from the possibility to measure uncertainty. Knight names measurable uncertainty risk, because in becoming measurable it is not uncertain at all. Uncertainty is restricted to cases of the non-quantifiable type (Knight 1921/1940). Luhmann (1991) considers Knight's definition as ossified into a dogma so that any further development of the term risk is confronted with the reproach of not having understood the term sufficiently (Luhmann 1991: 9). He claims that there is no definition of risk which would satisfy scientific demands and proposes an unusual difference instead. Regarding the fact that any risk presupposes a decision which has damage as a possible consequence, the contingency of the damage is clearly referred to and the double contingency of the decision comes into focus: the contingent damage is caused by a contingent decision. Taking another decision would have prevented the damage. Certainty as the opposite for risk is misleading. Not deciding always means preventing risk *and* chance. The better difference is between risk and danger. This presupposes an uncertainty on future possible damages. Either the damage can be ascribed to a decision, then it is called a risk; or the damage is caused externally, then it is a danger (Luhmann 1991: 30). Risks are the consequences of decisions, but we are exposed to dangers.

After globalization – living in the globalized world

What about locusts then? They are a natural phenomenon which belongs to the fauna in many regions and are even seen as delicate food. Where they appear in masses, as a locust plague, they are a danger to which we are exposed. This plague is not attributable to a human decision. Therefore they cannot be a risk. Seen from the two perspectives, as a biblical punishment and as a natural danger, the metaphor of locusts pouncing upon companies and doing them to death, as was claimed in the election campaign, can be seen as poorly chosen and misleading. However, playing with the meaning of the word for locust in German, *Heuschrecken*, may reveal the connection between investors and locusts.[2] When we separate the word into its two ingredients we face *Heu* – hay, and *Schrecken* – terror, horror. Hay in German has a close connotation to money: 'he has money like hay' means that this person owns immeasurable[3] amounts of money: the Dagobert Duck phenomenon. Exactly this, the overwhelming liquidity of the financial markets plus the anonymity of money as a neutral medium of exchange provide the feeling of unease turning into horror, when the own employer is affected by actions of hedge funds or private equity funds. The growth of the financial markets is indeed breathtaking. One of the most important markets today, the financial derivatives,[4] were so unimportant – and in fact most of them illegal in the early 1970s – that no reliable figures about their volumes exist (MacKenzie and Millo, 2003: 109). According to the Triennial Central Bank Survey on foreign exchange market activity (BIS 2010) the global *daily* turnover in this part of the derivatives market rose to US$4 trillion, marking a 20 per cent increase compared to 2007.

The interesting fact about the comparison of hedge funds, private equity and locusts is the origin of hedging as an instrument of risk management. Risks shall be hedged by adequate strategies of distributing them on markets. Originally derivatives were developed to deal with specific economic risks, e.g. the changes in currency rates. Typically a company in Europe exporting goods to the USA would, once a contract about a certain delivery is fixed, sell the expected amount of US currency for a fixed rate to its bank. The company wins the certainty of its future turnover value on the one hand and accepts the price for the instrument and the loss of the chance to get more in local currency if the rates change accordingly on the other. These businesses called swaps have been in existence for a very long time. Traditionally banks served as agents and tried to find corresponding companies looking for euros. Today banks still take over the risk and try to equalize them with corresponding risks themselves. Due to the growth of the market and the instruments becoming more and more abstract, i.e. that they can be traded without underlying business, there is no need for an exactly matching counterpart on the business side anymore. Nowadays international currency markets represent a volume many times over what is demanded by 'real' business. That instruments are traded above what is necessary for covering other businesses provides the market with the liquidity for those deals demanded by industry. There is no lack of counterparts. These abstract products, called derivatives, are not restricted to foreign exchange. In fact they can be and have been developed for almost every security or product of the banking market. Once instruments for diversifying risks inherent in concrete businesses, derivatives transformed into products with their own risk structure. The markets are characterized by a deep belief that these risks can be calculated and a portfolio built which diversifies the risks in a way that profits are certain. The strategies of hedging can also be used for portfolio management and a portfolio created just consisting of derivatives. Besides the more traditional strategy of trading in long and short stock and bonds, this is a strategy of hedge funds. These funds are restricted to a limited number of investors who are able to invest huge sums with speculative interest. Assets under management total a sum about US$1,300 billion in 2006 (Schmidt 2007). The assets are multiplied by credits. Combined with the leverage effect of the financial derivatives, the liquidity pooled by hedge funds has an immense effect and influence on international financial markets.

The business model of private equity companies is different, though it is also a result of existing liquidity looking for more attractive investments than straight shares and bonds. They aim at buying complete companies, which they think can be sold for a much higher price in the short or medium term, often via going public. Initially these funds aimed at medium-sized companies with problems, at least with a turnaround fantasy. Private equity found funds to collect money from investors, but the takeovers are run with high amounts of credits. With the takeover they explicitly aim at influence on the management. Usually a restructuring combined with a downsizing is seen as the appropriate means to increase the value of the company. Besides the loss of jobs, their activity is often criticized due to the financing of the initial buying. The credits are taken by a company founded for the takeover, which after the successful takeover is merged with the acquired company, including the debt. In effect the company being taken over is financing the takeover. This proceeding increases the pressure on profitability and makes job redundancies more probable. Hedge funds, in case they invest in shares, also massively try to influence management's decisions. They aim at seats in supervisory boards to opt for restructurings, sales of parts of the company, or even buying back their own shares. The intended effect lies in a sharp increase in the share price.

Both forms of investment quote returns of at least 15 per cent a year, often much higher. Unlike banks, there is no regulation and supervising authority and therefore almost no transparency. Given the influence these funds have, and the effect their strategies have on local employment markets in case of private equity or the influence on the stability of international financial markets as in the case of hedge funds, the lack of external reporting and transparency, combined with the huge margins of the funds, as well as the immense salaries and bonuses of the traders, provoke a public reaction. This can be an economically informed analysis like former German chancellor Helmut Schmidt's long article 'supervise the new grand speculators!' (Schmidt 2007). Schmidt does not use the term *Casino Capitalism* (Strange 1986) to describe recent developments in financial markets, but his quote of the volumes to be earned gives a hint into this direction: in 2006 the five largest investment banks in New York paid about US$36 billion to management and employees. This sum is equivalent to the complete sum of new credits taken by the German treasurer in 2006 (Schmidt 2007).

So what we see in the case of the locusts is a profound mixture of images of different times and different classes. Nevertheless the metaphors work and unfold their effect. They transform an uncertainty into a well-known image of the past which is ready for interpretation as a biblical plague, of which everybody knows that they have lost their significance as a form of divine punishment. Locusts are not sent; after all, it is just a metaphor. The metaphor works as a representation of an abstract threat transformed into a danger which, potentially, can be prevented. But the metaphor of a locust plague also implies effects on the basis of living. It destroys a season's valuable work of farming. The catastrophe arrives from behind the hills, it is coming from abroad, and with the new forms of the financial markets the effect of a globalized world enters the stage. If not shipwrecked, the vessels returned, hopefully full of precious material, was the calculation in times of discovery. Return on investment is the movement of all movements to which all acts of risk action oblige. It gives every action of capital a nautical characteristic: by the return of the swimming capital from the long distance journey the madness of expansion turns into the rationality of profits (Sloterdijk 2006: 134).

Postsocial relationships: acting in a projected environment

On its voyage around the globe, risk and risk management have been abstracted and displaced several times to return in a guise hardly imaginable as risk or its management by those confronted with these strategies. The original, physical risk of being shipwrecked that the sailors had to face was transformed into an investment risk shared by investors. Their possibility of loss may ultimately lead to the loss of assets, but not to the loss of life. The pooling of investments to shares to be traded at exchanges furthered the abstraction. It is not the concrete investment for a special journey to take part in the profits of the concrete load brought back, it is the expectation of future profits of a company investing in vessels, and of course in other profitable businesses. The increasing abstraction and complexity called for special treatments of risk. Risk management should not only prevent accidents but also control the volatility of profits due to influences beyond the own production: change of currency rates, natural disasters influencing the price of raw materials, external influences on the price of their own products etc. Derivatives were introduced of which the value depends on an expected future value of an underlying asset. Risk is transferred from those parties seeking certainty for their production to those accepting the risk for a price. Trading derivatives means a displacement of the risk. It is transferred from the underlying asset to its derivative. On this way risk is also distilled and purified. 'This distillation of risk, from asset to future to option on future, produces an essence of risk, exorcised from assets that are now seemingly secure once more' (Lilley and Lightfoot 2006: 384). The sailors, however, have vanished from this scene. They were left to handle their physical risk and, if they failed, became part of the financial losses. What has been exorcised is not the risk, it is the financial consequence of risks becoming reality – for the investors, not the sailors.

This displacement (or, *différance*) of financial risk management from the underlying risk was accompanied by another development. Money, as Simmel (1907/1989) already stated, has become the central organizing principle and affects social relationships, the mental condition of those involved and the logical structure of realities. Knorr Cetina and Bruegger (2002a, 2002b) and Knorr Cetina and Preda (2007) drive this basic insight much further. They researched the world of traders in international currency markets and realized a change from concrete interactions with counterparts to an enactment of the world of trades on the screens in front of the traders. Any information about the market, any offer and any own activity, the generation of information by providers like Reuters', Bloomberg or Telerate, as well as the results of data collections of the individual banks, are completely represented on the screen. The market does not exist somewhere out there; it is created on the screen. Sales and Buys match on the screen and not in direct interaction of traders on an exchange floor, or by telephone. The business itself had already become virtual before. Therefore it can be claimed that the fact that representation on screens has replaced the reality is just an expression of the virtuality of the businesses themselves. A deal which refers to an underlying, but where every participant in the market assumes that a delivery of the underlying will never take place, lacks a direct link to traditional business which, after trading and negotiating about prices, will be delivered. The delivery is, or was, the *sine qua non* of business – and that is what ships were for. The displacement of trade from delivery has been a characteristic of many financial deals. The interviews in trading rooms led Knorr Cetina and Bruegger (2002a) to the conclusion that they researched business in a postsocial world. Currency trading is entirely exteriorized and embodied on computer screens. With the term 'postsocial relationships' they refer to new kinds of bonds[5] between humans and objects. One aspect of the change of the structure of relationships is the clash between the postsocial world of trading and the social world of those being traded as part of the objects traded. Although the activities of hedge funds and private equity funds go beyond currency trading, they share the postsocial quality.

The transfer of the markets on to the screens enables the traders to position themselves simultaneously inside the market when becoming players in the overlapping networks, 'and to relate to the market on screen as exteriorized other, a sort of master-being that observes all transactions and includes their contextual conditions and motivations' (Knorr Cetina and Bruegger 2002a: 164). The screen as master-being, displacing the trader into a different (hyper-)reality alienates the trader from social relationships, as indirectly they always have been when considering an investment into a company. But with the screen as opposite instead of a human counterpart, the consciousness of being part of a social relationship, of a necessity for responsibility and ethics, simultaneously vanishes completely. The screens' crucial role becomes ontological:

> the screens do not, in their core elements, *re*present a reality 'out there', but are constitutive of it.... The screen is a building site on which a whole economic and epistemological world is erected. It is not simply a 'medium' for the transmission of other interactions.
>
> (Knorr Cetina and Bruegger 2002a: 166–167)

Financial markets have achieved a peculiar independence. The screen creates a different reality. Participants of these deals on the screen become oriented to the projected reality to which coordination and action respond (Knorr Cetina and Preda 2007: 126). However, although they seem to be created virtually, only existing on the screen, there is an interface to the markets on which there is still trading, even producing commodities and delivering them. Ownership of these companies is traded with shares. The exchange is the link where both worlds meet. Postsocial consideration of balance sheets, value of brands, aversion to business models different from the ruling opinion etc. conclude profit opportunities in papers and paper form and propose changes according to convictions shared in financial markets. The decisions on investment are clearly postsocial as they only refer to paper, numbers and prospects, assessment and judgement according to theories shared in the markets. Traders and fund managers have agency, they trade and the decision how to trade is left at their discretion. The flip side is the pressure to win. They have achieved a positive, active life form but can only maintain it when making adequate profit. What adequate means is defined by the investors in the fund. Those affected by the traders' and fund managers' seemingly independent decisions, the employees of companies bought by funds to be reshaped and sold again are consequentially passive. They are victimized. The burden of any decision to make the company more attractive to that market where traders are agents, is theirs.

Are the locusts back? Or, are investors locusts at all?

To perceive globalization as a finished process and to consider the life in a globalized world, where effects of distant decisions affect the lives of people in Europe from where globalization once started, is, seen from a theoretical perspective, a nice feedback loop. Another aspect cannot that easily be perceived. It derives from the postsocial characteristic of international financial markets which sets actors on the market into a peculiar opposition to people not being actors in these markets. Displaced, distilled and exorcised from risk: seen from the perspective of employees affected by decisions of financial agents, i.e. the voters Müntefering addressed, the risk seems to return as danger. In face of liquidity, pooled in funds, multiplied by credits, following postsocial rules of markets different from the life world, the locust plague suddenly seems to be not that bad a metaphor, at least not that badly chosen for polemical use. When Neiman claimed that naming an action evil points at its capacity to shake our faith into the world which we need for orientation (Neiman 2004: 34–35), then the feeling of those affected by hedge funds' and private equity funds' decisions as being exposed to evil becomes understandable. The money seems to be coming from beyond the hills, or, from the other side of the Atlantic. It is alien, or so it seems. The everyday understanding of risk is severely challenged. Risk as experienced in Casino Capitalism is a very one-sided pleasure: no risk, no fun – but the fun is exclusively reserved for those with agency. The risk is still theirs, the fun is on the screen – and in the enjoyment of the annual bonuses. The loss is reserved for those who are part of the object of gambling. However, even if we understand the polemical use of a phrase, we have to insist here that the image of the locusts is misleading. We do not talk about natural evil, i.e. a danger, we talk about moral evil, something entirely human made. The reintroduction of a discussion on ethics into the market is necessary. The agency of traders and fund managers is a consequence of an absence: 'A more general indication of the agency traders retain is the legal and commercial deregulation of these markets, the lack of a social censor, one might say, who restrains activities and prescribes their direction' (Knorr Cetina and Bruegger 2002a: 174). This should be the task of politicians and regulators, not just riding the waves of public indignation with the use of a misleading metaphor.

5 From 'risk and responsibility' to the risk of responsibility

> *I know, I did it.* It (the title) was already created in springtime. It was his proposal, and all of us liked it, because it expresses this responsibility. That's what he always cared about. He kept saying: 'I want liability, I want responsibility, for me as a human and for my oeuvre. I'll stand by it with my body and with everything what I instigate and for the irritation I bring into the world'.[1]

This title looks like an all too cheap showmanship on playing with alliterations, but it aptly summarizes a development which will be discussed in this chapter. Risk and responsibility are two terms that are closely linked. Anyone who takes a risk accepts the responsibility for the consequences, be it the positive outcome, the profit if everything goes according to the assumptions of the risky action, taking the losses or paying for the damage if the risk is realized. At least this would be the layperson's assumption. Considering the global financial crises of 2008, or other earlier implosions of bubbles, this seemingly self-evident connection appears questionable. 'The financial crisis can also be understood as a crisis of responsibility' (Thomä 2009). What has become different, where can changes be identified which can provide explanations for a disturbed relationship between risk and responsibility?

Risk is a term so deeply embedded into our daily language that a consideration of its content usually does not occur while it is used. Already a short reflection, however, reveals the complexity. Risk is the potential consequence of a decision. 'Potential' addresses two dimensions: uncertainty and futurity. A decision is called risky if it is unclear what the outcomes will be, and if the intended outcome will be reached on spot or if the outcome will be better or worse. If a bank grants a credit, will the debtor/borrower be able to return the credit sum and the interest within the time frame agreed? The risk is the loss of the money involved, but may also result from a more positive outcome than estimated. Judging from the perspective of the reliability of liquidity planning it is also a risk if the client pays back earlier. In principle, the better result of the deal – getting the money back earlier, no loss realized – has the character of realizing a risk nevertheless: it means less profit due to less interest paid due to the shorter time, but also the risk of not getting new business of comparable terms. Therefore it is usually foreclosed in the credit contract as a means of the reduction of risk.

By the time of closing the deal, risk means that the consequences are always in the future. Risk derives essentially from a contingent future. The reasons of the realization of the risk, a failure to pay back the credit, may be a consequence of the client's wrong business decisions in the past, but the potential loss will realize in the future; and when, or if this will take place at all, remains uncertain.

Considering future as uncertain involved a decisive change in the wake of modernism. The fundamental attitude of humans has changed. Divination to explore the unknown future was replaced by the thinking of risk and risk management in the form of sharing potential gains and losses and, in an organized and formalized way, by insurance. Risk replaced fate, future's status changed from being unknown and determined to being uncertain. Probabilistic calculation to evaluate the chances, to make future predictable is a precondition for the nature [*sic*!] of risk as we face nowadays: the almost complete change from external, or natural risks to manufactured risks (Giddens 1999). 'Manufactured' points to the characteristic that most of the risks we are exposed to are a result of human progression, of the development of science and technology. Progress does not mean that there is a development to a safer environment; on the contrary, science and technology go on in creating as many uncertainties as they dispel. Referring to Beck's work on risk society (1986) Giddens shares the assumption that manufactured risks have become part of the daily life of people who cannot interpret it anymore according to a given mode of reaction, by a stable social environment led by shared beliefs. We live in a society after tradition, Giddens (1999) states, reformulating the fact that life is no longer lived as fate. The future is opaque, essentially contingent in any aspect of life.

If risks are manufactured, a result of human progression, they are a result of decisions. For a long time this statement was not as self-evident as it seems. Both Giddens and Luhmann set themselves into sharp opposition to the most influential definition of risk by Frank Knight (1921/1940).[2] Knight named measurable uncertainty risk. By becoming measurable, so his argument, it is not uncertain at all. Uncertainty is reserved for cases of the non-quantifiable type. Luhmann (1991) set the framework differently. Either a damage can be ascribed to a decision, then it is called a risk; or a damage is caused externally, then it is a danger, he defined. For him there are no natural risks. Considering the far reaching consequences of decisions in the age of global warming it may well be argued that there are no dangers any more. Almost any natural catastrophe can be attributed to human decisions, or an accumulation of decisions. Linking risk to decision or manufacturing makes the central characteristic of risk clear: its futurity. A decision shall influence a result in the future. In the presence it is by no means clear if the intended result can be achieved or not, or if unintended consequences come along with the realization of the decision.

Bank's services can be described in terms of credit business, the organization of payments, financing companies, wealth management, etc. Such a concentration on functional aspects almost hides the central aspect which lies in all of these businesses. As the example of giving credit already showed, the central aspect of banking is a management of risks. It is not only the management of the bank's risks, it is about the risks involved in the business itself. Payments via banks reduce the risk of money transfer; financing of companies organized by a bank should make the process more transparent for investors and lay open the risks involved; wealth management is not just about increasing the fortune, it is also about investment strategies to handle the risk of the future. Banks provide specially designed products which help to transfer risk from one party to another. Banking is about the distribution of risk. Who shall bear the consequences of a realization of risk? Given this close link between risk and responsibility, an elaboration of their dynamic deems necessary.

With the notable exception of Anthony Giddens (1999), whose contribution to the discussion is quoted in the first part of this chapter's title, the direct link between risk and responsibility, however, seems to be a bit underdeveloped. Another link, the 'organized irresponsibility', presented as part of the whole argument on risk society by Ulrich Beck (1986, 1988) will be part of the argument in this chapter and further developed for the banking industry with the term of 'structured irresponsibility' which was introduced by Honegger *et al.* (2010) as a book title, but not discussed in the necessary depth. The relationship between risk and responsibility is disturbed, is my starting assumption, and this is not just a temporary imbalance which can be restored, but indicates the need for a fundamental reconsideration. Luc Boltanski's work on the bearer of responsibility combined with Derrida's consideration of responsibility with the absolute other is used to give an image of the situation of the financial industry in a state of structured irresponsibility.

Responsibility

Giddens (1999) is among the few authors who discuss the link between risk and responsibility. Responsibility is always connected to risk, he claims (Giddens 1999: 7). So it could not have been used before risk entered language. Responsibility, in contrast to the word responsible, seems to have come into the English language only by the end of the eighteenth century. The term now gained additional meaning in two more dimensions. While responsible only referred to the person as the origin of an event, to the actor as author linked with causality or agency, responsibility also refers to an ethical or accountable dimension. As a third dimension it means obligation and liability – which makes it most interesting when counterpoising it with risk. Giddens mentions six consequences that arise from the change of external, natural risk to manufactured risk regarding this connection to responsibility of which two are of substantial relevance for the discussion of risk in the financial industry.

Manufactured risk has an inherently ambiguous nature, Giddens claims, so that responsibility can neither easily be attributed or assumed (Giddens 1999: 8). The consequences described are:

- The emergence of organized irresponsibility
- The precautionary principle
- The shift of collective risks to individual responsibility in case of damage
- The future of the welfare state
- The emergence of a litigious society
- The two sides of risk: risk as potential damage and energising principle opening new horizons

Referring to Beck's work on the risk society (1986) he agrees that there is a fundamental change in the attribution of responsibility. Beck's famous term *organized irresponsibility* describes the fact that there are consequences of risks which clearly originate in human or organizational decisions, but that no individual responsibility can be identified. The impossibility of attribution goes beyond the attempt of individuals to hide behind the façade of the organization and their claim that they are just a tiny cog in the machine. It is a result of the increasing complexity of production processes where it becomes more and more difficult to find the causes of damages in individual human failures. The disaster of the BP oil platform in the Gulf of Mexico in 2010 gives an excellent illustration for the complexity of arguments involved here. Who is responsible? The CEO as the representative of BP, which as an organization didn't have an adequate disaster planning to react to these kinds of accidents? The company which manufactured the platform which exploded and caused the disaster? Who is the individual in that company who can be blamed for the explosion? The authorities which didn't control deep sea oil-drilling enough or not at all? The politics which prevented adequate legislation to enforce an increased safety standard? The markets which enforce cost reduction and steady profit increases? Or the society, addicted to oil consumption which motivates the companies to get all the fossil energy out of the planet no matter how high the price of collateral damage may be? The problem is exactly the difficulty of exact formulation: Beck's (1988) point is that the basic problem is a confusion of centuries. The nature of risk, its emergence and its consequences have changed in the twentieth century. The legal construction of industrial liability is still founded in the legal tradition of the nineteenth century. The legal responsibility for incidents in the present Western legislation has to look for an individual originator, an author of the event. But in a world with contested knowledge in almost any field, in an organized world of global economy it has become impossible to identify this single person which could be held responsible and liable. This figure is further explored later in the context of the bearer of responsibility.

The precautionary principle proposes to take action if there is a potential of harm independent of whether this potential harm is scientifically proven or not, and independent of the probability of its realization. Of course this encourages the discussion about the prevention of innovation due to the higher costs of implementation of new technologies or addresses the anxieties of the public. The influence of experts increases in this debate. Their role in risk taking is crucial but seen strangely uncritical.

The shift of collective risks to individual responsibility is closely linked to the future of the welfare state and the emergence of a litigious society. Considering health risks the shift becomes transparent. Although individuals get ill without being responsible for it, e.g. in case of flu or due to conditions at their workplace, in other cases illness is related to lifestyle practices. Today, smoking and the consequence of cancer are increasingly seen as personal risk though the ultimate consequence is not yet taken that the individual has to pay the price of treatment. The welfare state was, according to Giddens (1999, drawing on ideas of François Ewald), additional to the fight against inequality, also created as a form of collective risk management. The crisis of the welfare state then is not just the problem of it becoming too expensive, of taxes not being paid or too low, it is also a result of a change in the character of risk. The welfare state intervened in cases of unemployment, illness, disablement or losing a home to protect the individual who was assumed to be a helpless victim of forces out of her control. Manufactured risks shift the borders between risk and responsibility. Manufactured risks and the inherent shift of responsibility make unconditional help by the state seem impropriate. Giddens does not acknowledge here that manufactured risk in combination with organized responsibility leaves the individual as helpless against the realization of risk as she was in the nineteenth century, which led to the forming of the welfare state. His observation is that the consequence of organized irresponsibility is the litigious society. The search for responsibility is transferred to the realm of courts. This is on the one side what Beck (1986) meant: although there is no individual who can be held responsible as such, the search for this person is straining the courts beyond their capacity without bearing any really satisfying result. 'Where a common "contract of responsibility" has broken down, culpability can appear everywhere. Here indemnity has effectively been separated from causality' (Giddens 1999: 10). His example that he might be held responsible if someone is hurt through slipping on his garden path, however, is more a cynical neglect of the dramatic consequences for the individual who is not in the position to fight his demands through litigations. It is also an expression of the massive shift of power to the disadvantage of the mass of people.

The bearer of responsibility

Even if these arguments are interesting in themselves, they gain their power for the present context only if combined with considerations on the changes in capitalism taking place during the past thirty or forty years. Bauman (2000, 2008) has written a lot about these changes. What he coined 'liquid modernity' are those changes in late capitalism which render the foundations of living and working for the people in these societies less stable and reliable in any aspect of their lives. Luc Boltanski's work gives valuable insight into the consequences of the changes addressed by Giddens, but taking it to a much more powerful and insightful position, driving Bauman's overview to a detailed level. For the purposes here the figure of the *Verantwortungsträger* is of special interest, although the translation of this term into the English language faces serious difficulties. *Verantwortungsträger* is one of these terms where the German language is at its best concerning the capability to make new nouns by the combination of two or more others thereby creating new or additional meaning. The side effect is that it becomes almost untranslatable. The normal translation would be a *person responsible*, but that does not catch the close link between the two nouns combined. The *person ultimately responsible* comes closer, but fails to adequately transport the second part of the German word: *träger*. The verb *tragen* translates as *to carry*. Carrying responsibility does not sound very familiar in English. Referring to another example – *eine Krankheit in sich tragen,* to carry a disease – comes closer to some connotations by using the absurd irony lying in this comparison. Of course responsibility is no disease, but carrying responsibility can be a burden. The person responsible has to bear it, to stand the consequences. So my proposal for the translation is *bearer of responsibility*. The important point that is made by this expression is the move beyond the individual perspective. The responsibility in the term *bearer of responsibility* is a generalized one, not one which can only be ascribed personally.

The emphasis on the difference between the person bearing the responsibility and what the responsibility represents is at the basis of Boltanski's argument. His term for that is the 'hermeneutic contradiction' (Boltanski 2008). The problem of institutions is their lack of embodiment. Only a being without a body is able to escape the limitations of a particular standpoint inevitable for a being located in space and time by a body to express what that 'what' is, is in reality. The definition and confirmation of the reality in question as opposed to the world is the institutions' task. Talking about reality like this assumes a background in which it is not completely dissolvable. Boltanski names this background world, to include everything what is the case in Wittgensteinian terms (Boltanski 2010: 92). We can perceive and describe reality, but describing the world in totality is beyond our capabilities.[3] As some kind of generalized referee, institutions must not serve particular interests. At the same time, however, this being without body needs to express itself with speakers like judges, civil servants, priests, professors, etc. But those are, even if they are authorized properly, normal beings with bodies, with all the interests involved due to their situation in space and time, following emotions and instincts and therefore bound to a standpoint. It is impossible for those concerned to judge with any certainty if the person representing the institution is just neutrally representing it or if she also presents her normal being with all the interests or prejudices involved. The hermeneutic contradiction is the basic tension in social life. Either there are only exchanges of standpoints with the risk that there is no conclusion of the discussion of these standpoints; or, it needs a delegation of the interpretations to decide 'what that what is', is, to a being without body. Then we have to pay the price of a permanent uncertainty, if the speaker enabling the institution to speak, does so correctly or is (also) following own interests.

Luc Boltanski and colleagues analyse the *new sprit of capitalism* (Boltanski and Chiapello 2003) based on work on justification (Boltanski and Thévenot

2007) and recently further developed into a sociology of criticism (Boltanski 2010). They realize subtle shifts in structure which are enormously effective. There is no ruling class any more in the traditional sense. There is a cluster of individuals who are able to use the conditions of the globalized capitalism to their own advantage. Boltanski's description is, in addition and continuation of a terminology he developed with Laurent Thévenot, that of a new *polis*, the project-based *polis* (Boltanski and Chiapello 2003). *Polis* is an apparatus of justification describing the characteristics and the legitimation for members as well as entrance rules and assessment criteria. In the research on the changes in capitalism and management during the nineties in comparison to the 1960s the *polis* defined in the earlier work turned out to be insufficient. Boltanski and Chiapello added the project-based *polis*. 'The project-based polis proves to be a system of constraints and requirements setting a net-based world boundaries' (Boltanski and Chiapello 2003: 152, author's translation). The keywords are project and net-based. The basic characteristic is a loss of linear stability as could be found in hierarchies or family-based, patriarchal structures. Social life in the project-based *polis* contains multiple, temporal contacts which, nevertheless, can be reactivated. These contacts are spread over social, professional, geographical and cultural distances. They form networks. The limitation is achieved by projects. Projects turn out to be the fixed points in reality which otherwise consist of loosely coupled relationships. Instead of a more or less clearly definable ruling class referring to birth, status, property, etc. this ruling class is determined by criteria which explicitly involve a crossing of boundaries. The most important criteria is mobility in more than the geographical sense. Of course, international travel and membership in networks is a point, but mobility includes the actual work. Projects replace long-term, stable employment with the realization of concrete tasks with a defined deadline. Loyalty to a concrete employer loses its significance. This can very well be seen as a reaction of that part of the employees, who – due to their qualifications – can rely on being employed in new projects beyond the actual employer, to the increasing instability of the labour market and the reduced job security granted by employers.

Boltanski and Chiapello's diagnosis at the end of the nineties did not go that far. However, they already describe a potential conflict between the members of the global network culture and the persons linked to a concrete organization. It represents an updated version of exploitation. 'Mobiles' have an advantage which they use to the disadvantage of the 'immobiles', i.e. those who still occupy a position inside a (customer) organization and act as a contact to the mobiles. One is immediately reminded of the role of external consultants of the big consulting companies. Without contacts into their clients' organization's they are nothing. The advantages, however, are almost completely on their side. Their salaries are higher and they are not affected by the changes they propose. During my own practice I could observe dramatic failures which nevertheless didn't prevent the consulting company involved from getting huge contracts with other clients in the same industry, sometimes even in the same company. The suspicion is that there must be a pattern of explanation beyond the normal supplier/customer relationship. The understanding of belonging to a shared community beyond the employers is a possible answer. It does not necessarily create the same interest in the concrete case, but the orientation to a project-based attitude also on the side of the customer's management may lead to a short-term perspective and career-oriented behaviour devaluing the interest of the employer. There is a common understanding, because the employer on both sides steps back in favour of an understanding of the needs of a global market and the use of its potential for the persons in question. An extreme form of loss of loyalty can be observed in the financial markets. It is the team which counts in investment banking, not the bank any more. Often it is not just the manager who changes the employer to develop a successful business model with the new employer. It is the whole team changing sides to go on working in the same way for a different employer.

On the background of the project-based *polis* the bearers of responsibility are able to act in two different spaces at the same time. It is this simultaneous fulfilling of functions in private organizations or public administration, and of financial, industrial and intellectual networks widely independent and autonomous of these organizations, which creates the autonomy of actors. Of course it also creates tensions. The crucial capability is to respect the rules of the official position and at the same time play with the diversity of different rules of the network, which are very often contradictory to the official rules in such a way that the fields of intervention are extended. Some kind of a superior feeling and condescension regarding the daily problems of the organization, and a feeling of independence, have their price in the tension to combine the potentially contradictory constraints of both worlds.

The convergence of the new elites rests more on a common understanding rooted in the world of economy and management and embodied in IT, legal and accounting formats (Boltanski 2010: 209). The mode of ruling is refined as a result of groundbreaking changes. Boltanski defines two modes of ruling: a simple and a complex one. The simple mode deals with keeping a closed order which has to be kept against experiences of the world. New insights are seen as disturbing. This is the crucial difference to the complex mode which Boltanski (2010) names the management compliant mode of ruling. Change is the basic fact of reality, so is the central assumption. Changes cannot be prevented. They will become effective in any case, so it is better to manage and consider them as a chance. The central argument is the formal autonomy of the human and the formally equal access to the options which can be chosen or not. The latter will be interpreted as failure. This is a transfer of responsibility to the individual and can be recognized by the increasing labelling with 'self': self-responsibility (Günther 2002).

Instead of preventing change, it will be used to rule by change; necessity as will and representation (Boltanski 2010: 188). The process of permanent change is unavoidable and at the same time desirable. Boltanski uses a formulation which unfolds a nice irony in combination with the banking business: the 'fatefulness of the probable' (Boltanski 2010: 210). We have to rely on experts, on the results of prognoses calculated in IT centres.

Risk management in banks is a gigantic calculation, an excess of data and processing (Pelzer 2007). Necessarily relying on data of the past, this calculation provides a trajectory from the past into the future. It is, in fact, a continuation of the past. Does this unmask the talk of permanent change in a central part of capitalistic action, that part where it is just capital accumulation without production, as just being a rhetoric? At the very centre of dealing with risk, of transferring it from one party to another, from one form into another, where the abstraction of risk almost leads to its disappearance – this is at least the illusion – one characteristic of the simple mode of ruling reappears: the obsessive avoiding of change. Where change can be expressed in positions which can be traded, nothing changes. It should not change: the status quo secures influence and possibilities of income.

On the background of change Boltanski places the bearer of responsibility in her role as member of the ruling class. With the necessary expert knowledge and with management-oriented methods change can be mastered and poses no threat. As change is necessary and unavoidable special management knowledge is required to channel change in such a way that the necessary sacrifices turn out to be lower than without. This kind of rhetoric could already be found in the management discourses of the 1990s (Boltanski and Chiapello 2003). The bearers of responsibility take themselves out of the firing line. As the changes are unavoidable, because they are desirable as such, they cannot be ascribed to a certain class.

The expert as an instance of argument is used to exclude other opinions. Expert knowledge is privileged as a neutral instance, quasi objective; it serves as a reference for interpreting the problems in question. The quality of expert knowledge, writes Boltanski (2010: 201), is that the expert has shown the things 'as they are', completely transparent, so that the 'facts' are presented in all their relentless necessity. The critical question is, if the statements contain no arbitrariness, what would indicate any interest or alternative? Quantification is the method to achieve this. The result is benchmarks. To improve the position needs the maximization of the indicator and a change in behaviour into its direction. This is also a tiny though important shift in the meaning of objectivity. Three different modes of objectivity existed from the eighteenth century on: the legal, combined with the image of neutrality; the political, combined with personal indifference; and the scientific, combined with the separation of subject and object, which should enable the observer to produce timeless and reproducible judgements (Daston 1992). Subsuming public discussion in state and legal system under management, compliant arguments taken from its expert knowledge produces a problematic tension. If the state is seen as a company that has to manage resources and use them economically, it subjugates itself to an alien logic: under pressure of competition to other organizations it will produce profits. The field of argumentation is reduced to an economic perspective. It only accepts arguments which have a positive consequence on the development in this area, while ignoring quantifiable and not quantifiable costs of other areas.[4]

Crises serve the ruling class is Boltanski's slightly disenchanting insight (2010: 210). The argument unfolds its complete perfidious logic here. The fact that a crisis occurs proves that a reality exists which does not rest on a constructed reality but is a reality which has a logic of its own, independent of the ruling class. The crisis, it could be said, acquits the ruling class. Even more, the crisis confirms the necessity to which the bearers of responsibility refer. Their role as rescuer in case of crisis is out of the question. In the crisis they can again prove their abilities, albeit seemingly modest. Their form of modesty is that they acknowledge reality, i.e. they have their actions formed by those powers that they fight.

The suspicion that this is a form of setting a fox to guard the hen coop is, at least seemingly, rejected and the role of the bearer of responsibility is strengthened. It is the markets that are so overwhelmingly powerful. They do not consist of the single members of the project-based *polis*, whose decisions determine that state of the markets, which is considered as crisis. Of course crises are not made intentionally. Markets are too complex for that. But the argument points into the direction that crises are not any more an opportunity to hesitate, to reflect on what has gone wrong and introduce improvements or corrections. Historic possibilities range from reform to revolution. Under the reign of the project-oriented *polis* the potential of reform boils down to a 'keep on going'. Revolution, even non-violent, but radical rethinking of how things are done, is completely out of range.

For the topic discussed in this chapter, risk and responsibility, it is less interesting to discuss, if it is justified or not to organize a state according to market principles like a company to avoid maladministration. The point in the exclusive use of management rhetoric is that it creates the necessity and the unavoidability of measures. The question, if the claim for objectivity on the side of economic experts is justified at all, cannot be focussed adequately any more.

It is this *rhizom*, as I am inclined to say, which renders the hermeneutic contradiction invisible, at least not open for attack. The bearers of responsibility are representatives of necessity which independently of them defines reality. They are the only ones who are able to take necessary action to use the chances of the changes and to master the crises emerging in this reality. The reference to an independent reality renders the old approach of conspiracy theories useless. A conspiracy to produce desired outcomes has become unnecessary.

Absolute risk and the market: the aporia of responsibility

Taking a reflection of Jacques Derrida on responsibility, the role of the bearer of responsibility can be seen even clearer. Derrida gives two introductions to his thinking of responsibility, created roughly at the same time, referring to each other only by the quotation of a chapter title of his other book (Derrida 1995; 2002b). Both, as to be expected, deal with the aporias which immediately turn up when digging a bit deeper, when deconstructing the meaning. Starting from the grammar of the term responding, in the French form of *répondre*, the term has three different meanings. *Répondre de*: to take responsibility, be responsible for, to be liable for, to vouch for, to guarantee something. *Répondre à*: responding, answering someone or on something (a petition, a plea). *Répondre devant*: to justify something to someone or an institution. These modalities cannot stand separated, they implicate each other. One accepts responsibility for oneself or for something by justifying to an other, a community, an institution, a law. We take responsibility for (ourselves, our actions, our discourses) and are responsible to, by initially responding someone or to something (Derrida 2002b: 338). Therefore this modality seems to be the most fundamental and therefore unconditional one. The crucial difference lies in who is addressed. To respond usually addresses an other, a concrete person, the justification happens to an institution, the law, an instance which is authorized to represent the other in an institutionalized form as a moral, legal, political community. The other term which immediately comes to mind when talking about responsibility in such a way is respect. Taking responsibility is a consequence of respecting the other or the law. However, there are two forms of respect involved in the mutual implication of respect and responsibility. To respect the other is a social relationship, may mean to offer friendship, but there is no friendship for the law. It is the difference between an example of respect for a moral law as in the case of the friend, and the cause of moral respect as with the law (Derrida 2002b: 341).

Comparing Derrida's three modalities with Giddens' three dimensions of responsibility it can be stated that two of them roughly correspond. *Rèpondre devant*, to justify to someone or an institution, has an ethical or accounting dimension. *Répondre de*, i.e. to take responsibility or to be liable for, corresponds to Giddens' dimension of obligation and liability. *Répondre à*, responding to someone, answering, shares some connotation with the meaning of being responsible as an author, but there is also a fundamental difference regarding the starting point. For Giddens the dimension longest in use is perceived from the standpoint of the actor: 'Someone who is responsible for an event can be said to be the author of that event' (Giddens 1999: 8). This is linked with causality and agency. The actor takes initiative, he is the origin of the event, and therefore responsibility can be subscribed to him. This is the difference: Giddens emphasizes action; Derrida reaction, no starting point. The perspective of agency, of causing an event carries the image of an origin, which the responsible person initially acts. Derrida emphasizes the responding as part of the word responsibility. He immediately concentrates on the relationship. Responsibility is always directed to an other.

That this difference is far from being trivial was already concluded from Derrida's other reading of responsibility, his careful elaboration of the biblical parable of Abraham in his book *Gift of Death* (1995). Dealing with the absolute other proves in the extreme what is at stake when responsibility is linked to the duty; in this case the absolute duty, to an other. Seeing it as his duty to obey his God he was ready to accept absolute responsibility to him and follow any instruction, including killing his dearest. God, satisfied with this unquestioned loyalty, prevented him from cutting his son's throat at the very last moment. This parable describes the extreme, but it is valuable for demonstrating the basic problem of responsibility, in fact the aporias.

> Duty or responsibility binds me to the other, to the other as other and ties me in my absolute singularity to the other as other ... but of course, what binds me thus in my singularity to the absolute singularity of the other, immediately propels me into the space of risk of absolute sacrifice.
>
> (Derrida 1995: 67)

Following the duty to an other, accepting the responsibility for it, always and undeniably means sacrificing other others. Thus holding someone responsible, taking responsibility, is not such a straightforward action as is often assumed:

> As a result, the concepts of responsibility, of decision, or of duty, are condemned a priori to paradox, scandal, and aporias. Paradox, scandal and aporias are themselves nothing other than sacrifice, the revelation of conceptual thinking at its limit, at its death and finitude.
>
> (Derrida 1995: 67f.)

Either one accepts absolute responsibility to the single other representing an absolute singularity herself, or one answers to a family, a community, an organization, etc. One has to sacrifice the one for the other, is Derrida's conclusion. If I am responsible to one other, I am automatically irresponsible against other others. This insight can and must be generalized from the extreme of obeying the absolute other as in the case of Abraham. It is an aporia of the concept of responsibility as such. One source for the aporia is language. Absolute duty and absolute responsibility require singularity. It is the duty to a concrete other, excluding the relationship to other others. As soon as I talk to someone, singularity is replaced by a social relation, singularity becomes impossible, and alterity is the consequence. It becomes possible to respond to different others. The ethical order becomes problematic. Being responsible to a concrete other means at the same time the impossibility to be responsible to others. The extreme is the duty to the absolute other. What it means to turn away from the others to a single other, is the refusal of the ethical order, means sacrificing ethics. Taking responsibility inevitably creates sacrifice. This argument gains sharpness when introduced into the discussion of risk and economy.

Orford (2004) elaborated the foundations of trade agreements from the perspective of the responsibility of the national law maker and the relationship to the market using Derrida's interpretation of absolute risk in the *Gift of Death* (1995). As described in more detail in Chapter 2, the logic of the negotiations can be deconstructed as the constitution of the market as the absolute other. Responsibility to the market as absolute other becomes absolute, too, with all the complications identified by Derrida; especially the unavoidable sacrifice to other others. The sacrifice is not just a religious feature as might be assumed from the source of the parable, the Old Testament. It can be generalized. If every engagement with the other necessarily means neglecting another other, if every dealing with the absolute other means sacrificing a lot of others, the placement of the market into this central position means very concrete sacrifices and becomes a critical ethical issue. A concentration on the market as the foundation of thinking not just of economy, but the whole of human relations, is one source for the changes in the characteristics of responsibility discussed here. Thinking the figure of the bearer of responsibility as shaped by Boltanski, together with Derrida's reasoning on the aporia of responsibility, already provides a disturbing consequence. Before this consequence will be discussed, the special form of organized irresponsibility in the financial markets will be introduced.

Structured irresponsibility

One of the few systematic attempts to get information about the events of the global financial crisis in 2008 from inside the banking industry beyond the statements of experts and bearers of responsibility was a study done by a group of researchers around Claudia Honegger, Sighard Neckel and Chantal Magnin (2010). Based in the three German speaking countries, they were able to organize a broad selection of interviews with people of different tasks and hierarchical positions in a variety of international and public banks. They chose a qualitative approach to present their results. The interviews were transformed into sociological portraits, i.e. a mixture of a description of the person and her position and task within the bank and direct quotes. The result is a richer and more multilayered view on the business than the image of 'the banks' or the 'bankers' and the public discussion suggests. Inside the banking industry there is a lot of diversity between the business lines concerning attitude to the market and background of employees.

This holds true not only for the differences between the departments oriented to the markets and the supporting back office or technical departments but also for the business lines. There are huge cultural differences between the employees in retail banking, corporate banking, investment banking and asset management. Honegger *et al.* did not draw the boundaries exactly around the business lines, but they defined different types of typical attitudes, world views and conditions of acting. They named these categories fictive scopes of thought and action and identified four of them.

- The *playground* is the world of 'quants', those people who construct sophisticated models and products. They do not consider themselves to be bankers; they form a special breed, experts who calculate models their colleagues do not understand anymore. What happens with the models after the creation is of no interest any more. They seem to be the only ones who are enthusiastic about their work and who were able and ready to talk about their work on a content level.
- The *racetrack* is the martial art zone of investment bankers and other financial hazardists that Honegger *et al.* (2010: 30) state with almost astonishing openness. They mostly met young men: acrobats, gamblers, magicians of money accumulation, seeing themselves at the forefront of the financial system and being in permanent stress and competition. Lehman's bankruptcy

created a shockwave among these people where the 'objective' conditions of this area and the subjective concerns coincide. A peculiar mixture of arrogance and dejection, aggression and worries were expressed in the interviews.

- The *staged decency* is the room where moral scruples against certain business practices were expressed. Also those considering themselves as decent, as bankers of the old school who offer solid advice to their clients were subsumed here. They all suffer from the declined reputation and trustworthiness. In contrast to the racetrack, where only two women were interviewed, most participants in this scope were women. Opposed to the cynicism of the experts and traders, thoughtfulness and fatalism were expressed here.
- The *grey zone* is reserved for the precipices of banking. The wording for description becomes almost poetic. The authors met dubious types, bankers who know how to cultivate their craftiness, the abilities of a sly fox; the virtuosos on the back stages of the financial world who appear to be the more open the more hidden the worlds are in which they operate.

Structured irresponsibility (*Strukturierte Verantwortungslosigkeit*, 2010),[5] the title of Honegger *et al.*'s book, is more than a rhetorical move. It is the special form of organized irresponsibility in the banking industry. Therefore it is worthwhile to have a look at its peculiarities. Despite the fact that the term gave their book its title, it is not developed beyond the heading of an essay about financial scandals as a product of structured irresponsibility and in the conclusion. Biegler (2010) interprets these scandals as a result of a lack of supervision by financial authorities and legal control. The scandals described are in fact business crime. While these are certainly a consequence of deregulation leaving authorities without adequate means to perform prevention or take action, I see fraud as almost a side effect of a more fundamental development. Risk and responsibility, according to my assumption, are subject to the changes described above along the arguments of Boltanski and Derrida. In the banking industry we face a crucial intensification due to the fact that risk and the transfer of the responsibility for that risk is the core competence of this business. Banking is responsible for taking the responsibility themselves or for the distribution of the responsibility of risk to other market participants.

Also in the conclusion a careful consideration of the term itself is avoided. It is treated as obvious. Although responsibility within the four scopes is discussed, any discussion of parallels or further developments of organized irresponsibility is missing, and no reference to Beck (1986) is made. Structured irresponsibility is treated as a given to reflect on responsibility in this background. The authors identify two general patterns by which responsibility is moved away from the individual actor. The first is a generalization of greed. It was not the bankers alone who acted greedily, it is a more fundamental, anthropological characteristic of humans, so it was expressed in most of the interviews. As such it served as a general driving force for the crisis and exonerates those in the financial industry who now can claim they only provided a service and were only doing what anybody else would have done in their place. Public criticism on the banker's behaviour then is envy. The second pattern which mentally supports structured irresponsibility is delegation. It was always the others who triggered the crisis: investment bankers, financial engineers, rating agencies, clients, men, top management, Americans, politics or the state with the 'market' being the greatest exculpation machine. It determines one's own action like a natural force (Honegger *et al.* 2010: 306).

To name these patterns is valuable, but does not serve the purpose of defining what the term 'structured irresponsibility' may mean. Nevertheless the results of the interviews also give a deep insight into the interviewees' very different understanding of responsibility for the global financial crisis. This understanding was quite different in the four scopes of thought and action. The quants on the *playground* do not see any responsibility on their side. They develop the instruments. How to use them lies in the discretion of management, although the engineers claim that management does not even understand the complex constructions or the far reaching consequences of the instruments.

The traders on the *racetrack* also do not accept any responsibility. They are just performing their job, and if they would not do it, there are others to take over. The responsibility for what they do is with the bank, or politics, or even the society as such.

Those bankers subsumed in *staged decency* are more reflective than their colleagues and are annoyed by the increasing dominance of investment banking and the extreme forms of mathematization and the uncritical belief in science. But they clearly see that their reservation is not an adequate attitude in the financial industry any more. Above that the division of labour in a bank has developed in a way that no one really understands the business of the others and no one can really take responsibility for the overall business politics. This holds especially true for the board members, so it was often claimed (ibid.: 308). The attitude towards the job changes in the middle levels of hierarchy. The duties are fulfilled, the salary taken, but at the same time plans for a more meaningful life outside the banks are planned and often realized.

Those in the *grey zone* consider the situation much more pragmatically. The task is to optimize profits, taxes and products and to test the boundaries of business models up to the limit of legality. Responsibility lies with the system, capitalism, or human nature which has always been deplorable. Refraining from the game would be just idiotic. Even more extreme: it would be irresponsible not to take the chance to make that much money in such a short amount of time (ibid.: 309).

The picture of the actors in the financial crisis painted here is more complex than a reference to the 'bankers' assumes. The mistrust expressed by the staged decency against the board members – as those who are assumed to be informed enough to take decisions on the long-term business politics of the bank and individual large deals eventually threatening the stability of the whole bank, in other words to hold responsibility for the actions of the bank – is a telling example of the level that everyday mistrust inside these institutions has already reached. If they are right, and several of the crashes of banks during the past years indicate that the board responsible for decisions didn't actually consider the consequences, i.e. the risk, contained in their decisions, these bearers of responsibility are part of the problem, and not of the solution.

Greed as a generalized human characteristic, a widespread delegation of responsibility to others as generalized patterns, and the attitudes and behaviours of actors inside the banks give an idea of what is at stake with structured irresponsibility. What is the quality of structured irresponsibility which makes it so attractive as a book title, that the authors think that they can do without a definition of the term? The combination of the terms does its work in a context where *structured* has become a sign of dangerous banking products and the behaviour of bankers is publicly judged as *irresponsible*. But beyond that, what is the difference which makes it worthwhile to talk about *structured* instead of just *organized* irresponsibility? The lack of understanding the business of other business lines is already a prerequisite of the organized version. It is exactly the impossibility of finding the responsible person as the responsibility evaporates between the roles of the producers of risk.

The global financial crisis of 2008 was triggered by the collapse of several minor banks, the failures and enforced overtaking of major investment banks by larger banks, and finally by the collapse of Lehman Brothers as a consequence of an overheated market of securitizations. 'Simply nobody followed the thought to the end, that, if a lot of people are making money out of it, the money has to come from somewhere. And that has just somehow gone simply slightly wrong', as a risk manager expressed it afterwards (Honegger *et al.* 2010: 57). Just, somehow, simply, slightly: expressions of helplessness and amazement of a risk manager for the credit business when considering the attitude of colleagues in investment banking.

To judge how far the situation in a bank has moved away from responsible action, it is useful to remind of the ideal situation as understood in Derrida's three dimensions of responsibility: Who is responding to whom? To which law or institution the decision or action has to be justified? Who is taking responsibility, accepts liability, is held accountable for what? In a basic one-to-one situation, a single person selling a financial product or service and a client, the situation is straightforward. The single person answers the client, he has to justify himself to the law, and he accepts liability for the product or service. As soon as we enter the organized world things become more complex. The single person turns into a sales representative who does not sell his own products, but that of the company which employs him. He still answers the client, but the organization[6] has to justify itself against the law, and he does not accept personal liability as long a he did not violate the law in the sales process. The modalities of responsibility which Derrida claims that they cannot stand separated, that they implicate each other, are separated in the first step of organizing a risk transfer. Further complication derives from the fact that with selling a product in the financial industry, a risk is transferred. The transfer of risk is the basis, the intention of almost any financial product. The sales person can be the representative of the organization creating the product and with that offering a product handling a risk or it can be an intermediary which helps to transfer a risk from one party to another. This is again with the help of products enabling risk transfer and payment. In the first case the organization is the counterpart of the risk transfer; in the second case it is enabling the transfer, with the counterparts of the risk transfer being independent clients.

Organized responsibility as responsibility by concrete persons in an organization fails immediately as the person does not have the control of the whole chain of developing, of calculating the products, of the delivery. If forced by objectives to sell a certain amount of products in a given time frame, the sales person is implicitly forced to sell products to clients who do not have the correct profile to judge about these products – responsibility to the other changes into a sales responsibility. The sales person is responsible to fulfil the objectives set by his boss. The boss faces the same fate, reporting to his superior. These figures are of course only part of an overall sales plan to calculate the plan profits of the organization. Just briefly looking at this chain makes the term *organized irresponsibility* credible. The individual has become the wrong address for requests of liability. This is well demonstrated and put to public attention with the struggle of courts to prove liability of individuals in case of realized risks, i.e. concrete damages. If there is no obvious fraud, it is almost impossible to come to an adequate judgement. The proof of liability is almost impossible to achieve under the rule of law. The direct link from damage to responsibility is lost in the process of organizing and division of tasks.

Can aspects be identified which make it necessary or worthwhile to name the organized irresponsibility in financial institutions structured irresponsibility? My tentative answer would be yes. Several of the reasons are discussed in the following: the commodification of risk (1); the virtualization or growing abstractness of the risk involved, i.e. the changing character of risk (2); the financial institutions' role of an intermediary building up a market, if not to say an exclusive playground for themselves (3); the financial markets independence and dominance of other markets (4); the products (5); structural greed (6). In all these areas crucial changes in the nature, the visibility, or transparency of risk take place.

1 Risk in the economic world is the potential failure to pay, the rise or fall of prices of raw materials, changing currency rates in international trade, the volatility of exchange rates, changes in interest, etc. All of these directly or indirectly affect the profitability of companies. The most crucial difference between financial and commodity markets regarding risk is that risk is not involved in the trade of goods, the quality of services, i.e. as a potential of their use. It is risk itself which has become the 'good' to trade, it turned from a characteristic of a good or service into a commodity itself. A logical step for the product portfolio of banks then was to develop instruments to make the result of a concrete business more predictable for the company producing goods. The name of these products, 'derivatives', makes it quite obvious that something is traded here which by construction is derived from something else. The derivative is linked

to an underlying. Its value is connected to the expectations about the value of this underlying. It represents an assumption about the development of the underlying's volatility: do the prices or rates go up or down, and by how much? With derivatives the risk of changes in the value of the underlying can be traded. On globalized markets one of the risks, which a production company cannot influence, is that of currency rate changes. The financial instruments invented for transferring this risk are called futures. Futures are contracts in which one side contracts to buy and one side to sell a given quantity of an asset or a currency at a set price on a given future date. The seller achieves certainty about the exchange value of his turnover on a given date in the future independent of the actual currency rate on this day. He is willing to accept a premium and to give up the chance of getting more if the rate rises accordingly. He also gains the certainty of not losing money if the rate falls below the agreed level. A certain, clearly defined risk was taken off the company and transferred to another party. The idea is different from insuring a risk. Insurance steps in in case of a realization of a risk. It pays for the damage. The financial instrument places the buyer in the situation as if the risk does not exist. He cannot be affected. Whatever the currency rate will be in the example, he gets the rate agreed upon. The risk is taken by his counterpart.

Risk is commodified and this is exactly the purpose of these instruments. I still think that it has to be acknowledged that the current regular use of derivatives in international trade is a reaction of companies to the increased uncertainties of the global competition. They intend to reduce risk to those parts of business which they can influence and where they are not completely dependent on external market forces. The use of derivatives is not generally evil. The decisive change takes place somewhere else.

2 Before the step to the emergence of the market which massively influenced the power relations between the markets is taken, a look on the growing abstractness of risk deems necessary to get further insight on the consequences of its commodification. The risk in organized responsibility is still identifiable. However, the link to the decider, who takes the risk, is not perceptible any more. The realization of the risk can still be physically experienced, it is embodied. The meltdown of Chernobyl which was one of the causes for Beck (1986) to rethink the topic differently, made the direct threat by large scale plants, a feeling which was almost lost behind phrases such as reliable command of technology or rest risk, immediately imaginable for everyone. Even if this catastrophe had been adequately insured and all damages could have been paid for: the victims remain dead, the cancer of the people who lived in the area remains real decades after the accident. This drastic example highlights the difference between the quality of risks in the real economy and the financial markets. It is the difference between embodied risk and the kind of risk which can be calculated economically. The corporeal, sometimes even existential quality of a realization of risk is what might be insured, but cannot be traded away. Financial instruments which transfer risk deal with economic, monetarized aspects of a concrete business transaction. In the early times of the change from fate to risk,

described above in Chapter 2, the difference could be experienced. The crucial change was that of the ownership of the vessel turning into an investment of people who remained on land. The sailor's risk as owner of the vessel is always a double one: in case of shipwreck he loses property and life. The investor loses his investment. The return of the vessel with traded goods is a return *of* the investment, but also the return *on* investment. The embodied risk is cleansed of the smell of rotting bodies, it is abstracted into the world of numbers to be exclusively realized as financial gains or losses. Displaced risk solely serves as a connotation of business relationships.

The increasing abstraction and complexity called for special treatments of risk. Derivatives were introduced of which the value depends on an expected future value of an underlying asset. Trading derivatives means a displacement of the risk. It is transferred from the underlying asset to its derivative. On this way risk is also distilled and purified. The character of risk changed. It has become an essence which can be traded independent of the underlying asset. This was the fundamental point making financial markets of trading risk with an independence of commodity markets possible. It opened the opportunity for banks to move beyond their role as intermediary and service provider to an active role of constructing and dominating markets.

The risk taken in the financial industry is an interesting one from the perspective of the difference between natural and manufactured risk. Financial instruments are created to transfer risk from one party to another. At the beginning of these were the risks of going to sea and discovering new worlds to return with valuable goods. Going to sea meant being exposed to the imponderabilities of weather and the power of nature. The products developed for taking the risk of losing the investment in the ship are clearly manufactured. They and their trading have inherent risks themselves, which is another level of abstraction from the original risk. Trading these instruments in a way that has only negligible connections to an underlying, i.e. a real existing commodity or asset, takes the manufacturing process to yet another level.

3 As long as banks transfer the risk from one party to another by offering special products called derivatives, they act as intermediaries and service providers. They help to transfer the risk of one party who is not willing to take it to another party accepting it against a premium. Derivatives, however, can also be used to make profit directly from assumptions about the direction of the market. The logic of a future, i.e. an agreement to buy or sell a security or an amount of commodities at a fixed price on a fixed date in the future, can be seen as an instrument to predict the future development of prices, if these futures are traded in a market. The price agreed upon mirrors the opinion of risk seller and risk taker about the future development. A new market of expectations is created in a generalized form. Expectations of price developments are traded. As these have to be paid for by the participants, it is assumed that this gigantic price finding machine is acting seriously.

To understand that a decisive change is involved at this stage, it is perhaps useful to rephrase what has happened here in the terms of an author who is only rarely quoted in this context (with exceptions like Macintosh *et al.* 2000; McGoun 1997; Pelzer 2007). Baudrillard's 1983model of simulation, although a bit provocative, helps to understand the complexity of the situation. The model was used in the chapter looking for aesthetics of risk, where risk was said to have entered the level of a simulacrum, on which a risk is only referring to itself without the need for an underlying at the end of the process of securitization. To describe the change discussed here, we have to move back to the levels two and three of simulation. Phase one is the reflection of a basic reality. This is the initial stage where the entrepreneur is dissatisfied with the situation of his business concerning the risks not directly involved in the production of goods like the risk of changing currency rates threatening to render his calculation useless. With the solution offered by banks, phase two is entered to transfer the risk to another party. The derivative masks and perverts a basic reality. It is masked as the risk now is still there, but no longer connected to the business from which it was derived. The derivative separates the risk from the business or asset. The underlying, though referred to, the derivative derived from it, appears to be free from this concrete risk. A perversion is strong to claim this, but the basic reality of the business is seriously distorted, at least for a traditional holistic understanding of business that should not be divided.

The purpose, however, leads the market into a completely different direction. This is the threshold where the difference between a trading of risk and a casino (Strange 1986) gets blurred. The underlyings purely serve as a reference for the price of the derivative. There is no intention to deliver the good at the date agreed. The date exclusively serves as accounting date for the margins. The amount of derivatives in commodities markets without link to a concrete business has reached a share of more than 95 per cent.[7]

4 The direction and intention of the market is reversed. The part of the market for which it was created and which still has a connection to the commodity markets has become entirely dependent on a business which has its own logic. This business was mirrored by the demand of a growing liquidity looking for investments. The gigantic sum of US$42 trillion, just of private capital, was looking for investment (Deutschmann 2008). Financial services became an industry beyond the realm of banks. Funds in all their diversity from government and private pension funds, state funds, hedge funds, investment funds, offer their services as wealth management institutions and function as institutional investors. Their activity is not restricted to the exchanges. On the contrary, most of the activities of the international financial markets take place over the counter (OTC), i.e. directly between the counterparts.[8]

The result is that the speculation dominates the terms on the real markets. Volatility risks in the real markets now have to be separated from the products, because they are dependent on a new type of development, a new type of risk: the risk of price changes resulting from predictions of participants of the other market, the financial one. Financial institutions now provide the market against which all other economic activity is judged. This development was supported by the deregulation of financial markets. As a result societal control moved to the markets and societal crisis tendencies must be seen as a consequence of the functioning of the economy (Beckert 2009).

With the volumes of derivatives traded many times over the volume of potential underlying businesses, phase three of Baudrillard's model of simulation is reached. In case of a derivative as an investment to speculate on these underlyings, there is no concrete basic reality. The derivative still derives from an underlying, its calculation refers to the underlying, although there is no direct link any more to a basic reality, to the physical commodity or business. The derivative now masks the absence of an underlying. The boundaries between the phases two and three have become blurred in the financial markets. They both exist parallel in the same market. Their relation, however, has become anything but equal. What we see here is the creation of a new market on which banks and other financial institutions allowed to act in these markets[9] are dominant. The markets of derivatives have still not completely reached the phase of a simulacrum, that they are their own reality, or, that they bear no reality at all. The fundamental change is their dominance: the virtual financial market takes the rule over the real market which almost seems to disappear in its perspective. The direction and intention of the market is reversed. The part of the market for which it was created and which still has a connection to the commodity markets has become entirely dependent on a business which has its own logic. The result is that speculation dominates the terms on the real markets. Volatility risks in the real markets now have to be separated from the products, because they are dependent on a new type of development, a new type of risk: the risk of price changes resulting from predictions of participants of the other market – the financial one. Financial institutions, banks, funds in all their diversity from government pension funds, state funds, hedge funds, investment funds and others, provide the market against which all other economic activity is judged. An independence is achieved which made the dominance of financial markets possible.

The derivative is, in Baudrillard's (1983) terms, already an evil appearance in the order of malefice. The level at which that change of ruling takes place, is of the order of sorcery. Of course it is not claimed here that we fell back into the times of witchcraft, which enabled the financial markets to take over. The terminology, in all its exaggeration, serves to highlight the quality of change taking place here. It is quite provocative, but perhaps also illuminating to formulate the change like this. The argument will unfold its persuasiveness when combining it with those about the bearers of responsibility.

5 Structured products are the group in which the catchy phrase of 'structured irresponsibility' comes closest. These are investment strategies based on a combination of several different financial products of which one has to be a derivative. The phrase 'investment strategy' is telling. A structured product is not about handling the concrete risk of a concrete business; it is more than a participation in building up a market expectation on the development of volatility of a specified underlying, in other words speculation. With that move almost any financial strategy can be calculated which has a link to the financial markets. It is an investment strategy, i.e. it has become part of an increasingly commodified

wealth management. Structured products can be used as a strategy to secure a portfolio, to hedge it, finely adapted to the investments the client has. But it can also be claimed to be the last step into the retail market for banks. Certificates, index related papers, etc. aim at the private client in the retail market. It has become possible for anyone to speculate, even with 'safety belts': one of the conditions of the paper can be that the paper is paid back by 100 per cent at the end of the investment duration, independent of whether it was profitable in the meantime or not. Structured products mark the transition from a professional market to a mass market.

Securitization is another term with a telling double meaning. On the one hand it is the process of transforming single contracts involving some kind of regular payment into a security, tradable independent of the underlying contracts. Due to the mix of different qualities of the underlying contracts the security has a rating different from the underlyings. It is a mixture of the average of the underlyings and the creditworthiness of the issuer. On the other hand, the terms 'security' and 'securitization' themselves turned out to be euphemistic (Koslowski 2009): the securitized papers were by no means made more secure; on the contrary, the whole process became less transparent. At the beginning of the century securitization was a major means of banks to reduce their volume of problematic credits by securitizing them. By that time it was a business between professionals. The bank offered the buyer a package, e.g. a hedge fund made a due diligence to clearly calculate the value of the package and the deduction was negotiated. The bank was able to remove the package from its balance sheet and won new possibilities to gain new business – hopefully with a different risk structure. The buyer took over the risk of failure of payment and speculated on a better possibility to exploit the package than the price agreed.[10] Risk was completely – at least as completely as possible with the instruments of risk calculation – transparent.

With the CDOs (collaterized debt obligations) the sheer growth potential of the products enforced addressing a wider range of clients. Growth was possible on both sides, the credit contracts to be securitized were mortgages, the target clients a much broader selection of banks, funds and also clients in private banking. The risk on the mortgage side was increased by accepting homeowners with little or no creditworthiness and mortgage constructions that relied on rising real estate prices (Mian and Sufi 2008). Nevertheless the securities created gained a favourable rating. The growing real estate bubble heated by the fact that the banks granting the mortgages could immediately hand over the risk to others and with that got their balance sheet free for new business, remained unnoticed, or to put it more accurately, ignored. One can even speak of a multilevel risk evaporator. Those who had a direct access to the risk, the failure of paying the credit rates, systematically lost interest in continuously checking as they immediately handed over the risk to another bank. This other bank thought in averages and shares of contracts with different risk levels. The created security needed a positive rating to be successfully sold. At this point the responsibility linked to risk changed profoundly: it became a sales responsibility. Once the mortgages were accepted to be securitized, the intention is not to keep them, but to construct a package that can be traded away. Securitizations are very often constructed with several layers of assets with different creditworthiness and a hierarchy of priority payments becomes part of the security's construction. Rating was meant to produce some kind of transparency of the investors. In fact the rating hid the increasing complexity in the construction of these securities. Risks could not be judged any more by the investors.

The dynamics in this field is intensified by the internal objectives and competition among the quants. The mathematicians in the product development were under permanent pressure to prove their abilities. As a head of sales and solution management remarked, if one had not developed a new product after six months, he was out (Honegger *et al.* 2010: 144). This is part of the job's logic: high income, but developing products for sake of product development without any background or a market demand beyond the demand for ever more exotic products.

6 Greed has already been identified by Honegger *et al.* (2010) as a general pattern by which responsibility is moved away from the individual actor. It can be seen as one of the main justification motives of the bankers interviewed. The system produces greed, the clients all too easy follow the promises, and so it can be interpreted as an external need from which nobody inside the banks can withdraw. They are following the markets. A risk manager claimed that emotion, urge for recognition, being regarded as important and striving for personal merits excessively intensified on the side of clients and of investment bankers, was the subject side of the greed which had driven everything (Honegger *et al.* 2010: 51). But beyond individual greed, so it can be argued, some kind of a structural greed emerged. Longing for ever more also became part of the aims of the organizations in the financial markets in the form of a relentless race for the most ambitious profitability. Only a multiple yield was considered a financial success. A 25 per cent return on equity became infamous as the declared aim of Germany's largest bank, which claimed that this is a necessary aim to meet the requirements on international financial markets where the competitors aim for even higher rates (Freiberger 2010). That this could only be achieved by a huge leverage and the corresponding increase of risk was denied as long as the hedging strategies seemed to work. Keywords like shareholder value, short-term perspective, quarterly reporting, the pressure to increase profits immediately at almost any cost are examples for expressions of a structural *ever more*, mirroring the dominance of financial markets over the real economy.

> The longing for success, judged exclusively in terms of money and status, became the mental equivalent to financial capitalism, to the subjectivation of a society of competition, in which a ranking on the first places could develop into some kind of a private religion.
>
> (Neckel 2010: 6, author's translation)

Organized irresponsibility, as a result of extreme division of labour producing complex results, is a phenomenon that can be watched in any organization and also inside banks. It seems useful, however, to make the distinction to the special characteristic of financial institutions, which makes the reasoning even more complex than in the general form. I propose to talk of structured irresponsibility when we talk about products exclusively dealing with the transfer of risks, which do not belong to the risks of the bank as an organization. These are those risks that the bank takes over from clients on its own account or in order to transfer them to other counterparts. This enables to clearly distinguish the issues related to banking from those which are endemic of organizing as such. The result, however, is similar. Risk is commodified and becomes increasingly abstract on each level of its commodification. The result was an emerging financial market, which made the financial industry independent of the real economy, and even reverses the relationship. Financial markets dominate the real economy. The real economy has to react to the demands of the actors of the financial markets. Many of these requirements can be termed structural greed. In this changed context responsibility, interpreted as a unit of responding, justifying and being accountable on the basis of the single, clearly identifiable individual is not part of the system. With the widespread use of securitization not just in the market of mortgages, as it has become well known during the past years, but with any type of credit business already before, the majority of the banking business is affected. Banks can transfer the risk immediately after accepting them, even in that part of the business that, traditionally, was their core competence: financing business in the real economy by giving credit. This leads to a form of moral hazard, as one participant of Honegger *et al.*'s interviews stated: 'Since the bank transfers the risk completely, there are no adequate checks any more, and the quality is lost' (Honegger *et al.* 2010: 116). As the bank does not have to face the consequences of the risk, because it is no longer part of its own balance sheet, the amount of business can be increased without being affected by the responsibility for the risks taken.

The bearer of responsibility: an example

Structured irresponsibility takes place exactly at the point where it has become possible to handle risks without being liable. Taking responsibility bears no consequence in this world. This can well be read from a short interview by ABC News' Claire Shipman (2010) with Goldman Sachs CEO, Lloyd Blankfein, after the subcommittee hearings of the US Senate. She asked, if Goldman Sachs bear any responsibility for the financial meltdown. His answer:

> Yes we do. It embarrasses me to say it. But of course we do. The financial system failed and Goldman Sachs is a very influential member of the financial system. So we have to share – we have our share of the burden of that.

This seems to be a clear statement of acceptance of responsibility. Blankfein acknowledges the fact that Goldman Sachs is a member of the financial system which failed, and a very influential one. But even as an influential member it is the system, something independent of the bank itself that failed. Without using the word 'responsibility' he admits that they have a share of the burden. He represents the bank as the bearer of responsibility which is seen as a burden. The responsibility is transformed into a burden that hit everyone independent of guilt. So everyone who is hit has to carry the burden. Despite the clear beginning of the answer – Yes, we do – in the course of this short statement, the responsibility – as it is understood in the threefold concept of responding to an other, to justify and to be liable – already vanishes. It is a careful avoidance to accept any individual liability.

The answer didn't satisfy the interviewer. Shipman insists:

SHIPMAN: Listening to a lot of the people who work for you and some of your testimony, it seemed to me there was a real coordinated effort not to say certain words like 'I'm sorry, I have regrets, I apologize'. That there were just certain phrases that people don't want to utter. Wouldn't it just help to just state the obvious? We're sorry, we apologize, yes we.... It seems there was just a bit of hedging about.

BLANKFEIN: I don't think that's the case. I think, look, we had different groups, the first panel are four individuals, by the way, two who are out of the firm now, but four individuals really engaged in market making and I don't know if they have been challenged or asked about these issues before. But I think in the senior people you talk to, I think they were very reflective about their responsibilities and their role.

The obvious expected by the public is not that obvious for the bearer of responsibility. If there is no liability for an individual bank, if it can be proven that it didn't violate laws, that there is no individual failure which caused the crisis, the bank's role changes from an actor playing an active role in the constitution of the market's reality to a victim of market forces which hit the bank as it does with any other part of the economy. Blankfein claims that he does not know if the four individuals really engaged in market making were challenged or asked about these issues before. Within the context of a senate hearing, one can assume that it has not been the case. These kinds of hearings take place after the crisis has already occurred. But what does it mean that the market makers have not been challenged or asked before? Is this an indication of how risk management inside the bank operates? That risk management does not have the task to cast doubt? This assumption would be in line with the observations by three interviewees in Honegger *et al.*'s study (2010: 70, 108, 124) that risk managers who warned that it could not go on as being practised, who asked for more prudence, were fired.

And what does it actually mean that the senior people were very reflective about their responsibilities and their roles? If apologizing for being a major player and therefore part of the problem that led to the crisis is not an adequate reaction, a different understanding of responsibility and the role may well be the cause. In a context just described, responsibility then does not mean responsibility for the risks taken, but for the merit of being the most profitable bank in the market.

But Shipman still insists:

SHIPMAN: Listening to your testimony, you sounded very logical, very much talking about the way business are done. And maybe business is done that way at Goldman Sachs and maybe it does make sense.

But can you see why a lot of Americans would look at a situation where there is a lot of money being made. A lot of glee being expressed as Americans are losing their homes and think there is something wrong with that. Or look at a situation where you hear that, well wait, we knew this deal wasn't great, but we're selling it anyways. That doesn't seem right. It might be legal, but doesn't feel right.

BLANKFEIN: No, look, we're not solving for a minimum. Our firm has been a client-oriented firm for 140 years and, by the way, very successful in an industry where you can't be successful unless you have the support of your clients.

And we have been on the top of that for many years. The way we treat our clients has been with Goldman Sachs for a very, very long time.

This is the crucial issue: Blankfein thinks of clients, Shipman asks for the public who most probably have never seen Goldman Sachs from the inside and who most probably would have never been accepted by Goldman Sachs as clients. Americans loosing their homes exist in Goldman Sachs' terms only as part of the securitizations traded. Clients with bad ratings cannot afford the bank's services. They do not have enough money or no money at all. Shipman tries to get Blankfein to admit this difference and consider his responsibility:

SHIPMAN: I'm not necessarily talking about your clients. I'm just talking about Americans at large who look at what happens and for better or for worse say, those investment banks really did not do us any favours. They're blaming you. They don't understand why anybody should profit from something that hurt so many Americans.

BLANKFEIN: I understand that. I understand that reaction. There were things that were taken by people out of context. Look, there were some people, again, in the market making business, there are people who are long and people who are short and people who are making an observation that when something went down they were making money. They could have been – they were expressing a thought about their PNL.

But I tell you, we are all citizens and family people and taxpayers and members of our community. The fortunes of Goldman Sachs, just like the fortunes that we all have as individuals, are totally in line with the interest of the public.

There is no Goldman Sachs unless we have the support of our clients, who are the public. Frankly, there is not success for Goldman Sachs unless there is growth, people financing, people will to invest and that is also in line with the interest of the United States.

Blankfein claims to understand this reaction, that the people blame him, the representative of a bank which profited from something that hurt so many Americans. But 'there were things that were taken by people out of context'. Yes, there were things taken out of context. But who were these people taking things out of context? Are they really the ones blaming the market – Blankfein hides the argument behind the market here, not mentioning that his bank is part of it and he describes exactly what his traders are supposed to be doing – for doing business in long and short sales as a consequence of their expectations of how the volatility of prices will develop. Or are these the bankers themselves who took the risk out of the context of the single home loan to transfer it into another context, the context of financial trading and speculation? Taking things out of the context then means the whole process of the commodification of risk, from mortgages of whatever value to selling the mortgages as a package to another bank, which repacked them to create a security that can be traded independent of the individual value of the single mortgage? Taking the risk out of the context of the original home loan means a financial innovation that could support a politics of an increase of home ownership on the one hand, but the creation of moral hazard on the other. The risk taken out of the original context cannot be valued adequately any more, and almost no one feels the need to do so. Moreover, after, and perhaps even during securitization it becomes impossible to understand the risk structure of the whole package (Hellwig 2008, Weitzner and Darroch 2009). A new risk is added instead: the risk that the quality of calculating the exposure is diminished. The P&L of the bank and its clients only realizes what is at stake when the crisis occurs and the hedging fails. Only after justifying the restricted perspective of the traders, and after very briefly stepping out of the role of the bearer of responsibility by including himself into the general 'we' of citizens, family people, tax payers and members of a community he manages to relate to Shipman's question. But this is just for a moment, a rhetorical move in order to include his bank into the whole the nation. Here he demonstrates clearly his restricted view: '...our clients, who are the public.' This inclusive remark denies Shipman's question and ignores the sacrificed. Instead he turns it into an all too well-known phrase. We heard that before of General Motors, and experienced it in the same context again during the same crisis that Goldman Sachs is one source. Goldman Sachs is totally in line with the interest of the public and, therefore, also in line with the interest of the USA, Blankfein claims. No mentioning of the bailout, no gratitude that the public as taxpayer has saved the market so that the business can go on.

The link between risk and responsibility as the core competence of banking became increasingly questionable. With the evaporation of risk in the system, the feeling of responsibility and strategies to prevent risk from realizing got out of sight. In the interview with Lloyd Blankfein the reasoning of a bearer of responsibility can well be understood. In the world of financial markets the bearers of responsibility took over the role of Abraham, granting the market the role of the absolute other. The other others, the real economy and those dependent on it, are sacrificed. There is a difference, though. Abraham knew what he was doing when he accepted the responsibility to the absolute other. He was conscious of whom he sacrificed: his family. This is, as Derrida explained, not just an exception in an extreme case, it is the most common, everyday experience (Derrida 1995). Taking responsibility inevitably creates sacrifice. Exactly this is not understood, or in his role as bearer of responsibility not admitted, by Blankfein. He tries to keep business and the responsibilities for the business and the public separate.

Lloyd Blankfein's statement is another example of how the bearers of responsibility understand responsibility: responsible, but not liable, a representative of structured irresponsibility.

The bearers of responsibility in the world of structured irresponsibility

It almost suggests itself to combine the arguments about the bearer of responsibility, the market as absolute other and the special condition of the financial industry concerning responsibility. The bearer of responsibility, so it was said above, is a role model that goes beyond the boundaries of organizations and institutions. The changes in liquid modernity have created a new ruling class whose basic characteristics are a project-based *polis* and the membership in networks replacing the traditional loyalty to an organization. The hermeneutic contradiction which has always been in place when a concrete person represents an institution and claims to speak for the institution, reaches a new quality in a complex setting of domination. This is the interesting interface: the transition from a simple to a complex mode of domination includes that the reality the bearers of responsibility refer to becomes, at least seemingly, independent – an objective reality to which one has to react. This view clearly leaves the bearer's contribution to the production of this reality out of sight. The market has won independence from those who act on these markets and also from those who may be suffering the consequences of developments on this market, or rather, these markets. The discussion around structured irresponsibility has shown that it is useful to speak in the plural, not just to indicate that there are very different markets for different goods and services, but that the financial markets have won an independence from the other markets. The financial markets followed the trade of goods and services anywhere. Globalized, financial markets' participants created products that developed the basic idea of risk transfer into investment strategies. With that, just following ideas with product innovations and developments, the financial markets developed an independence from their underlyings, the businesses whose risks following from the globalization of trade were at the beginning of banks' engagement. The creation of a market like that for mortgage-backed securities (MBS), so eloquently described by Michael Lewis (1990), is from the outset about autonomous products of the banking industry developed exclusively for the financial markets. MBS are created to transfer risks of an anonymous amount of home owners to an anonymous amount of investors.

Banks and other financial institutions take part in creating markets, but so also do investors looking for a higher return on their investment. The market as the other consists of those who refer to it as THE market. The bearers of responsibility refer to the market as an absolute other, which can only be influenced to have a positive outcome by reacting to the market in a way the market digests. A client rep put it straightforwardly:

> Now, both factors, risk and profit, depend on perception: What is perceived as risk? And if it runs smoothly for some time, the cow goes dancing on thin ice.[11] And the banks have to follow the cow, as the cow is the market which is to be milked.
>
> (Honegger *et al.* 2010: 288)

The market was clearly perceived in a difficult, if not dangerous situation, but the banks followed their sources of profit. They did not perceive themselves as part of the market, as co-creators of what was happening; they observed it developing as one watches the beast – very interested, but detached from the scene. The client rep meanwhile, sells the milking equipment in the form of the latest inventions by his colleagues, the quants. He doesn't have to understand the products; he just has to sell them. The banker in this case made no reference to the absolute other and a parallel to the parable of Abraham seems to be ridiculed when using a cow as a reference to the divine. Nevertheless the argument points to the same direction. The market seems to be separate from the actors on it. It seems to have a life of its own which can be predicted as long as everything goes along the trajectory the statistical data describe from the past into the future. If not, the system and its participants are taken by surprise.

Structured products are investment strategies by which it is possible to represent the investor's own estimation of the future and buy certainty, some kind of a tailor-made insurance strategy to cushion negative economic developments, so is at least the expectation. It is a form of future management. 'It is impossible to prohibit to manage the future in a market society' is the opinion of a head of a bank. No banker can withdraw from the markets. Everyone has to rely on functioning markets to invest money, he adds (Honegger *et al.* 2010: 206). Even for reflected bankers – this one was categorized as part of the staged decency – the market is the absolute other without which surviving in a globalized economy is impossible. A more disillusioned remark is quoted a few pages later. The loss of reality at the top and their dependency on managers lower in the hierarchy and their information are part of the reasons for the failure of the banking industry. That CEOs of banks only say in public what others have told them, is the somehow devastating judgement of a colleague (Honegger *et al.* 2010: 211) who is at least conscious about the effect of large organizations.

Perceiving the market as the other, from the outside, helps to describe the events as unpredictable, as something beyond imagination, and one's own bank as victim. It was the unpredictable collapse of the market which brought the bank and its subsidiaries into such a difficult situation, a head of sales and solutions department explains. Looking at the interest management and refinancing of the bank he describes the usual behaviour of banks to refinance long-term engagements as short-term. If the risk takes place as an event, i.e. no refinancing can be achieved in the market situation of the crisis, current risk management is helpless, but not worried: 'Basically it is legitimate, because I can assume – and we all assumed – that the short-term market was liquid. This was the principle. That it became "illiquid", no one could assume that this would happen' (Honegger *et al.* 2010: 144).

The market as an independent force shows that unpredicted behaviour is one pattern of explanation. If one has to acknowledge a contribution of one's own bank's top managers, the network comes into play with an interesting twist. 'High finance' is a 'closed network, no one can blame the other or place the other in a difficult situation, because he exactly knows that the other has as much material as he has'. No one asks the question about responsibility and guilt, 'because everyone has a skeleton in the cupboard', a business analyst is quoted (Honegger *et al.* 2010: 63f.).

This short overview of banker's different opinions after the crisis can serve as an illustration of the role of the bearers of responsibility in the world of structured irresponsibility. Considering the global financial crisis of 2008 and the following events regarding the rescue of banks, the explanatory power of these arguments is overwhelming – even depressing. *Market's opinion is*. This sentence can be understood as the beginning of a statement. But it can also be seen as an almost ontological statement. Such is the power of the market that the bearers of responsibility can only react to it. They are, however, the most experienced actors and therefore able to interpret what is happening and to advise the remedy. The remedy of the 2008 crisis was the massive bailout in several states. Just to repeat the figures (Panetta *et al.* 2009): eleven countries helped their financial sector with very different amounts: Australia, Canada, France, Germany, Italy, Japan, the Netherlands, Spain, Switzerland, the UK and the USA. The bailouts total is €4,994 billion in commitments and €2,006 billion in outlays, which represent an average of 18.8 per cent and 7.6 per cent of the GDP in these countries. The engagement varies significantly. While the UK's commitments represent 54 per cent of the GDP, USA 22.3 per cent and the Netherlands 44.6 per cent, Japan's figure is only 2.7 per cent. The figures were used for recapitalization, debt guarantees and asset purchase and insurance. Eighty-five financial institutions obtained government assistance.

The generalized figure of the bearer of responsibility describes the mechanism of strengthening their own position by a failure that gives the cause as acting like the bearers of responsibility, supporting the reality to emerge as it emerges, sometimes in the form of crisis or catastrophe, with not being individually liable. With the market as absolute reference, the bearer of responsibility feels responsible to it as his absolute other. He gains the advantages from this relationship. At the same time this makes him irresponsible to any other other. The network shares his attitude of prioritizing the market.

After the arguments above the consequence is of no surprise. The top bank managers were responsible for the strategy of the banks leading into the disaster.

After the crisis occurred, they slipped into the role of government advisors and their interpretation of the reality, which has occurred as the realization of the accumulated risks of these strategies left no other solution than to draw on the lender of last resort, the state. With that it provided the same top managers, or, to put it more bluntly, they provided themselves, the means to revitalize the same system to go on as if nothing has happened. That the bearers of responsibility were the same people, that almost no personal consequences were taken, only exceptionally fired or held legally accountable, is a confirmation for Boltanski's figure of the bearer of responsibility. The network proved to be stable enough to carry its members through the crisis and dispose of the price for the crisis somewhere else. The refinancing of the banks almost exhausts the combined means of nation states. Seen from this perspective the optimistic view of a re-entrance of the state as actor on the stage of economy is proven wrong. The state's reaction is exactly that, a reaction, and not an action with a clear objective in mind (Beckert 2009), it was steered by the bearers of responsibility who were able to make use of public assets for private gains.

The bearers of responsibility, therefore the conclusion out of a discussion of risk *and* responsibility, represent the risk *of* responsibility. They represent the exact opposite of what Christoph Schlingensief meant in the quote introducing this chapter. He expressed his understanding of the responsibility for the things he did shortly before his untimely death as: *I know, I did it*. But he was a theatre and opera director, an artist.

6 'Who's afraid of red, yellow and blue'[1]

Towards an aesthetics of risk

Robert Cooper (1991) emphasizes the value of aesthetics as a necessary counterpart to the practical-useful, the managerial view to which the professional study of organizations is heavily biased.[2] The reign of instrumental rationality must be counterbalanced with a perception via the senses, as the idea of aesthetics suggests, to reveal a complex world that is hidden from us when we rely uncritically on the practical-useful, the managerial attitude (Cooper 1991). Conditioned to see institutions almost entirely in functional terms, a good example being the banking industry with its formal structures and calculations, it is difficult to see that human institutions also rely on aesthetic logic like forms, structures, representations, symmetry/asymmetry, etc. Of course Cooper didn't stop with these basic insights and we will come back to his arguments when debating the examples.

Since Cooper's initial remarks on the topic of aesthetics and organization there have also been critical remarks on the inclusion of art, artists, or generally aesthetics into the public appearance of organizations. Taking Marcuse as a point of reference stating 'in a situation where the miserable reality can only be changed through radical political praxis, the concern with aesthetics demands justification', Warren and Rehn (2006: 81) start a special issue on the other side of the use of aesthetics: as justification of bad practice, denying creative spaces; in short, as oppression. Böhme (2003) reminds us that the critique of aestheticization is by no means new. *The Dialectic of Enlightenment* (Horkheimer and Adorno 1971/1944) presented a sharp refutation of the excesses of the culture industry, an argument that has been renewed several times since then. While this is fully acknowledged, the focus shall nevertheless be on aesthetics and the sublime, but trying to develop its critical potential.

Aesthetics can say a lot of things about attitudes on and towards this special form of risk banks are taking, especially beyond the boring credit and retail business, and is the assumption in this chapter. This qualification, boring as opposed to exciting other activities like trading or asset management, is already an aesthetic judgement. Trading in banks is basically the conscious trading of risk instead of the risky trading of goods. The basis of the trading is the uncertainty of the future and in this area the volatility of prices for all kinds of commodities, securities, carbon certificates, even weather. Traded are not only these goods themselves; current favourable trading is with derivatives, i.e. products that have a link to an underlying commodity or security, but are traded independently and not necessarily with the purpose of delivering the underlying. The result is an opaque market whose participants are not only specialists – as in any other market where one needs special knowledge of the products, their qualities, or other actors. They need an abstract knowledge of mathematical rules with which the products operate. This picture, however, may be more complex. It is not the trader herself who needs the knowledge. It must be available in the bank to develop the products traded. Trading can then take place on the usual financial markets. We will try to understand the aesthetics of risk to appreciate the special status and fascination of this banking activity[3] from a different perspective.

It is in this world where the City Lives project of the British Library,[4] probably one of the best resources of insight into trader's world, took place (see Courtney and Thompson, 1996, for a brief account of this resource as well as some of its highlights). The interviews with participants contained within are exemplary in the ways they tried to get access to trading in the financial world and motivated the participants to reflect on their position inside the institutional context in which they worked. Two general aspects will be highlighted with the help of this and other ethnographic material. The beautiful and the sublime are the aesthetic terms used to get access to the terms of trade, to realize that admiring the beautiful can well lead to miss essential points and trading under the influence of the sublime, or trading the sublime, has consequences.

A taste for coffee

Coffee surely is a substance which activates perception via the senses and provides a connection to the beautiful. In the following example it can also be shown that tensions can be perceived even if the imaginary smell of good coffee almost overrules other aspects of the report. There is a difference between the aesthetic quality of goods of which a story is told, and aesthetics as a framework to judge the circumstances and help to understand what is going on. Both dimensions are addressed during this interview.

Jack Spall (interviewed by Cathy Courtney in October 1991 and January 1992) was a dealer in coffee futures. Besides all the insights on the nature of trading or on the moment of exchange (Lightfoot *et al.* 2009) this interview offers an insight into the importance of aesthetics in an otherwise extremely abstract business. The distance since the time Spall remembers for the interview is already a clear sign for the basic tension between the two worlds of commodity and futures. He recalls his visit to Hamburg back in the late 1950s. The coffee futures market had opened in London, and as a preparation for coffee trading his employer sent him to Hamburg to learn to taste coffee; literally an official educational trip to learn the variations in different kinds of coffee by drinking coffee. Spall demonstrated how it was done and the similarities to wine tasting are surprising. Even the description on paper gave a deep impression of the aesthetic pleasure of the old trader when remembering the golden times of trading.

A connoisseur who is lucky enough to have his area of delight as a trade, one could assume, or at least a well-understood training for traders who better know what they are dealing with to judge price differences of the varying types of commodity. However, as soon becomes clear, there are light years between the futures markets and the experience of taste Spall so vividly tells of. He knows the differences between robusta,[5] the kind of beans instant coffee is produced from, and the higher quality of Kenyans, Columbian or other Latin American coffee and can tell a lot about their special aromas, and therefore has a profound basis for his disgust on the robusta. It is a description of traditional commodity markets, where producers and traders meet, judge the quality of the goods and negotiate the price, ideally finalizing their agreement by handshake.

Two worlds met here, and it was still possible at the time that they met: the world of actual commodities, their materiality, and in the case of coffee its taste, smell, its sensual qualities. Perception is required to become a member of the markets. Especially in Hamburg coffee and tea trading was a matter of the senses. The famous *Speicherstadt* in the harbour of Hamburg with its spectacular architecture, the smells of fine commodities, which were at times even in the streets, and the corporeal experience of tasting with the correct ceremony added to the impression of being included into a very special world. It's just a selected few who are able understand the important differences which keep the trading going. The memory of a time, where all the senses had to be included to make business, expresses a certain nostalgia. The basic tension can clearly be read in Spall's report. Two types of coffee, related to the different markets, spot and futures, express not just the difference of aesthetics involved, but also the trader's esteem. When talking about robusta, there is openly expressed contempt in his description – *pretty lousy, pretty awful, but that's the stuff they use* – just stuff, not really worth drinking. But robusta became the centre of trading on the futures markets where trading is devoid of the aesthetic qualities of coffee anyway: it is not yet produced, but already sold and bought. Regret is only implicit, but telling the interviewer about his experience of tasting in such detail emphasizes a feeling of loss.

The trade, however, is as expected at markets, even at futures markets. It is about buying coffee early, before it is actually harvested, making a price for some time in the future, of course assuming that the price will rise, and already selling it before physically having it, delivering it at the time in the future for the agreed price, independent of what the price at that time is on the market. One can buy or sell a year ahead, taking into consideration potential damages to the crop, like frost in an important region, wiping out large amounts of the expected harvest. Except for a margin, payment is also due in the future by the time of delivery.

The fascinating point in this interview is that a crucial change in trading – i.e. from trading commodities with concrete counterparts and terms and conditions connected to different qualities of a commodity to an abstract market represented on screens – is the background of the interview. It is the difference between spot markets and futures markets, between concrete goods with identifiable quality and immaterialities, between selling and short selling. 'Why on earth', so Lightfoot *et al.* put their bewilderment into words, 'does one need to know how high quality spot traded coffee tastes in Hamburg if one is actually trading dust in London?' (2009: 113). Spall was witness to the old world at a time when the changes were already largely implemented in terms of abstraction of products, but not yet in the form of postsocial relationships (Knorr Cetina and Bruegger 2002a). We will return to this phenomenon later.

The interviewer is trying to get the point:

> So selling it on the Futures Market is taking a risk about whether you're actually going to be able to bring it in for less than everyone thinks, or whether you're going to lose.
>
> Yes. That's a very simplistic term, yes. There's a good deal more to it than that, but, but, but that's it in general.
>
> (Lightfoot *et al.* 2009: 114)

'A good deal more', yes, but what might that be, except perhaps the glaringly obvious:

> So that's the point, really, is to make money?
>
> Yes.
>
> By everybody thinking it's going to be worth more than it actually is?
>
> Or worth less.
>
> But that, but that's what, but that's why you would sell it on the Futures Market?
>
> You would sell it on the Futures Market, you can either do it, as I say, so you have a properly hedged situation, or, you can just punt, and say, 'Now, I think that the output from Angola, Mysore, Uganda, is going to go up this year, and by August of next year, the whole market will be awash with coffee. So, when the price of coffee is at 300 pounds a hundredweight, or whatever it is, and so I'll sell it at 300 pounds a hundredweight, and I'll just wait until it goes down to 250 or 280, and I'll buy back my August contracts, and then I've made 20 or 30 pounds a ton, er, hundredweight, or whatever it is, on it.'
>
> That's ludicrous, isn't it?
>
> (Lightfoot *et al.* 2009: 114)

The interviewer doesn't follow. The description of what is known as short selling deems the interviewer as ludicrous. Selling the commodity before buying it is strange behaviour outside the world of trading. For the trader it isn't. Besides the obvious, making money, it is just the reversal of thinking the normal path of trading goods to arrive at the logical reverse step needed for trading. If one has the opinion that prices on the market will fall and others in the market are of the opposite opinion, a short selling is the correct instrument. This is the trader's view. Any potential systemic risk is not involved. One must have a very special attitude and view this market from a perspective beyond the commodity in question to understand that the link to the commodity exists, or has formerly existed, but it is becoming increasingly rare:

> No. Not ludicrous. The thing is eventually backed by coffee. But you could trade a million tons on a futures market, and only have a hundred thousand tons, or ten tons delivered at your physical making and taking delivery on the Futures Market in the end.
>
> There's this peculiar mixture of the abstract and the literal.
>
> Yes.
>
> (Lightfoot *et al.* 2009: 114–115)

This peculiar mixture of the abstract of dealing liquidity, just money, only eventually backed by coffee, and the literal which in this case is coffee, this game of placing bets and influencing the real world of coffee producers and consumers has, as have all of the financial markets, shifted very much to the side of the virtual. Only a fraction of all deals in the futures markets are actually delivered in the end. The majority is cash settled. It is, as Spall explains, margin trade which gives the trades on these markets such an enormous leverage. The interviewer gains an impression of what it is really about, not surprisingly any more in our days:

> So it's a sort of game, really, isn't it?
>
> Yes. They're all games, yes.
>
> (Lightfoot *et al.* 2009: 115)

At this point Lightfoot *et al.* (2009) stress the seeming impossibility of satisfactorily disclosing to an outside interlocutor what it is precisely that is going on here. Spall's answers are a demonstration of the intransparency and ungraspability of the markets. The failure to explain satisfactorily to an outsider may be part of the game, the magician increases the fascination of the audience by explaining parts of his tricks, leaving other parts in the darkness of imagination. Or, the participants of the markets themselves have only insight into fragments and, therefore, must systematically fail to explain the system. And perhaps this is exactly part of the preconditions for the markets' functioning: it cannot be explained completely, otherwise it would be just business, predictable, boring, nothing to be proud of.

In explaining the world of commodity trading to an outsider, aestheticization has, or shall have, the effect of sharing the fascination for the activity itself and taking the situation over otherwise disturbing perceptions. However, a fissure remained and the interviewer put her finger on it. In this chapter, what cannot or should not have been explained – the source of fascination – will be interpreted with the concept of the sublime. But first another aspect of risk taking will be highlighted using an example from a high risk leisure activity: mountaineering.

Risk is taken or avoided

High standard Himalaya climbing is a risky occupation. Among the riskiest activities, to be sure: the chances of being killed are 1 in 8 or 1 in 10 per expedition. The reflections of an anthropologist who himself is a dedicated mountaineer can prove to be very illuminative in the context chosen here as well. Michael Thompson (1980) insists that it is necessary to research the aesthetics of risk in mountaineering instead of the economics of risk to understand why and how people come to accept very high levels of risk. There are several ways to climb Mt. Everest. The first one, originally chosen by Hillary, is no longer favoured by leading climbers due to improvements in equipment, or climbing activities of large parties supported by helicopters. To do this means to do less with more and to render the outcome a foregone conclusion. The interesting fact for Thompson was that not just his party reacted to this kind of behaviour by ridiculing it, but that also the local Sherpas entered the aesthetic framework and characterized the original route as 'The Yak Route' indicating that this is the easier and safer route which even these big animals can take. 'The aesthetics of high standard mountaineering are such that a proposed route is only felt worthwhile if there is considerable uncertainty as to its outcome' (Thompson 1980: 278). The convenient assumption is that Nepalese perform their job as Sherpas by carrying the loads and sometimes even the Sahibs, doing it simply for the money. The shared joke all of a sudden reveals that there might be more commonalities than the common conviction of the different cultures of East and West would allow. The challenge of the route, the perception of its risk, and the evaluation of this sort of risk as the 'right' one, is shared.

Thompson embeds this anecdote in the research about two completely different patterns of behaviour of peoples regarding risk taking in the region. Owing to the landscape and different types of food that can be grown and animals that survive in the different climate zones south and north of the Himalayas, there can be profitable trade between the regions, granting the potential traders a comfortable, though risky position due to the harshness of the landscape and the trickiness of the routes. History shows that it was the Buddhists who took the risks and moved, and the Hindus who refused the risks and stayed. All explanations ended up in a circle: 'Do they move or stay put according to whether they are Buddhists or Hindus, or do they become Buddhists or Hindus whether they move or stay put?' (Thompson 1980: 275). Both are right, Thompson claims, but they can't both be right at the same time. For an answer he introduces risk taking and risk avoiding as the leading difference between Buddhists and Hindus, and between serious, traditional mountaineers and high-tech followers. The risk taker's response to uncertainty is positive. He acts boldly, hoping for rich reward. The strategy occupied is that of risk narrowing, i.e. he disregards those possibilities that lie outside his immediate concern. The risk avoider's response to uncertainty is negative. It is better not to act as everything is connected and one thing may lead to another. The strategy becomes risk spreading. The reason for these very different strategies has nothing to do with cultural differences but with social context. The difference is simply if there is somebody around to share with. If there is no one to share the risk with, the risk can be taken individually and the profit can be gained. The one taking a huge personal risk does not want to share the profit with risk avoiding fellows in case of success. Social context makes the difference. The difference is a learned one. Due to the practice in the group, learning from success and failures, the attitude towards risk is locked into behaviour. It is possible to change groups, but with considerable effort in changing the investment structure, in fact ignoring past experience.

With Jack Spall, we witnessed the business becoming abstracted from its underlying. This may well be considered as outdated, having been recorded in the early 1990s. A parallel and most important development was the increasing computerization of the working places of traders which led to a major change on the screens. Today trading rooms look much different and surprisingly uniform: a narrow working space for the individual, crammed with four or six monitors and the phone enabling to shift between connections. The screens are not just carriers of information – latest news and rates on everything that might be connected to securities, currencies or commodities traded – but also trading platforms which connect market participants for trading anything that is not traded at an exchange. 'Over the counter (OTC)', as it is called, with the counter being provided by the ubiquitous and unavoidable intermediaries Reuters and Bloomberg, plus a few others. They provide the form and content of the screens, present in every work place in every trading room in the world.

Knorr Cetina and Bruegger (2002a, 2002b) and Knorr Cetina and Preda (2007) researched the social relationships in the trading rooms of banks acting in international currency markets. Their fundamental finding was a change from concrete interactions with counterparts to an enactment of the world of trades on the screens in front of the traders. The image still provided by the evening news – when they connect to their correspondents in the exchanges, with the background of hectic trading on the floor between humans to give their report of the developments of the day on the financial markets – is misleading. The trading floor in exchanges is just kept as an image for the outside world. The trades themselves have moved into the systems and the majority of trades takes place outside exchanges, between traders directly, OTC.[6] Any information about the market, any offer and any own activity, the generation of information by providers like Reuters', Bloomberg or Telerate, as well as the results of data collections of the individual banks, are completely represented on the screen. The markets do not exist somewhere out there; they are created on the screen. Sales and Buys match on the screen and not in direct interaction of traders on an exchange floor, or by telephone. The virtuality of the business finds its expression in the representation on the screens. The interviews in trading rooms led Knorr Cetina and Bruegger (2002a) to the conclusion that they researched business in a *postsocial* world. Currency trading is entirely exteriorized and embodied on computer screens. It has become a human-machine interface.

The screens' crucial role becomes ontological:

> the screens do not, in their core elements, *re*present a reality 'out there', but are constitutive of it.... The screen is a building site on which a whole economic and epistemological world is erected. It is not simply a 'medium' for the transmission of other interactions.
>
> (Knorr Cetina and Bruegger 2002a: 166–167)

Financial markets have achieved a peculiar independence. The screen creates a different reality. Participants of these deals on the screen become oriented to the projected reality to which coordination and action respond (Knorr Cetina and Preda 2007: 126).

The relationship to an other shifts. Traders position themselves simultaneously inside the markets as participants of global networks and they 'relate to the market on screen as exteriorized other, a sort of master-being that observes all transactions and includes their contextual conditions and motivations' (Knorr Cetina and Bruegger 2002a: 164). The screen as master-being, however, displacing the trader into a different (hyper-) reality alienates the trader from social relationships, but is also the representative of the market.

This seems to be in contrast to Michael Thompson's argument that social context is the decisive difference in risk behaviour. However, postsocial relationships between humans and objects are embedded in social contexts consisting of the group itself and its inner structures and in its difference to other groups. Traders share assumptions about the world they act in, they share narratives, or at least realize the relevance of narratives of the markets, as Valerie Thompson reports, and they trade narratives (Lilley and Lightfoot 2006) both in the market and about participants in the markets. Valerie Thompson gives a nice example of how traders are enacted into trading. In the 'City Lives' interview she reflected on how she became a trader and on her initial difficulties. Following time served as a telex operator and subsequently assistant and recorder of notes to a currency trader, Thompson herself is invited to trade. After initial doubts as she didn't have any education for the new job, she accepted. Obviously no formal qualification was asked for. The candidate was placed into the context and left to survive or not, training on the job by having her try to learn how to do it herself. Spall's notion that there is a good deal more to it than the interviewer seems to understand, is also a hint to the belief that there can be no formalized education to learn what is really at stake when trading. Thompson's description of her inquiries with colleagues, asking ridiculous questions and getting unsatisfactory answers gives the impression that the kind of opaqueness of the business that Spall seems so eager to keep is a common feature of the industry, perhaps even in the interest of the actors (ibid.).

Information is far from being clear, no accurate definitions are provided, just context which may mean different things on different occasions. The answers completely confuse. And they even may be intentionally so. It is also by no means clear, if the basic intransparency is only mirrored in the answers of colleagues, or if it is a defensive move against a new colleague to protect the own position in an opaque environment. Thompson became a successful trader by collecting bits and pieces of information from colleagues, by trying to understand the social context she was in and adapt to it. 'So ... I started, I made money. I don't think I, you know, I ... I learned how to do it, and I made money' (Lightfoot *et al.* 2009: 115).This is a mutual process. She receives information about what is going on, but this information is not an input processed to an output; the information also changes the actor. This is the crucial difference of what an aesthetic approach adds. Information is always part of the system. Referring to Kant, Cooper claims that the actor is decentred. She does not collect information to use it, to transform it to a success. She is enacted by the information, i.e. the actor is in-formed/en-framed (Cooper 1991: 6) instead of being a centre to which information comes and is processed with the centre left unaffected.

Risk taking in trading relies on the stories told in a social group enacted by the information shared. Either one shares the opinions about the Yak routes and the relevance of avoiding them for the big successes in trading, or one doesn't belong to the group. They belong to that group in the bank that is responsible either for the big profits or the huge losses trading the most abstract products in a virtual market which only exist on the screens.

Thrown into a completely virtual world with a different ability of perception needed, for the aesthetic quality of the world they live in, a difficult search for the meaning of this postsocial world starts, or simply a justification for the outside is required.

The sublime

Barnett Newman created the painting the title of this chapter is referring to in 1966/1967.[7] The painting is huge: 2.45 m high and 5.44 m wide, composed of three colour fields. The overwhelming part is red with a blue stripe of 15 cm on the left side and a 2.5 cm stripe of yellow on the right side. The borderline between the yellow and the red is slightly irregular, while the red and blue are separated more distinctively. Despite its size and the homogeneity of the colour red it is a canvas painted in oil colours.

Newman's painting is quite unusual. Its purpose is not just to challenge expectations of form and composition. It should enable the adventure of an experience beyond any well-known experience (Imdahl 1989). Newman gave an instruction of how to present the painting. The viewer should only be able to see the painting at close range, so that she will be concerned and completely overwhelmed by its size, experience the size as hugeness. There is an obvious tension between the maximum space given to the red and the minimum space given to blue and yellow. The stripes are small, but differ in size. Therefore the red is slightly eccentric to the whole of the painting. This is not without effect on the viewer. She tries to take a central place in front of the painting, but is prevented from an exact position so that she is, at least when she positions herself as advised by the artist, unable to perceive the whole rationally. This emotional irritation is what Newman aims at.

His intention is to go beyond any conceptually, mathematically, geometrically or aesthetically determinable order which the viewer might bring along to draw on absolute emotion as an elementary human capacity. Emotion is meant as the experience of the sublime which links to an experience and exaltation of the own self as an appeal for human independence, self-development and self-realization (Imdahl 1989). The painting refuses everything that is familiar. *The sublime is now!* as Newman (1948) declared in a short, programmatic text. The viewer becomes the centre of interest. The painting aims at the experience of presence of the viewer who is isolated from all of her familiar images and situations: 'I became involved with the idea of making the viewer present: the idea that "Man is Present" ' (Newman, as quoted in Imdahl 1989: 237).

The sublime is a concept that gained new significance in the wake of enlightenment to counterbalance the idea of the beautiful. Edmund Burke draws the line between the beautiful and the sublime through attention to feelings of pleasure and pain. Whatever is fit to excite the ideas of pain and danger, whatever is in any way terrible or operates in a manner analogous to terror, is a source of the sublime. The ideas of pain are much more powerful, have much greater affect on the body than those of pleasure. Pain is the strongest emotion (Burke 1998/1757: 86). Though the feeling of nothingness – the fear of extinction – is connected to the sublime, the sublime is also, Burke argues, a source of delight.

Lyotard (1984, 1989; Lyotard and Pries 1989) reformulates the crucial point in Burke's concept. The sublime is called upon by threatening to disrupt the continuation. Burke's examples always deprive the subject of something: the horror of darkness is deprivation of light; the horror of loneliness is the deprivation of the next; or, most important, the deprivation of life by death. For achieving their essential characteristic for the sublime, these horrors have to be displaced in a crucial way. They are mediated. To combine this kind of pain, the horrors of losses with pleasure, needs a certain distance to annul the physical threat. The shudder, the eerie feeling is produced but from a safe distance, so that it is mixed with a feeling of relief and is able to create pleasure. Displaced, second-order horror: the viewer is deprived of the direct threat of loss of light, language, life. Art and literature were the first means to achieve this kind of delight. The aesthetics of the sublime enables us to go beyond the mimesis of beautiful ideals. The artist wants to create the event, that something takes place instead of a discontinuation. This is Newman's central message: *The sublime is now*! (Newman 1948), taken up by Lyotard to emphasize a decisive sequence. Our thinking starts after something has happened with the question of what has happened. To ask this question, the event must already have taken place. *That it happens* precedes the question of *what* happened. *It happens, il arrive* first is a *Does it happen? Is it possible?* Only then the question mark indicates the question if it is this or that which happened, if it is possible that this or that happens? (Lyotard 1984: 152). It is a boundary which marks the possibility that nothing happens. Nothingness lurks behind the boundary. This waiting triggers impatience, nervousness, perhaps even despair if it is the artist in front of the empty canvas, the writer staring on the white sheet of paper while realizing his own incapacity to express that which waits to be expressed. But waiting can also increase the lust for the unknown and the pleasure of being. The feelings at this boundary are contradictory and this contradiction is expressed by the sublime. It is about the expression of what cannot be expressed, right here and now.

Cooper (1991) makes clear that it is not just the artist's waiting for *the* moment at the beginning, staring at the empty canvas, but every time something has to be waited for, is expected to continue – or not.

> The sublime, the beyond, the inexpressible aspect of the Event or the 'Now' is not something that resides in the 'beyond' as another place or time. Newman's point is that it is the 'it happens' is what is happening here and now – it *is* the paint, it *is* the picture itself, not some representation of an external reference … the sublime is ordinarily the sub-liminal – what's continually staring us in the face but which we never see.
>
> (Cooper 1991: 11–12)

The sub-liminal means 'up to the uppermost threshold' (Pries 1989: 12).

Kant (1974/1790) accepted the sublime as a new category of aesthetics, but changed Burke's more empirical concept to a transcendental procedure. His intention was to build a complete framework for connecting mind and reason by the sensual capacity of imagination. While the beautiful connects imagination and mind, the feeling of sublime results from the interaction of imagination and reason. For Kant the sublime is a term of judgement (1974/1790: §25). This categorization places the sublime inside the subject. It is not, like the beautiful, a characteristic of nature; it is a judgement about what is perceived in relation to the subject's experience. This is the crucial point: to transform the sublime into an experience in which mighty nature shrinks to almost nothing in face of the intelligible self-confidence. The respect evoked by the sublime is not of nature but the superior self of humans (Böhme 1989: 139). This is a clear manifestation of enlightenment. Before the sublime was the experience of a border which separated the tiny, subjected human from frightening and admired beings. Now it is a quality of the human, containing the fear. For Kant the sublime's task is to overcome archaic fears of nature. It is the aesthetic form of the modern programme of the subject's empowerment and subjection of nature (Böhme 1989: 126).

Risk taking is fun, seduces: perfect waves and bends

Mark Stranger (1999) looks at the 'aesthetics of risk' in surfing. His insights result from an intensive research of the Australian surfer community including own experience and interviews. High risk leisure is a feature of contemporary society, he claims. The thrill in risk taking in sport is an embodied experience. The sublime rests in becoming one with the wave, an ecstatic union with the power of nature, a power greater than the surfer. It doesn't destroy the surfer, but there is only a fine line: 'Apotheosis and annihilation are separated by the narrowest of margins' (Martin, quoted by Stranger 1999: 271). He observed that the thrill of surfing can be experienced in small surf, but that it becomes harder to replicate when the skill level improves. It needs ever stronger waves to achieve the intense thrill the surfers are looking for. One of the interviewee's answer is indicative: 'It's like a drug. You get the thrill fairly easy at first, but then it becomes harder and harder to achieve and you have to ride larger and larger waves in order to get that feeling again' (quoted by Stranger 1999: 267–268). Looking for a more intense thrill the surfers do not strive to increase the level of risk,[8] but it is seen as a by-product by chasing the most intense thrills.

Media have their share in increasing the risk levels. Surfing becomes ever more aestheticized by constructing and reinforcing the sublime in photos and videos. A wider audience is infected with the desire to share the transcendent moments of the perfect wave. The images in magazines and electronic media do their work: 'Increased levels of desire help to counter greater levels of fear, and in this way the surfing aesthetic and the surfing media help facilitate greater levels of risk taking through the aestheticization of risk assessment' (Stranger 1999: 273). The activity becomes meaningful without need of further justification and rational risk assessment is replaced by unreflecting desire.

Another activity where people are seemingly ready to take a great risk is motorbiking. Driving a motorbike is a dangerous way of moving with pace. No safety belt, no airbags, no steel around the driver, just a helmet and a few plastic protectors – if these are worn at all. Taking the common place 'thing to be avoided' model of risk one might assume that this mode of transport would be given up as soon as it becomes possible to drive a more comfortable and safer vehicle. But the bikes are still here, faster and more powerful than ever. Perhaps because motorbiking embodies play with and experience of the enormous acceleration, which is afforded by a vehicle-driver assemblage that is incredibly light in relation to the power its engine can generate. Ruling this power is one motivation to ride a bike. Showing car drivers the back wheel, seeing their image becoming smaller and smaller in the rear mirror – provide a prosthetic feeling of superiority. Two quite different modes of fascination for this kind of conscious risk taking will be introduced.

John Berger, the novelist and art critic, who wrote the influential book '*Ways of Seeing*' (Berger 1972), still, at the age of eighty, rides a motorbike. His description (Berger 1992) demonstrates the experience's aesthetic value in a fascinating way. He admits that biking is dangerous but denies that it is a flirt with death. Perhaps, he claims, bikers take a certain distance from everyday life but not to start a dance with the death; they want to be carefree, want to follow their own look. After a few hours of driving the feeling prevails to have left behind more than just a few cities and villages. More important the all too well-known constraints of everyday life have been left behind and open up the mind for a special perception of freedom, resting between oneself and the space. It is connected to the image of a target, both subjectively and concerning the space. The eyes are the target mechanism while driving. Wherever you direct your look, you and the bike will follow. Basically you steer by looking at something and not with arms or body. And it works in both directions. Your look leads you, but what you set your sight on, also drags (Berger 1992). You are drawn and the body and the bike follow the distant target, the one which seems to be interesting right there and now, independent of the constraints one usually feels. Risk is no topic here. It is present, acknowledged, but the feeling of freedom overrides all reservations.

Of course there is an ongoing stability, but it is the result of a continuous adjustment as a consequence of what you perceived fragments of a second before. This perception is visual, but also tactile and rhythmic. Often the body realizes faster than your head (Berger 1992: 41). Biking is a corporeal experience.

The novelist and journalist Hunter S. Thompson[9] gives a taste of what is at stake beyond the carefree ride, if the experience is a flirt with death:

> [W]ith the throttle screwed on there is only the barest margin, and no room at all for mistakes. It has to be done right ... and that's when the strange music starts, when you stretch your luck so far that fear becomes exhilaration and vibrates along your arms. You can barely see at one hundred; the tears blow back so fast that they vaporise before they get to your ears. The only sounds are the wind and a dull roar floating back from the mufflers. You watch the white line and try to lean with it ... howling though a turn to your right, then to the left and down the long hill to the Pacifica ... letting off now, watching for cops, but only until the next dark stretch and another few seconds on the edge.... The Edge.... There is no honest way to explain it because the only people who really know where it is are the ones who have gone over. The others – the living – are those who pushed their control as far as they felt they could handle it, and then pulled back, or slowed down, or did whatever they had to when it came time to choose between Now or Later.
>
> (Thompson 1965: n.p.)

Going over The Edge is a telling metaphor for the risk involved – the risk of death, destruction or, at least, some fairly debilitating disability. The moving experience of driving down the Pacific highway, of going too fast – faster than the law allows – has a dark side as Thompson admits by beginning his article with consideration of the wreck that was once his motorbike. Hunter Thompson is well known for excessive experimenting not just with biking, but also with drugs to explore the boundaries between life and death, consciousness and unconsciousness, of sanity and insanity. Stephen Lyng (1990) takes his notion of *The Edge* as a reference point for his framing similar kinds of high risk leisure activities as 'edgework'. Edgework activities involve a clearly observable threat to one's physical or mental well-being: sky-diving, rock and ice climbing, auto and motorcycle racing, downhill skiing, or scuba diving are among Lyng's examples. Thompson's nonchalent statement describes quite well, what Lyng is pointing at: 'You have to be good when you take nasty risks, or you'll lose it, and then you're in serious trouble' (Thompson 1974, as quoted in: Lyng 1990:

858). Edgeworkers have an extreme elite orientation. They see themselves as having a mental toughness which makes them master the most extreme situation in their activity. They have the ability to maintain control in situations which most of the people would regard as entirely uncontrollable. Testing the limits of the machine or the abilities and mastering the difficulties leads to an attitude that those who sadly enough had an accident have proven not to be real edgeworkers. They simply didn't have it. A feeling of omnipotence is a consequence, also a feeling of being one with the machine. Their commitment is to get as closely as possible to the edge without going over it.[10] There is a tendency in searching for ever more purified forms of edgework with even artificially increasing the risk involved.

What the notes about motorbiking make clear is that there is more at stake than just the appreciation of being in the nature. Risk as game with extinction, drawn on and through the foil of the beautiful. The continuous attempt to find the limit, the boundary between the maximum speed possible through a bend, and its mastery to remain exactly on the ideal line; the ability to stay on the limit without being thrown off the bend into the abyss: that is the sublime suspense of motorbiking,[11] the aesthetic aspect of edgework's meaning. It is the aspect of ruling, of power that can be interpreted as a modern realization of Kant's take on the sublime, that it is an overcoming of archaic fears of nature. High risk leisure can be taken as exemplary for the subject's empowerment and the subjection of nature.

Looking for the sublime in the trading room

By carefully reading Burke's, Kant's and others' texts on the sublime it soon becomes clear that the conclusion trading is sublime cannot be put as straightforwardly as it initially seemed. Something doesn't fit, sounds wrong, when risk is described as sublime. We have to be more precise to catch the point.

Three high risk leisure activities were introduced for an explanation of the influence of the sublime. To see how far an analogy with trading and the risk in trading may reach, a look at the structure is helpful. There are at least three components in which the sublime unfolds. These are an action, the risk taken, and an aspect of nature. In surfing it is riding the wave, the risk is collapsing into the wave and potentially drowning or being thrown on to a reef, the aspect of nature is the power of the wave, THE wave and being able to master it. With motorbiking it is the driving, the risk is being seriously injured or killed by going over the edge of the bend, the aspect of nature are the centrifugal and centripetal forces which keep the otherwise instable vehicle on track, or the appreciation of the landscape. Mountaineering involves the risk of being killed by falling off the track to get up the highest mountain. Nature, or the laws of nature, are sources for the fascination, the trigger of the sublime. The overwhelming feeling derives from the greatness and incredible power of the wave, the subtle balance of physical forces able to destroy the bike and the driver, and, the prototypical example of Burke and Kant, the mountain. The risk involved is being consumed by the sublime forces; the thrill is being able to master the challenge. There is, however, a crucial difference of these high risk leisure activities to the Burkeian model of the sublime: the loss of distance. The aesthetic concept of the sublime insists on two steps. The initial terror, perceiving the frail body threatened, fearing the pain, extinction, and the relief turning into pleasure following from realizing that there is no real, physical threat. In all the high risk leisure it is possible, if not probable, that the actor moves beyond the edge. It is a game with the powers of nature, and the intention is to prove its mastering. I can ride the mighty wave; I can take the bend with the highest speed possible; I can master the highest mountain on the most difficult route. This goes far beyond the nice thrill of Gothic novels, even if these are the masterpieces of its genre with contemporary settings which make the reader tremble, as if she is the heroine in the novel. Similarly in the arts: The overwhelming feeling created by the RED in Newman's painting gives just a distant, displaced idea of what the sublime of taking the risk itself actually creates. Stranger (1999: 271) analysed the loss of distance involved as a de-differentiation: '[S]urfers *experience* the sublime in unison with the object of the *appreciation* of the sublime.' This leads to a serious distortion of any rational risk assessment. Desire is added to the experience. The surfer wants more, an ever higher wave. De-differentiation leads to a sublime synthesis of emotions and 'the likely outcome from such aesthetic judgements of risk is a sublime appreciation *of* the object and the desire for engagement *with* it' (Stranger 1999: 272, emphasis in the original).

What is the thrill in trading, the 'what' that makes it so desirable? The assumption in this chapter is that there is an aesthetic quality in trading, that the risk involved or the nature of the business itself has the quality of the sublime. This quality cannot be described properly to an outsider, there is more to it, as Spall put it. Selling short, i.e. selling something that the seller does not have, is one kind of trade which makes these markets special and opaque for outsiders, makes it worthwhile for traders:

> I think the first thing that you're taught, and perhaps [...] it's the most difficult thing for people to understand, is that you can sell something that you haven't got. And sell short. [...] And that, really, it's paper trading. Quite exciting, and very nerve-wracking.
>
> (Lightfoot *et al.* 2009: 115)

It is nerve-wracking if it has to be accepted that the own assumptions on an investment strategy are opposed by a stronger force, which wipes out the own position, a larger investment house, or a central bank with an opposite opinion about certain securities. This kind of nerve-wracking quality is put clearer by these statements of bond traders:

> Until you take your first position home and try to go to sleep at night and wake up the next day with a loss staring you in the face, you never know if you can live with it.
>
> (Abolafia 1996: 240)

> The mentality of being able to take a loss is a very unusual trait in people. To be a trader you must have it. To be able to go home every night and know that one of the nights you lost maybe half a million dollars and get up the next morning and come to work. That's tough. That's tough on the body and tough on the mind. You have to be a special kind of person.
>
> (Abolafia 1996: 239)

This is how the risk taking in trading comes closest to a corporeal experience. It's tough to go home with the consciousness of the possibility of a financial loss in one's position. The absence of a physical threat to the frail body is the crucial difference to high risk leisure. Nevertheless the images used to describe the feeling in the trading room give a different impression. They tend to be heroic, emphasize the risk involved. The trader's view is on one-to-one challenges, he concentrates on his positions and the speculation of the motives and moves of the counterparty. The trading floor is a place to win:

> There is an adversarial relationship in that the trader is not a fraternity type of brother. It is you against him. You would love to make money at his expense and that's all over the street.
>
> (Abolafia 1996: 242)

Abolafia (1996) collected male-oriented images like gun-fighters, fighter pilots or professional athletes as self-images. '[Trading] is like catching bullets with your teeth' (Abolafia 1996: 240). Although the edgeworkers researched by Lyng (1990) explicitly denied gambling as edgework, as this involves circumstances that cannot be controlled by the risk taker, several of the criteria of edgeworking are present here. It is a threat to one's mental well-being; the one taking the risk has to be good or he will lose it; the extreme elite orientation; the ability to maintain control in situations that most people would regard as uncontrollable; the attitude that those who fail simply didn't have it.

Considering eighteenth century aesthetics in literature Poenicke (1989) comes to an almost sardonic conclusion which, nevertheless, provides us with a valuable hint to the situation in trading rooms. The sublime is a jump into the abyss of something overwhelmingly threatening, immediately followed by a feeling of redemption, because the self has saved herself and feels up to the danger almost titanically. The immediate pay off of extreme fear is the opposite: extremely increased power. Poenicke (1989) concludes that we, therefore, actively look for opportunities to meet the sublime, as it is some kind of a power drug. The dark romanticism following the aesthetic understanding could then be seen as a drama of a procurement addiction. More of it, and ever more from different realms is required.

This level of threat, however, is on a different level than the threat for the individual trader. The power of the whole market never comes into sight: 'I have a first rule of survival: not become too personally involved in the market. Otherwise you can get caught up in fighting this thing and you can't win', is a statement by a trader (Abolafia 1996: 240). Is the market the source of the sublime?

The market as the source of the sublime

One profound irony of the situation at the beginning of the twenty-first century is that we learned from postmodernists to mistrust in metanarratives, that metaphysics is suspicious, but at the same time saw another absolute other emerge. Where risk replaced fate, money replaced God in the relationship with time and eternity.[12] The theological fixation was removed in favour of a monetary fixation. The failure of theodicy of providing a proof for God's existence, in the time of the development to a globalized return on investment, gave way to replace the idea of God with the more mundane idea of a symbolized global exchangeability, i.e. money. The exchanges take place on the market, which is globalized in a crucial double meaning. We live in a globalized world, included into the global market in a way that it has become very hard to distinguish between the two; and it is a generalized idea. Despite the fact that there are many different types of markets with many distinctions for industrial or consumer goods, for mass markets or individualized ones, and marketing intends to segment them further, these share a generalized idea of the market. Markets are not local any more. Competition is expected to come from everywhere and goods produced and delivered everywhere. The market transformed into an absolute other: THE market. It is not seen as a result of the actions of its participants, but that the participants have to serve the market's logic. The market has won an independence. It seems to exist outside and above its participants and is able to regulate itself. Trade liberalization, the standardization of rules to prevent system frictions from national rules are nowadays institutionalized. Orford (2004) analysed the development of international rules and regulation known as GATT (General Agreement on Trade and Tariffs), GATS (General Agreement on Trade in Services) or the WTO. Her conclusion is that this process has consequences which go far beyond the securing of international trade. The constraints set instead by existing local rules and regulations, procedures or decisions are potentially extremely far reaching in that they go beyond trade agreements and become more governance agreements. A similar move can be watched in the financial markets. At the preliminary end of a forty-year period of deregulation in the banking industry, beginning with the end of the Bretton Woods regime of fixed currencies in the 1970s the financial markets have won an impressive independence. Not only are they freed from many former regulations, they have also won independence from other markets to which they were formerly connected. They completely turned the dependence: financial markets make the prices for commodities as a consequence of the trading taking place in derivatives. Haas (2008) tried to give an image of the relationship between the trade in derivatives and the economy it is built upon. This shows a remarkable turn of relationships. Once created to manage the risk of price volatilities of producing companies and their value being a friction of the value of produced goods and services, it now looks as if the production has become an almost negligible part. Haas used the estimated Gross World Product of 2007 (as estimated by published reports of the CIA), US$65.61 trillion, and the total value of all shares of stock issued that is available to trade on all stock exchanges of the world, i.e. a figure coming close to the world's capital base by the end of 2006, US$53.51 trillion with the figures of the Bank for International Settlements (BIS), the bank of national banks which provides statistics of international financial markets on derivatives by the end of 2007: US$680.29 trillion. Haas concludes that a loss of less than 8 per cent of total derivative exposure would wipe out the world's capital base.[13] This is an interesting figure: Basel II, the international banking regulation[14] stipulates a coverage of 8 per cent of base capital for all risks of losses for a bank. If there is an argument for the sublime of the market, it is the size and the threat originating from the annihilating potential for the world economy. No coffee beans left.

Looking for the sublime of risk or in trading is in some contrast to other areas discussed so far and to aesthetic theory. Incorporating the market means a crucial replacement to these other concepts. Following the structure given for high risk leisure we can identify the potential ingredients of the sublime in trading. The action is trading, the risk is the loss of money, and the overwhelming aspect is the market. The market, however, has a very different character as to what it replaced in this structure, nature. But the effect seems to be similar. The market has replaced nature as the opposite for humans, as the entity to be mastered. No complete view can be achieved, it is always greater than the individual can perceive. The 'market is a nebulous type of animal', a bond trader is quoted (Abolafia 1996: 238). Or, even clearer in the following dialogue between a researcher and a currency trader:

LG: You know it's an invisible hand, the market is always right, it's a life form that has being in its own right. You know, in a sort of Gestalt sort of way () it has form and meaning.
KK: It has form and meaning which is independent of you? You can't control it, is that the point?
LG: Right. Exactly, exactly!
KK: Most of the time it's quite dispersed, or does it gel for you?
LG: A-h, that's why I say it has life, it has life in and of itself, you know, sometimes it all comes together, and sometimes it's all just sort of, dispersed, and arbitrary, and random, and directionless and lacking cohesiveness.
KK: But you see it as a third thing? Or do you mean the other person?
LG: As a greater being.
KK: ()
LG: No, I don't mean the other person; I mean the being as a whole. And the being is *the* foreign exchange market – and we are a sum of our parts, or it is a sum of its parts.

(Knorr Cetina and Bruegger 2002a: 169, omissions in original)

A life form that has being in its own right, no control possible, a greater being: the market appears to be an independent reality, a given to which the individual is at mercy. Human made entities consisting of nothing but human actions, decisions or regulations seem to acquire an existence independent of the humans who keep the market going, who constitute it by taking part of it by buying and selling. Transcendent qualities are subscribed to it. The viewer is perplexed. In a completely rational environment where calculation seems to reign, where the aim is to gain the highest profit possible and the participants are sure that they have the rational chance to win, all of a sudden metaphysical, religious formulations are used to describe what is more to it. The market is the overwhelming other, although it is clearly seen that it consists of its participants. The market is seen as an independent entity, opposed to the individual trader, able to annihilate the position, but also provides the 'power drug' (Poenicke 1989). The successful trade means being up to the demands of the powerful market and the self feels up to the danger almost titanically. The increased feeling of power can be interpreted as the reward for permanently taking the risks on the market.

The preconditions for the sublime taken from high risk leisure – the wave, the centrifugal and centripetal forces in motorbiking, the mountain – are parts of nature. The market is entirely human made. Nevertheless it is possible to ascribe to it a fascination, a power similar if not equivalent to that of nature. I will come back to potential interpretations and consequences in the last sequence. Before that the structure of the risk in financial markets will be perceived with the help of Baudrillard's ideas on representation and simulation.

The sublime simulacrum

The business has become virtual and takes place on the screen. Together with the speed – 'real time', indicating that there is no time lag between pressing the button 'confirm' and the actual effectiveness of the trade – these are defining factors for the technical sublime (Bartels 1989). Starting from early nineteenth century, nature as the principle source for the sublime increasingly became replaced by human made artefacts. Kant (1790: §25ff.) already made the difference between raw nature as the source of the dynamic sublime and cultivated nature as source of the mathematical sublime. The mathematical sublime is the starting point of the technical sublime. It refers to architecture: the pyramids, cathedrals and other huge buildings. Adding the movement of huge machines and cogs is a consequential step in the industrial age. The artificial infinity created by huge buildings is combined with the sublime of speed. Trains, planes, war, where the technical sublime of huge machines became one more time physically threatening, are steps to a hyperkinetic sublime as the result of the addition of the dynamic of flying, the dynamic of war and the dynamic of photographing. Put to the extreme we arrive at the replacement of nature; artificial nature, simulation, creates the feeling of the sublime instead of nature (Bartels 1989: 308). Nowadays, Bartels (1989) claims that the microcomputer has taken over this role of hyperkinetic sublime. Despite the fact that his article, which was published only about twenty years ago, seems to concern the predicted consequences of the microcomputer almost struck with a portion of naivety, given the more provocating contributions to a representation of wars on screens by Baudrillard (*The Gulf War Did Not Take Place*, 2002), it points to a central issue here. The screens have become the artificial nature that creates the sublime. Aggravated to a post-social relationship the representation on screen is not just detached from nature, it creates a world of its own. There is no nature as a given reference point any more. The durability in time and space, which gave reference points in nature, is lost. Bits and pieces of information are delivered on the screen. It is the creation of the trader's reality in the moment of delivery. It is a process, but of a different quality as the image of one action taking place after another to create a meaningful result. It is 'an infinite succession of non-identical matter projecting itself forward as changing screen' (Knorr Cetina and Bruegger (2002c: 398). This is the source of the sublime. Riding the wave of an infinite succession of non-identical matter, waiting for THE wave.

The artificiality of the screen's reality is also stressed by the fact that the trader may feel his position threatened but the frail body remains safe. It is not just the virtual displacement of bodily danger. He is trading risks, not taking risks. The trader is never directly endangered; it is a series of numbers which she deals with – in the double meaning of the expression – which affect a position, again in the double meaning of the term: the financial position and the position of the trader in the bank, including bonus payments. It can be called a simulated experience of the sublime, although it clearly affects emotions.

Referring to the work of Jean Baudrillard, entering his version of hyperreality, unveils an otherwise hidden aspect. What McGoun in his paper on 'hyperreal finance' (1997) writes about the status of money or stock prices in the four phases of simulation, can also be used for the description of the changing role of risk.

> This would be the successive phases of the image: – it is the reflection of a basic reality – it masks and perverts a basic reality – it masks the absence of a basic reality – it bears no relation to any reality whatever: it is its own pure simulacrum. In the first case, the image is a good appearance – the representation is of the order of sacrement [*sic*]. In the second, it is an evil appearance – of the order of malefice. In the third, it plays at being an appearance – it is of the order of sorcery. In the fourth, it is no longer in the order of appearance at all, but of simulation.
>
> (Baudrillard 1983: 11)

In the first phase risk reflects a basic danger. The risk of going to sea is losing one's life, the risk of mortgages is the failure to pay the rates. In the second phase the basic reality is masked and perverted. Risk is calculated and distributed to groups of investors. The individual sailor's risk is masked, not visible any more. In the third phase the basic reality is absent. Risk is transformed into a derivative and hides the needlessness of an underlying. It may be traded because of the underlying, or not. This is no difference for the derivative. In the fourth phase the sign bears no relation to any reality, it refers to hyperreality, i.e. there is no representation anymore. This is a perfect description of a derivative at the end of securitization. Risk is separated from the product; it is an ongoing process of purification of risk. Risk is distilled, from asset to future to option on future. During the development of products answering to ever more fine tuned requirements of hedging risk, an essence of risk is produced, exorcised from assets, as Lilley and Lightfoot (2006) have observed. A risk referring only to itself with no need for an underlying. Given the original intention of trading the risk away from the asset, it seems that the assets are now secure again. The financial markets take over the risk and leave a secure business environment, at least free of those risks alien to the entrepreneur.

What can a sublime simulacrum be then? The dynamics of the international financial markets, existing on screens; looking for the thrill of trading; consuming the power drug and doing edgework; riding the wave of an infinite succession of non-identical matter means taking part in the process of the creation of the market of which the individual trader is part of. In Baudrillard's terms it is acting in hyperreality, i.e. a reality substituted by the signs of reality. Risk is the simulacrum in the sublime market, a purified essence of infinite range. In the market trading takes place for the sake of trading. This is the hyperreal characteristic: trading simulacra of risk for the sake of trading in the sublime market. Despite all the hedging efforts, risk can still be realized. Even if the position is properly hedged, second-order dangers (Holzer and Millo 2004) remain possible, as the global financial crisis of 2008 has proven. Securitized mortgages hedged by derivatives proved McGoun's (1997: 117) conclusion wrong that hyperreal finance may have only negligible effects on other parts of the economy.

Trading risk evokes the sublime, but…

In this final sequence the result of the aesthetic analysis will be linked to a few other aspects. It must be clearly seen that this kind of trading is a consequence of a conscious decision in favour of free markets. The line of thought developed for the market as the sublime needs to be extended to realize an intrinsic consequence of setting the market as absolute other. Jacques Derrida (1995) read the biblical parable of Abraham as an example of the relationship to the absolute other. Dealing with the absolute other – in the case of Abraham this was God – proves in the extreme what is at stake when responsibility is linked to the duty – in this case the absolute duty – to an other. This parable describes the extreme, the sacrifice of the own son by the order of the absolute other, but it is valuable for demonstrating the basic problem involved, the aporia of responsibility. 'The story is no doubt monstrous, outrageous, barely conceivable', admits Derrida (1995: 67). 'But isn't it also the most common thing?', he continues. An orientation to an absolute other, as in Abraham's case, accepting the responsibility for it, always and undeniably means sacrificing other others. But this holds true not just for the relationship to God, it is the most common thing in the relationship to any other. Either one accepts absolute responsibility to the single other representing an absolute singularity herself, or one answers to a family, a community, a nation etc. One has to sacrifice the one for the other, is Derrida's conclusion.

Setting the market as absolute other for any economic relationship thus means sacrificing others. If the free market is the point of reference, deregulation becomes a must as regulation means to distort the forces of self-regulation inherent in the markets and binding the markets to values external to it. This opinion about deregulation is not uncontested any more, to say the least (representative for many Klimecki and Willmott 2009), and complaints about regulatory holes come from prominent sources (e.g. Cox 2008) after the very obvious failures of the markets recently. Derrida, however, provides a profound philosophical reasoning for a critique on setting the market absolute. Judging from this perspective the dark side of concentrating solely on the market becomes clear. Trading for trading's sake becomes possible without the responsibility for damages outside the markets. The thrill of taking risks in a sublime market and the exclusion of responsibility are justified.

Looking through this glass another play of images and projections starts. Freeing the markets from regulation led to a greater freedom for the actors on these markets. The completed globalization offers almost endless opportunities to move capital around the world and also labour. Bauman analysed the profound changes which accompany this development. Modernity, he claims (2000, 2008) has become liquid. His keywords are deregulation; abdication of politics; individualization and fragmentation; immediacy as the irrelevance of time in crossing space and getting satisfaction; the proliferation of an elite in the form of exteriorized nomads; a shift in the significance of the masses from producers to consumers; the replacement of leadership by the spectacle, of surveillance by seduction. Long-term aims have become impossible to follow. All these slight or massive shifts result in an increasing uncertainty, instability and vulnerability of contemporary life. Fear is created without an identifiable source. Independent of origin, pressure is built that looks for an adequate valve. As the sources of uncertainty cannot be addressed directly, the pressure finds its way to the individual security in the immediate environment. The feeling of uncertainty is increased by the retreat of the state from formerly self-evident tasks. In this context, the shift of the responsibility for old age pensions, at least partly to private forms, could be quoted as one example of these crucial changes. State guaranteed pension schemes are now only part of the of old age income. The rest has to be done privately or by pension funds which invest the money in financial markets. The individual who is not an actor on the financial markets, and in their majority do not intend to become involved, is nevertheless becoming dependent on the developments in these markets.

In this situation the individual looks for certainty and security. This may set a projection in the scene in which an aestheticization and the valuation of trading might play a role that is not completely overt. Besides those who were always fascinated by gambling and the impression of easy money at stock exchanges, besides the attempts to increase private investments in stocks and other activities to grant a better accessibility of the markets for the 'Joe Smiths', a need to inform and worry about own investments is part of everyone's reality now. This driven interest is served – or co-created? – by the media with long columns of rates and comments on the outlook of the markets in newspapers, by the daily reports from the exchanges on the estimations and rumours of traders on actual developments, etc. Special magazines describing investment strategies, publishing technical analyses like those done in banks, discussing fundamental values of stocks and giving recommendations serve a similar role as those special magazines for surfing and motorbiking. They co-create a public image of the topic in question. The image is that it is rational to invest in these markets and the decisions taken are rational and explainable as well. It is a matter of calculation and the sophisticated models, which the banks develop, are a mandatory part of risk management. This is a serious business, capable of containing the fears of future, the public image can, or shall be interpreted.

Of course the public image is also influenced by fictional characters in novels or movies, sometimes turning living persons into figures which might well have been invented, or vice versa, of course: the invented figure becoming all too real. Steve McCoy, the master of the universe, bond trader with a salary like a telephone number, was an invention in Tom Wolfe's novel (1988) shaped by the expectations of the readership. Gordon Gecko in the film *Wall Street* by Oliver Stone (1987) became the synonym for the ugly trader. Eric Packer in *Cosmopolis* (DeLillo 2003) as the stunning example of what was seen as the result of the exaggerations of the nineties at the stock exchanges gambled away his billions, but kept his philosophical attitude. André Kostolany made his living as an individual speculator and gained public attention in Germany as a positive example of making a very good living from the international markets. He wrote books (Kostolany 2004) and appeared in TV shows, presenting him as a nice, successful and wise old man. John Meriwether, inventor of Liar's Poker, was a real existing bond trader at Salomon Bros., appeared in a book by a Wall Street insider, Michael Lewis (1990), and later founded a hedge fund together with two Nobel Prize winners that became a landmark of spectacular failures. LTCM aimed at risk-free profits (MacKenzie 2003b), but also can be analysed as unbounded irrationality and organizational narcissism (Stein 2003). The dot com bubble was first accompanied by a hype and, after bursting, by a damning in the media. In these different academic as well as popular publications, do we see a peculiar mixture of fact and fiction, a desire for certainty and an idealization of dealing with the risk? This is not intended to mean that MacKenzie or Stein and the other ethnographers cited so far are trapped by LTCM and their managers, but that the images found contribute to an overall impression about the trades in question and their protagonists oscillating between fascination and disgust.

Realizing the implications of a god replaced by money, the market set as absolute other, the audience is shocked about the sacrifices to be made and projects its disgust on the traders who just live in a purified way what market-orientation has made possible: trading away uncertainty, insecurity for huge amounts of money. Money is the defence against the threats of life, so is the idea of insurance. A loss can be evaluated in terms of money and this loss can be replaced. The risk is insured by a company which itself has to hedge the risk. It does so at re-insurances and the international financial markets. Money's grip on all aspects of life seems ubiquitous, its power institutionalized. 'The institutionalized power of money', concludes Shafer (2001), 'is a defence against rapidly increasing powerlessness and diminished faith in personal and institutional authoritative leadership. Money is currently over-valued, to protect us against unpredictability.'

The current over-valuation of money to protect against unpredictability and uncertainty is the common factor of life in liquid modernity and the expansion of trading activities in financial markets. In a world of uncertainty it is reassuring that risk can be traded away, that it can be hedged. At the same time risk taking is not reserved for trading. The interesting observation here is that the rise of high risk leisure to a mass phenomenon and the extreme increase in trading derivatives developed in parallel. The basis of both is the mastering of uncertainty and risk. Lyng (1990) concludes that voluntary risk taking is a type of experiential anarchy in which the individual moves beyond the realm of established social patterns to the very fringes of ordered reality. Edgework challenges the limit between order and disorder, form and formlessness and therefore is a thoroughly aesthetic concept. The fact that many people find this alluring and seek to repeat it as often as possible is an important critical statement on the nature of modern social life (Lyng 1990).

In the world of trading risk is the sublime simulacrum, referring just to itself in its own hyperreality. That this hyperreality does not affect other (hyper-)realities has been proven an illusion. 'So it's a sort of game' was the interviewer's question to Spall. 'Yes. They are all games, yes' was the answer. Prices go up or down and the game is about 'you against him' (Abolafia 1996: 240) and the emotions of defeat, of felt violence and attack are present all the time (Knorr Cetina and Bruegger 2002c: 400). The threat, represented on the screen, seems to come from everywhere and nowhere specifically at the same time. The reference to the market as a greater being is telling, it is overwhelming. The traders, it can be concluded, struggle with the same anxieties as others living in liquid modernity, but they have found a field on which to fight the anxieties created by the uncertainty with the perspective – or the illusion? – to momentarily gain the certainty of a success on exactly that field which creates the uncertainty for everyone by mastering the risk of the market. The nice side effect is that they also earn the money to buy them certainty in real life. This is an extremely privileged position for which traders are envied as long as everything is running smoothly, and hated when they create an even deeper uncertainty by the actor's inherent tendency to exaggerate, by their desire for an ever larger wave.

One should not forget that the privilege goes even further. Traders can lose their job, if they are not successful enough, however the measure of success inside the institution is set. Beyond that, their risk is limited. They do not participate in the risk they take for the institution they trade for, as a female broker told Honegger *et al.*:

> One reason for the disaster is the asymmetrical risk profile that many people have. If something goes wrong, nothing happens, but if it turns out to be

> great, I cash in fully. Inside the banks there should have been a lot of people with brutal responsibility, but they didn't see it. In the middle management, you can brutally earn money. The responsibility is with the bank.
>
> (Honegger *et al.* 2010: 136)

If aesthetics' role for organization theory would consist just in reminding us to research organizations beyond functional terms and giving us the means to do so, something would already have been achieved. To develop aesthetics' critical potential, however, needs to avoid the pitfalls of concentrating on the beautiful and neglect its other, the sublime and with it its fascinating, but also dark sides. This chapter 'towards an aesthetics of risk' is an attempt to use the sublime to look for a possible explanation of the obvious – the oscillation between fascination and disgust while following the events on the global financial markets.

7 The risk to come – a different way of thinking risk

Towards a risk to come

Risk and the management of risk (re)entered public attention during the global financial crisis and the years since then. Before that, in times of continuously rising yields, the old wisdom, the higher the yield, the higher the risk, which informed the decisions in the financial markets for centuries, seemed to have miraculously lost validity. The ambition to create risk-free profit by calculation (MacKenzie 2003b) seduced market participants on both sides, traders and salespersons in the financial institutions as well as private investors including those in the retail market. Some kind of generalized greed (Honegger *et al.* 2010) seemed to have filled the system. There was a hunt for ever more profitability of investments not just on the side of traders and salespersons in the banks and in the funds, but also on the side of private customers investing into the products of banks and funds. The immense liquidity in the international financial markets was looking for ever better returns. Warning voices were silenced, either by ignoring them as single opinions without relevance for the insiders,[1] or they were fired, as several interviewees of banks after the meltdown told researchers (Honegger *et al.* 2010: 70, 108, 124). Even the Chief Risk Officer (CRO) didn't have a chance to insist on a critical estimation of the risks involved, as Otto Steinmetz, the former CRO of a large German bank, told in an interview:

> Perhaps they've [the CROs] trusted in their internal models too much?
>
> STEINMETZ: Perhaps, at least that's what BaFin[2] believes. But what would have happened to a risk manager who said two years ago that he wanted to build the bankruptcy of a major American investment bank into his models? And if he'd stated on the record that he couldn't back the risk?
>
> He could have left.
>
> STEINMETZ: Then he's seen as a bad leaver and loses his variable pay, share options, even his pension entitlement. And who'd give him another job?
>
> (Pfeil 2010: 27)[3]

What, today, is included in stress tests developed by regulating authorities was seen as so absurd before the Lehman bankruptcy that a calculation of the consequences in the risk models would have rendered even a CRO an outcast. There is no doubt about the fact that investment banking and risk management have to clash, Steinmetz confirmed (ibid.). In times where investment banking was responsible for the majority of profits in a bank, any doubt expressed was seen as a cog in the profit generating machine.

Risk management that tries to control risk by influencing investment decisions, i.e. prevent investments of or into incalculable risk, is seen as an obstacle for the generation of profits. As indicated by Steinmetz and proven during the stress tests, such cases can easily be calculated. The increasing capacity of IT provides the basis for ever more sophisticated mathematical models shaping the risk profile of the complete exposure. Risk management in the banking industry takes the form of the calculation of an enormous amount of data, which can already be interpreted as an excess of data (Pelzer 2007). The conflict in practice between traders and risk management, as significant and telling as it already is as an example of the fragile security in the banking industry, however, tends to cover rather than reveal a fundamental flaw in the thinking of risk. Even an excess of data does not lead to an adequate reading of the situation. There is a shortcoming in the assumption of calculation itself.

Taking risk, financial risk that is, can be evaluated, and the probability of a loss predicted, is the core assumption in mathematically driven risk management. This is not a statement which concrete business will fail, but a statement of the probability of losses for all the risks taken. This is an attempt to make an otherwise unpredictable future present. It is in the nature of risk that the uncertainty expressed by it can turn into losses. If and which loss is realized will only turn out in the future. Risk then can be interpreted as a form of considering possible futures, evaluating them and acting accordingly. Risk, as it is seen here, is not just an expression of uncertainty, of what may go wrong, but the so-called rational expression of dealing with an unknown future made known in the present as artificial, produced reality. Seen like this, as a tool for risk management, risk is order. Risk orders future by making it present.[4]

George Shackle, based on the Keynesian concept of uncertainty, already made clear that the consideration of the future is not that simple, as rational theory implies. It is impossible to know the consequences of one's own actions before they are performed (Shackle 1967). Information about the future is necessarily incomplete as it cannot predict the exact results of one's own actions. Shackle redefines the crucial difference between possibility and probability. Probabilities still show the signs of gambling where it was introduced. They aim at present futures while possibilities aim at future present. Possibilities describe the situation of an actor who needs to decide in the context of an uncertain future. Shackle's use of the terms 'time-to-come' and 'choices-to-come' as something not predetermined and predeterminable[5] are expressions of a potential surprise. Potential surprise of what is to come is a nice preparation for discussing the paradoxes involved in risk and risk management. Arguments developed by Jacques Derrida around what is 'to come' will be used to elaborate on that side of risk that cannot be considered by calculation.

What is 'to come'? Democracy (2006), justice (1992), the university (2001), the invention (2003), friendship (2002) are among Derrida's examples and it is very clear that there is a difference between an event taking place in the future and the examples which are 'to come'. The event which will occur, or not occur, is im-possible, as we have already noted. It is unexpected, singular and unconditional. Once it occurs, it has become possible, can be repeated and thus immediately belongs to the context and changes it at the same time. In this changed context decisions can be and will be taken to structure the future to be again surprised by an event. The examples Derrida gives to explain what is to come have an even more complex construction. We know all of the concepts he uses for a long time. At least we think we know them, we ascribe meaning to them. We have a clear image of what they may mean. We have an image of how the ideal could be or how it was conceived during the history of its use. We can analyse what is realized and how big the difference is. Deconstruction as a method helps to find out about the developments of the concepts throughout history, understand how they were introduced and immediately changed and distorted in its first and the following usages, e.g. out of a very one-sided understanding of friendship (Derrida 2002), so we can become conscious of the difference still there. And that the difference will never be overcome. But this description implicates that there is something like an ideal, a regulative idea, perhaps even a utopia. Derrida not just denies the necessity of any teleological or ontotheological concept which he considers as distorting. Instead he insists on withstanding the aporias he unveils. One of his difficult thoughts here is his construction of the future to come. What is to come is not something fixed, a whole that is just not yet achieved, but an other that will never be achieved completely, as both sides are changing in the process of realizing what is coming. What is realized changes what is there and offers new opportunities. The difference to what is still to come remains, not as an additive whole in which one side gains what the other loses, but with a redefinition of what can be understood in the process of coming. Future points not just to the coming of the other, it is directed at the invention *by* the event (and not *of* the event) (Derrida 2006: 126). The coming, anything to come (*à venir*), doesn't only have no requirement for regulative ideas. Democracy to come doesn't necessarily mean a future of a democracy, which will come or should come. Nothing concrete is announced. Democracy to come does not mean 'the democracy will come'. To remain coming, failing to appear, unfulfilled, pending and withdrawn from any dependency on an ontology – what can be the status of democracy? The modal status of the 'to' in 'democracy to come' lies in the oscillation between two possibilities without ever being able to decide: imperious order (a performative demand) and the patient '*perhaps*'[6] '(a non-performative ascertainment of what is coming, but also may not come or even may have already occurred)' (Derrida 2006: 130, emphasis in original, author's translation). The first would be the analytical part, considering the contents of the term democracy constatively. Using the term one has to know what was written into it, how it was used and what the dimensions of its meaning are. As a performative statement, because of the absence of a full meaning, a final definition, because it remains to come, it is necessary to believe in it. Both attitudes may alternate, may address you one after the other or haunt you both at the same time, leave each other and become an alibi of the other. Oscillating between the possibilities, without ever coming to rest on one side, means using another word – *undecidability*. Derrida believes that this undecidability which is part of democracy as well as of freedom itself, is the only radical possibility of decision; of having (performatively) it or her happen or rather (metaperfomatively) admitting it or her as event. It opens a completely ambivalent and unsettling experience of freedom, threatening and threatened (ibid.: 130).

The potential of what is described here as 'to come' is large and promising. It denies a fixed, objective, constant future for concepts like democracy. It is the philosophical foundation of a thinking which assumes that the possibilities in both dimensions, what to achieve and what to lose, changes on the way into the future. There is no such thing as a zero sum game here. Any step taken in the direction of democracy does not mean that another tiny part of what an ideal democracy is will be realized and that the rest will be achieved piece by piece in the future. It is a moving target and it will always be. With any step taken, the understanding of what can be achieved, even the definition of what that is which can be achieved, changes. The understanding of what democracy means opens the field for more expectations, or at least for more possibilities, which can then be aimed at, achieved, or not, and on that way, in discussing and fighting for realization, any image of what an ideal may mean, of what can be achieved, is constantly developed.

Derrida didn't work with the term risk as explicitly and intensively as he did with the others discussed here so far. He mentioned risk in interviews, which give an impression of the depth of the term if it is thought by the somewhat annoying combination with the adjective absolute: *absolute risk*. He also mentions it at a central point of his thinking about the relation to the absolute other. The *Gift of Death* provides a few remarks which hint at the direction which he might have taken if he had developed this term further: 'a venture into absolute risk, beyond knowledge and certainty' (Derrida 1995: 5). The absolute is the norm if we consider the consequences of aiming at the im-possible, of moving beyond the horizon, of triggering the event. All these terms aim at the space beyond knowledge and certainty, a very uncomfortable place, where no experience helps and uncertainty on the way is the decisive feeling. It needs to take absolute risk to decide, to go through the ordeal of undecidability, to face the other.

Derrida's arguments are used here to describe a dimension of risk which is necessarily ignored by a risk management that relies on data from the past to calculate the probabilities of the realization of known risks in the future. The risk described here is, on the one hand, the risk of taking decisions beyond what is known, decisions that are more than a choice between alternatives. This would be 'a venture into absolute risk, beyond knowledge and certainty' (ibid.). However, such a form of decision happens quite rarely. Nevertheless it is a form that is not covered by routine risk management. But these kinds of decisions, so one could speculate, are an interruption of the everyday decision making of managers and, therefore, get the recognition beyond routine which might cover the risk involved. The risk to come is not covered by this. Derrida turns our attention to a dynamic involved in any social interaction. The risk to come is the necessary contrast to risk as understood in risk management. It is exactly the difference between the calculable, the processing of programs, the following of the trajectory of the well known that needs to be contrasted. The perhaps strange move taken here is the turning of the phrase 'to come' from something to be longed for, something from which to achieve the full potential, is entirely desirable, to something where the fruit of achieving the full potential is at least a doubtful pleasure. It depends on how risk is defined. Is it just the negative impact of a decision, or is the volatility included, that is, an outcome can be better or worse than expected? But even this remains inside a framework of the expected. Any evaluation of risk that considers what can be expected and what has to be avoided deals with the calculable, with what is already known as potential consequence of deciding and acting. Any management of these kinds of risk will inevitably fail to grasp the event. It doesn't aim at the im-possible. It only takes the possible into consideration – into calculation. The term risk helps to draw an image of the future. It makes future present and with that known. Such a future can be calculated, it is possible to count on it. However, we can only take into calculus what is known today, or what has left traces in the past, something which has already occurred and can therefore be followed on the time arrow into the future. 'Probability', as Cooper mentioned, 'is a form of prediction or prior awareness which defends the system against the strange and the unknown' (Cooper 1987: 397). What remains to come, haunts the present from the future.

Trading away future

In her ethnography of Wall Street, *Liquidated*, Karen Ho (2009) describes basic attitudes and mechanisms of investment banks and their employees which she also considers as key elements having led to the global financial crisis of 2008. The results of her study, however, explain this crisis as just one crisis, or, less a crisis for the investment banking itself, but rather the result of normal ups and downs of the markets. Wall Street takes pride in being one with the market and, therefore, following the chances of the market as long as possible. Being one with the market means getting out immediately when it turns out that there are no chances any more. This includes the firing and rehiring of large quantities of their staff without prior announcement. Speed matters: getting out of projects immediately is mirrored by getting into other projects as quickly as possible. Being one with the market means mistrust against planning, almost an open refusal to do so, as one of her informants expressed: 'How do you plan when you never know what the market is going to do?' (Ho 2009: 276) The dynamic of Wall Street is to make money immediately, to make use of the chance presenting itself right now. Efficiency in the sense of developing products over time, improving them, is sacrificed for immediate rewards and the next new thing. Ho's expression for this proceeding is 'strategy of no strategy' (Ho 2009: 274). She does not criticize these banks for being without strategy, as if they just don't consider a long-term orientation to the future as part of the development of the banks. She claims it to be a constitutional factor of this kind of banking. The actions and the behaviour of investment bankers exclude long-term thinking. Investment banks are 'institutionally unable to peer into the future' (Ho 2009: 279). Investment banks defuturize[7] future, they trade-off the future present for the present future, which is nicely incorporated in a form of derivative called 'future'. Futures are used to transfer a risk in the future to another party willing to accept it out of a different evaluation of the future development, so that for the party trying to get rid of the risk the present future is less risky. The potential chance of the future present being better than those estimated in the present future is given away in favour of an advantage here and now. This well makes sense for the management of an industrial company who, for example, wants to transfer the risk in the international currency markets. The risks in this market are not part of their business and limiting these risks is a rational move. The construction of the financial product 'future', however, is a crucial play with the different levels of future. It tries to transform the volatility of outcomes of present actions in the future into a product tradable in the present. By trading it now, the risk has acquired a form manageable within the horizon of the known. It could be taken as a warning that this special product, future, can have a plural form: of course there are futures.

This is exactly the point where Derrida's arguments become crucial. There is no such thing as the one, determined future. Only one concrete future will realize, but up to the realization many are possible. The argument, however, goes much further. This is not just a quantitative argument. It doesn't mean that there are more futures to be calculated. This would require that all these possible futures are known today, only which one will be the future present is undetermined. But this completely fails to take the event, that what is to come, into account – if that is possible at all, to take what is to come into account. It is exactly the characteristic of the event that it is im-possible before it has taken place. There is a part in risk which defies calculation, which lies beyond the teleological horizon, which is a result of the absence of fate, a result of the fact that any decision taken will inevitably trigger reactions which will alter the conditions of the decision and will help to realize an event, an im-possible event.

This argument in combination with Ho's characteristic of Wall Street bank's strategy of no strategy, the complete and only reaction to the here and now, precludes risk. Defuturized, the presence runs into the disaster without a means of stopping at the edge of the abyss. Trying to think the im-possible as a necessary part of reality, a part of a CRO's task as Steinmetz tried to describe it, becomes impossible. It is excluded from the radar of risk management, but paradoxically included by exactly this exclusion: the im-possible is that risk which is not just made possible by excluding the risk to come, it is even made probable by this move, and so is the consequence of thinking in Derridean terms here. No one is present who is ready to see the risk to come arriving; or, to be more precise, no one who has the authority inside the bank to warn or take action if an event takes place, no one left to care about the future present. This is not to say that risk management, however it may be organized and authorized, could identify the realization of a risk to come, the im-possible event, but the acceptance that the future present will be different from the calculation of the present future. This is the first and necessary step to reduce the effects of the risk to come to those risks which are really behind the teleological horizon and to make a difference to those risks which are only behind the horizon of ignorance: these risks could be identified if the denial to peer into the future would not have been institutionalized like in Wall Street banks.

Risk to come means that the character of the risk changes along the way into the future. A realization does not mean that it can be described sufficiently to deal with it in the next term. The dealing with the risk, its calculation and the trading of risk, of hedging against it, will inevitably alter the risk and provide it with the capacity to be realized in a different form. The risks we know may change, the volatility, the probability of their realization may change, or an event may take place demonstrating the incompleteness of the knowledge. Risk is a much more complex topic than risk management by calculation is able to cover.

8 Risk and regulation disseminate

The *pharmakon*

> To lose one's head, no longer to know where one's head is, such is perhaps the effect of dissemination.
>
> (Derrida 2004c: 17)

Dissemination is one of Derrida's terms rendering all attempts to fix meanings impossible. The book he wrote about is both explanation of the term and demonstration of the effect. Even more radical: the demonstration is the explanation. 'This (therefore) will not have been a book' Derrida (2004c: 3) starts his, well, what is it? The reader would expect some kind of a preface, an introduction. But with the first sentence the author makes clear that he has something very different in mind. The translator's difficulties had already started the page before, with the title of this preface refusing to be a preface. The text is deconstructing itself to demonstrate the 'simultaneous impossibility and necessity of prefacing', writes Barbara Johnson, the translator of the English edition, in her preface of *Dissemination* called 'translator's introduction' (Johnson 2004: XXXIII). The word dissemination is disseminated within a preface on prefaces and the first sentence represents several moves which will have been made: a presentation ('this'), anticipation ('will'), negation ('not'), recapitulation ('have been'), and conclusion ('therefore'), Johnson explains. It has to be seen as an anticipatory retrospection and internalized exteriority. Expecting what will have been in the future by reflecting on it as if it were already past; an im-possible, vertiginous move to subvert the normally assumed order, to make clear by a permanent movement of meanings that the meaning of texts, definitions can never be fixed. Dissemination is an attack on the notion that texts can be owned, controlled, limited or appropriated in the name of some legitimate authoritative source (Norris 1991: 112–113). This (therefore) will not have been a risk the consequence for this text could be circumscribed. Risk and regulation disseminate.

By saying dissemination 'is', however, we are immediately trapped. In trying to find out what it does to the terms we use we try to get a fixed meaning and oversee that the term dissemination itself is, of course, subject to dissemination. Defining what risk is then, becomes a fruitless attempt.[1] The wonderful (at least for the analyst, the deconstructive reader) effect is that any term is changing with its context, with its use and its users, the time passing and the space over which it is moving. It is easy enough to accept that risk means something different when it comes to judging the safety of a nuclear power plant or throwing the dice. We judge from the consequences. Can a definition be given that covers all the necessary aspects? Will the result be a definition so abstract and empty that it makes no sense to use it? Yes, but dissemination tells us more. A definition as well as the meaning of any text can never be fixed, it will always be immediately supplemented by the first use of the word.

Ortmann (2003: 14) expresses the consequence that if organization is understood as the work on fixation, ascertainment, determination of meanings, this work must be seen as always necessary, but never successful, never concluded. Risk as an eminent feature of organization makes no exception, although 'risk disseminates' is a strange expression. However, the passive version – risk is disseminated – is misleading. It would require an identifiable source, an actor, or a group of actors who start with a risk and then disseminate it for whatever purpose. The point is that risk, as any language structure, inevitably disseminates, although it does not disseminate itself. It is a result of the permanent supplementations in the process of existence starting with the identification of the risk. The identification of a risk can be seen as the attempt to fix the meaning of a concrete risk of a concrete business. But with the attempt to fix the content of the risk, its meaning, the understanding of the risk is disseminated by everyone and everything that has contact directly and indirectly or is just related to it by others. In the context of ongoing decisions (or running programs) inside the bank or outside, risk's context changes, it is interpreted, calculated, hedged, or counter measures are taken; actors react on its identification and the measures taken and so change the context. The risk may realize in a different way and somewhere else than anticipated: it will have been materialized differently.

> Indeed, if such a thing were justifiable, we would have to assert right now that one of the theses – there is more than one – inscribed within dissemination is precisely the impossibility of reducing a text as such to its effects of meaning, content, thesis, or theme. Not the impossibility, perhaps, since *it is commonly done*, but the resistance – we shall call it the *restance* – of a sort of writing that can neither adapt nor adopt such a reduction.
>
> (Derrida 2004c: 7)

Talking about a term like risk with its obvious inherent ambiguity – denoting chance and potential failure at the same time – an elaboration of the term with the help of Derridean thinking adds the necessary complexity to the notoriously blurred meaning of the term risk. Showing how risk disseminated, disseminates while talking (writing) about it, and will inevitably go on disseminating, is a valuable exercise when delving into topics of the international financial markets. To get this kind of practice Derrida's discussion of the *pharmakon* is especially useful.

The *pharmakon*

In 'Plato's pharmacy', the second chapter (or, the first chapter after the disseminated preface) of *Dissemination*, Derrida demonstrates what dissemination can mean on the concrete example of the term *pharmakon*. To be more precise, it is a discussion of the meanings of a family of terms: *pharmakeia*, *pharmakon* and *pharmakeus* which Plato already used in *Phaidros*, and *pharmakos* which Derrida adds to the discussion. *Pharmakon* sounds reassuring, it is the medicine and as such at first sight connected to the positive process of healing, of restoring health, of rebalancing a body out of balance under the influence of external forces. Derrida, however, insists that the term is notoriously ambiguous: 'There is no such thing as a harmless remedy. The *pharmakon* can never be simply beneficial' (Derrida 2004c: 102). It is a drug and as such has the potential of working in both directions, towards remedy and harm, curing an illness or causing detrimental effects. The effect is not restricted to pills, Derrida aims at texts:

> Only a little further on, Socrates compares the written texts Phaedrus has brought along to a drug (*pharmakon*). This *pharmakon*, this 'medicine', this philtre, which acts as both remedy and poison, already introduces itself into the body of the discourse with all its ambivalence. This charm, this spellbinding virtue, this power of fascination, can be – alternately or simultaneously – beneficent or maleficent.
>
> (Derrida 2004c: 75, emphasis in original)

The ambivalence is what characterizes the *pharmakon*, with no prescribed certainty about which direction its potential effect might take. To render the potentiality even more complex, it cannot even be said whether the effect goes in one direction or both at the same time. In the course of the visit to Plato's pharmacy it becomes clear that the effect is not restricted to the acknowledgement of the danger of measuring out a wrong dose or a wrong diagnosis. Derrida aims at a more fundamental problem raised by the introduction of text as a supplement of language as discussed in *Phaidros*. Socrates told the legend of a divinity, Theuth, who invented numbers and calculation, geometry and astronomy, even draughts and dice, but most importantly, writing. Because of his status as a demigod he offered his invention, writing, as a kind of present to Thamus, the king of gods. The reaction was not as Theuth would have imagined. He praised writing as an improvement of the memory and a contribution to the wisdom of the people. Derrida's view is that Thamus is faced with the *pharmakon*. The value of writing, estimated highly by its inventor, is nothing without god-the-king's approval. For Thamus writing is presented, it is not his own, it is coming from below, and he is asked to judge. He is sovereignly independent: he speaks, his word is enough. Thamus therefore rejects, belittles, abandons writing; the *pharmakon* presented to him. The present, the gift,[2] is not only not adding, for him it is subtracting. He sees the potential of harming what he evaluates highest – the living, knowing memory. Writing is good for re-memoration, recollection or consignation and for artificial devices such as 'inventories, archives, citations, copies, accounts, tales, lists, notes, duplicates, chronicles, genealogies, references' (Derrida 2004c: 109). Therefore Thamus cannot see any added value and condemns it as being of little worth. In his writing, his report about Socrates' lecture, Plato attacks the substitution of the mnemonic device for living memory, substituting the passive, mechanical by-heart for the active reanimation of knowledge.

Derrida interprets this present/ation as *pharmakon*. Even if the divine, sovereign attitude is removed, the detrimental effect remains. Writing is presented as an improvement for memory, a remedy against forgetting and in this represents the ambivalence of the term. Remedy against forgetting means an externalization of memory. Knowledge is transferred from the individual owner, or a group sharing the experience from which the knowledge stems, to an objectified medium where the relation to the constitution of the knowledge is cut off. The present of writing is double-edged: it can help, reduce forgetfulness, but it is also an impoverished version of what it archives. The text Plato produced to praise the superiority of speaking has been kept for more than two thousand years, but we have inevitably lost the context of both what Plato was teaching in class about this issue, and the context of Socrates' dialogue with Phaedrus. Recommending writing as a remedy, thus translating *pharmakon* one-sidedly is the attempt to reduce ambiguity. This is what Derrida aims at, insisting on the other end of the spectrum, the fundamental ambiguity of all terms, definitions: 'No absolute privilege allows us absolutely to master its textual system.... It cancels out resources of ambiguity and makes more difficult, if not impossible, an understanding of the context' (Derrida 2004c: 98–99).

Pharmacia (*pharmakeia*) signifies the administration of the *pharmakon*, but this term, too, contains a double meaning. It is not just the keeper of medicine, the institution or person informed about its use for the betterment of the ill, it takes over the ambivalence of medicine and poison contained in the *pharmakon*. Already in ancient Greece poisoning was a common meaning of *pharmacia*. In the Greek mythology Pharmacia was the nymph of a well with poisonous powers. It is remarkable that Platon uses an incident at this well at the beginning of Phaidros. Orithyia was carried off by Borea at this spot, while playing with Pharmacia. Or, less mythological: while playing, the boreal winds blew her into the abyss. Can it be coincidental that a story about an accident with the victim dying is placed at this point of the text? It remains enmeshed in the entire dialogue. It marks the potential negative pole. The well, perhaps with curative powers, perhaps poisonous, stands for the unsettling ambivalence of the *pharmakon*. Already before the introduction of Theuth and his invention of writing, the negative connotation of writing is discussed with the topic of the necessary capabilities of a true practice of medicine based on science. If anyone thinks he is a doctor, because he has picked the knowledge from books or blindly uses drugs, 'the man is mad' (Plato, in Derrida 2004c: 78). In the context of Socrates' dialogues writing is inferior.

Within the family of terms the *pharmakeus* can be expected to run the *pharmacia*, to prescribe, to use and to make use of the *pharmakon*. The play with ironies starts when Socrates as a philosopher is introduced as *pharmakeus* to describe its diverse connotations. Several sources addressing Socrates are quoted which all aim into a similar direction. His superiority is acknowledged and even praised, but it is also made clear that his capabilities are a source of anxiety for those who get under his influence. The effect of his arguments is compared to the viper's venom in their ability 'to penetrate and make off with the most concealed interiority of the body' (Derrida 2004c: 120). The *pharmakeus* is a magician, a sorcerer, a poisoner, provides the power for the priests, the medium for the priestly rites of sacrifice (ibid.). The irony, however, does not consist in rationalizing the *pharmakeus*' magical arts, in explaining away its effect by describing its functioning. 'rather, it reverses the *pharmakon's* powers and turns *its* surface over – thus taking effect, being recorded and dated, in the act of *classing* the *pharmakon*, through the fact that the *pharmakon* properly consists in a certain inconsistency, a certain impropriety, this non-identity-with-itself always allowing it to be turned against itself' (Derrida 2004c: 121). When performing the roles in the realm of risk, we will see what an ugly consequence this irony of non-identity-with-itself might have, or, recently showed.

Pharmakos is the term Derrida adds to Plato's discussion of the *pharmakon* (Derrida 2004c: 130). On the one hand it is a synonym for *pharmakeus* and not discussed in Plato's text. On the other, it had a very special meaning added by the Greek culture. Thus it can serve as an example for the enormous extension of the context influencing the actual discussion taking place between the protagonists and, passing by, it also opens the way for an important argument in the realm of risk in the financial industry. What was the role of the *pharmakos* in Athens' society? Sociologically it is a very interesting one. The Athenians had a special use for selected members of the underclass. Several of them were maintained at the public's expense. When critical moments occurred, like droughts, pestilences or famine, two of them, a man and a female, were chosen, led out of the city and sacrificed. It was a ritual, and although death was included, it was not the central point. The two served as a representation of the evil. Leading them out of the city, performing the ritual, can be seen as an act of purification. It is a reconfirmation of the boundary between the inside and the outside. '[T]he *pharmakos* represents evil both introjected and projected' (Derrida 2004c: 134). Again this aspect of *pharmakon* is ambivalent. It is both beneficial, as its sacrifice heals, and harmful as it incarnates the powers of evil. Basically the *pharmakos* is the conscious storing of outcasts as scapegoats.

Of course the irony cannot be left unnoticed that a discussion about the harmful effect of writing is presented as a text. Derrida takes up the text on writing to elucidate Plato's reasoning in order to substantiate his own thesis that even language is already the result of dissemination. Any expression of an object, an event, of an impression, always comes late. It is a reproduction and for Derrida a reproduction of something of which there can be no original. Language supplements. Without supplementation we cannot talk, let alone write. This is the effect of *différance*. Naming something adds and subtracts that which it names, it defers and differs. This difference – *différance* – between signifier and signified and the being cannot be bridged. With every use of a word what is signified is supplemented. What we perceive as a result is just the trace left by the process of signifying. Writing then is a derivative of speaking; speaking a derivative of what is assumed to be talked about. The derivative, however, has a meaning of its own. It supplements its underlying of which only a trace is left. The trace replaces what was considered to be the origin. Derrida puts it even more radically: he denies that there ever was an original (Derrida 1983). What we can perceive is an ever moving development of traces which are the result of using words in ever changing contexts. As time goes by.

The *pharmakon* risk

This family of terms can aptly be transferred to the realm of risk, risk management and regulation, so is the background for this delving into the discussion of the *pharmakon*. It is quite obvious for the term risk itself. Risk is a *pharmakon*. It is essentially ambiguous, as it always signifies both chance and potential failure. It denotes a difference from present expectations and future outcomes. The uncertainty involved in any decision is covered by giving a name to it, by rendering it calculable. Supplementing a decision with risk, however, has consequences. It is not just the insight that the term itself has two dimensions. It is also the effect in the course of deciding which unveils risk's character as *pharmakon*. Risk is order, so it was argued above, which intends to grasp the future event, the consequences of the decision. Risk leads the decider to believe she is in control of the consequences of the decision, that the potential danger of the necessarily absent, that beyond the horizon, the unknown, can be ruled. Risk as order is vulnerable against the detrimental effects of risk controlling. As it denies the im-possible, it becomes a risk itself.

For the role of the *pharmaceia*, the pharmacy, there are two candidates. They aim in the same direction: an organization of risk so that the consequences will not destroy the risk taker or the risk taking institution. Risk management of a bank aims at knowing the risk position the bank has. The intention is to make the aggregate level of risk transparent, which all the businesses of all different departments represent. This overall level is the focus of decision at board level. It defines the risk appetite of the bank. Risk appetite, however, is an expression of regulation. Regulation intends to set boundaries on the risk appetite of the individual bank so that losses from failed businesses do not threaten the existence of the bank, especially not of those seen as system relevant. Regulation looks at the stability of the banking system and aims at preventing failures which destabilize the banking system as a whole. Risk management and regulation then are the pharmacy of the market of risk taking. They provide the medicine, the remedy, but oversee the poisonous potential of the *pharmakon*.

The nymph of a well, *pharmakeus*, is in this case only exceptionally female. It is, depending on the level of perception, either the individual bank, or the individual trader. The bank is the focus from the perspective of regulation, the trader from the perspective of a bank's risk management. He deals with the products which are risk. Here a crucial doubling can be observed. The products which are used to transfer risk from one party to another are risky themselves. Risk and product become the same. The product traded is the risk to be transferred. Risk has inherent risks itself. Risk is risky. The *pharmakeus* should know about the dissemination of risk in the markets. How he is also taken away is the subject of Chapter 5, looking for an aesthetics of risk.

According to Derrida's observation, the *pharmakos* was absent in Plato's discussion, but cannot be kept separated. It belongs to the semantic field. The (re) introduction of the *pharmakos* makes the observer look to the casting. Would anybody take on the role of a trader or of an extremely risk-oriented head of a bank without knowing what the scapegoat is? The global financial crisis showed one thing perfectly clearly: the state and the taxpayers were cast in the role of the scapegoat. Bailing out is the name of the sacrifice. The actors on the markets act as if nothing can go wrong, as if the market always has the right answer. Some actors win, others lose. Any winning is due to the wits of the actors, any losing is the bank's accountability or externalized to the public. The trader may get a smaller bonus, or fired, but the assumption that the wheel keeps turning, is not challenged.

The *pharmakon* regulation

The ambivalence of risk is clear. It is a probabilistic statement about the chances of a future element. Therefore, what the risk is characterizing may turn out exactly as calculated: it may turn out to be better, or it may turn out to be worse. Trading the risk proves the ambivalence of risk in several dimensions. The trade itself contains a risk. The risk which is traded does not vanish. As part of risk management – to trade a risk away, to hedge it, is an active tool of risk management – it contributes to the success or failure of risk management. On each of these steps risk can be a remedy or a poison, it can help to prevent the potentially harming situation and it can be the ingredient of the action that leads to a loss. Regulation, seen as the pharmacy potentially containing the medicine to prevent the harm of risk taking, and an aggregated loss resulting from too many risks turning out to be poisonous, cannot deny its double-edgedness as well. Pharmacia, the nymph of a well with poisonous powers, gives the name for the pharmacy. The pharmacy is the collection and the knowledge about the drugs which may heal, which may give remedy. If the incorrect medicine is prescribed, if the dose is wrong, if there is no adequate substance or if the pharmacist oversees the illness, the contrary will be the effect. The ambivalence is inherent to both: risk and regulation. They interact. Risk gives the reason for regulation, regulation tries to shape risk and risk taking. The interaction of ambivalent terms renders the result almost unpredictable.

To describe the relationship between risk and regulation in their two dimensions of remedy and poison, a two-by-two matrix can be drawn. Such an image,

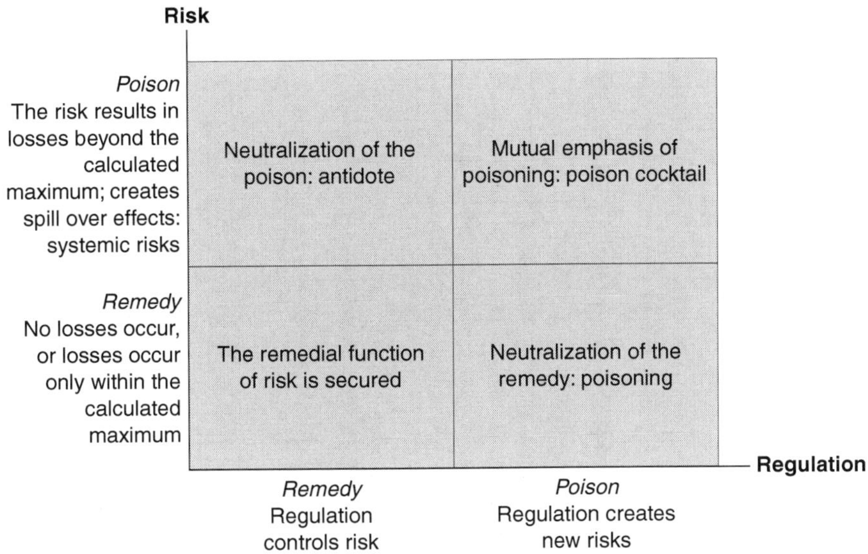

Figure 8.1 Risk, regulation and the effect of *pharmakon.*

however, has, despite its informative value, side effects. It contradicts its own message. Dissemination is the topic demonstrated by the *pharmakon.* Trying to grasp the *pharmakon* by a graphics looking like a mathematical representation, or even worse, like a consulting tool, the attempt is immediately transformed into that order from which the discussion of risk management suffers. Keeping this '*risk*' in mind, the result is the following.

The four squares indicate a dynamic relationship between risk and regulation:

- The remedial function of risk is secured: risk and regulation play out their remedial aspects. Regulation took precaution that risk management works in a way that the losses are kept within a manageable frame.
- Neutralization of the poison: antidote. Regulation's remedial aspects are able to deal with the poisonous effects of risk. Regulation was able to make the banks resilient. Even if losses are larger than calculated, spillover effects to other parts of the economy can be prevented. There is no danger that the financial system as such would collapse and the sector has to be saved externally.

These two squares describe the terrain regulators aim at. It is either the normal world of risk taking and risk transferring. The results are as expected by the market participants. Or it is the situation where good regulation is required to prevent the crisis. The next two squares frame the situations in which the intended outcome of regulation does not appear, or even the worst case.

- Neutralization of the remedy: poisoning. Regulation's poisonous aspects destabilize. This describes the utmost failure of regulation. The regulation is not just wrong, so that it does not control the poisonous aspects of risk. In this case it is the creator of additional risk. By following the regulation additional risks in the financial system are created, or existing risks are intensified in a way that they result in spillover effects to other parts of the economy.
- Mutual emphasis of poisoning: the poison cocktail. Regulation's poisonous aspects meet with the poisonous effects of risk. Regulation intensifies the effect of losses. It is not only not able to control losses which exceed the calculated buffer of capital, but it creates new risks or emphasizes existing risk in a way that other parts of the economy suffer from the risks of institutions they are not connected to.

Calling potential effects of regulation poisonous is perhaps irritating. Regulation will help to prevent negative effects. There is a positive bias which originates in the intention to prevent harm. By naming regulation *pharmakon*, however, helps to see that the result of the regulating process is by no means clear. This is more than to say that regulation may have a back side, that despite its best intentions it may also have unintended consequences. *Pharmakon* indicates a crucial 'and': it is remedy *and* poison. Despite the fact that some of the effects may not be predictable, there are aspects of regulation's effect that were predicted already during the discussion before implementing the Basel II accord and a small stream of publications warning about other effects since then. The comments either discuss the value of the tools, if they are able to fulfil their function, if the assumptions of the methods are correct, if the construction of the accord as a whole shows deficiencies; or, they question the validity of central ideas of the regulation. It is not my intention here to give a detailed discussion of the deficiencies of Basel II, but to provide a few examples of what *pharmakon* implies in the context of regulation.

A large bundle of criticism is about the regulation's quantification. The Basel accords heavily rely on risk metrics. The central problem for risk management in the banking industry is the knowledge of the overall risk exposure. Could the question be put, what is the Value at Risk at any given point in time? and with this the name of the central statistical figure also be presented: Value at Risk (VaR). Denominated in units of a currency, it is a measure to name the potential loss of the portfolio with a given level of confidence. It indicates that, under normal market conditions, there will be not more than a loss of x € with a probability of y per cent during the next n days. If such a figure could be given reliably, this would greatly enhance the stability of the financial system. Despite its almost ubiquitous use in risk reporting, VaR is not a proven mathematical rule but a probabilistic statement. It is just an estimation of future outcomes. Criticism of this figure is clearly expressed, questioning its value at such, or identifying concrete shortcomings which then are proposed to be solved by improvements of the existing metrics or by replacing them with different measures. Just briefly considering several of the shortcomings of VaR and similar risk metrics casts doubt on its validity:

- VaR is not sub-additive. It should be assumed of a coherent risk measure that the risk it indicates is the same when judged on the individual risk or all the risks taken (Danielsson *et al.* 2001). Sub-additivity is the reflection of the idea that portfolio diversification makes sense, because of the overall reduction of risk. From the perspective of the risk management of a bank, the criterion of sub-additivity has two sides. If the sum of the potential losses does not sum up to the same amount as an evaluation of the whole, the VaR does not reflect the risk position. Given that, it is also an incentive to decentralize risk measuring, e.g. into several subsidiaries, as the diversified risks require less regulatory capital (Basel Committee on Banking Supervision 2010).[3]
- This problem is incorporated into the architecture of Basel II. Each risk category is calculated individually. The capital requirement is the sum of the categories in Pillar 1 (credit, market, operational risk), plus the sum of risk categories in Pillar 2 (concentration, liquidity, residual and other risks). An integrated risk approach would calculate capital for all the risk simultaneously and account for the dependencies and correlations of the risks. The general judgement in the literature is that the bank's capital is mis-measured if risk interdependencies are ignored (Basel Committee on Banking Supervision 2010).
- Time varying volatility is a complex issue to be calculated in a risk metrics. It has to be carefully scrutinized at which level of the risk calculation and for which purpose it is considered. As a basis for regulatory capital it raises questions about potential pro-cyclically effects of regulatory standards (ibid.).
- The Basel accords set a confidence level of 99 per cent. This risk level is arbitrarily chosen. Although 99 per cent sounds very rigid, it means a violation of the VaR model every hundred days. Danielsson (2002) speculates that the level was chosen due to the availability of models. Forecasts with a higher confidence level may have been too difficult to model. If the risk level was defined for preventing a systemic failure, he considers the VaR regulations to be the wrong instrument, especially because a model which renders a violation statistically normal 2.5 times a year has no prognostic value for a rare event like systemic collapse.
- VaR numbers are prone to moral hazard. Already the non-sub-additivity opens the door for a choice to design the overall risk in a way counterproductive to the intentions of a coherent risk management and regulation. VaR also cannot account for trading strategies which aim at hedging an unacceptable high VaR. 'The reliance on a single quantile of the P&L distribution is conducive to the manipulation of reported risk' (Danielsson 2002: 1285).
- Most risk matrices fail to include the fact of non-linear dependence. The correlations between assets in an increasing market are lower than in mixed

market conditions and significantly lower than in falling markets. If stable correlations are presupposed in a model, it will systematically underestimate the downside risk (Danielsson *et al.* 2001).

- An early contribution to the discussion already came from Benoit Mandelbrot in the 1960s. Based on research on commodity and security markets, he especially doubted the normal distribution as the foundation of risk metrics like VaR. (Mandelbrot and Hudson 2004). Price movements, he states, are erratic and non-linear instead of following continuous paths. Over time small price changes follow small ones, but large changes appear with large ones, i.e. volatilities intensify each other. The consequence is that, in the long run, series of price changes do not oscillate around a mean value, but lead to fat tails on the margins. Fat tails is the name for the untypical feature of a bell curve, when the extreme points with low probability show a high realization. The conclusion of these findings is that there will be no predictable periodic movements over time.

Parallel to this kind of criticism on the models used, which can partly be healed by incorporating more sophisticated models, there are more fundamental points challenging the foundations of this regulation and even the intention of any regulation. There are two sets of argument: the role and the effect of regulatory capital, and the character of risk as perceived from a risk management perspective. Regulatory capital is in intensive discussion due to its pro-cyclical effect. That regulatory capital intensifies crises, is the conclusion of many authors (Danielsson *et al.* 2001; DiNoia and Micossi 2009; Hellwig 2008; Kayshap *et al.* 2008; Stiglitz 2008; Szegö 2010). According to Basel II, banks are required to hold at least 8 per cent of their exposure in base capital. This should act as a buffer in case of losses realizing in the portfolios. There is no methodological or proven statistical approach supporting this requirement. The figure 8 per cent seems to be an arbitrary result of negotiations (Szegö 2010). Above that Basel encouraged the use of more sophisticated models to calculate the risk exposure so that hedging and netting effects could be included. This often led to a risk coverage by base capital of only 2 to 3 per cent (Hellwig 2008). To put it positively, it enabled banks that were ready and able to invest in a more complex calculation and the development of more sophisticated methods to gain a competitive advantage. By using the models they could reduce the regulatory capital. They could use their capital more intensively, enabling more business. They had more leverage. This fact, as critical as it already is, covers the regulation's basic flaw. The 8 per cent, or whatever was left after recalculating, was meant to be a buffer, so that the bank could survive significant losses without going bankrupt. But the buffer is unable to serve as a buffer, because the regulatory capital is mandatory. A buffer necessarily needs to fluctuate. Once used it must be filled when the situation is getting better. There is a time lag. This is made impossible by the mandatory holding of regulatory capital. The boundary must be held at all times. So when a bank suffers a loss reducing its capital, it must immediately sell assets to fill the capital again. Capital can only serve as a buffer in this context when it is beyond regulatory capital. Hellwig calls this the paradox of banking regulation: 'Any position in the bank's balance sheet that serves as a buffer against unforeseen contingencies ceases to serve this buffer function when a regulator imposes a rule stipulating a minimum amount for this position' (Hellwig 2008: 48). The only function of regulatory capital is to meet the regulation. The effect is serious: it makes the regulation pro-cyclical. Losses on a large scale occur in downward markets. Many banks face the same critical situation. In a situation where a complete market segment breaks away, as happened in 2007–8, when the whole banking sector is involved more or less globally, mandatory regulatory capital means that to fill up the buffer immediately after realizing a loss a bank has to sell the assets which lose value in the crisis. These are the ones which have, according to the mark-to-market rule in accounting, to be marked down, meaning that risk coverage is reduced, which enhances the pressure to sell. The regulation increases the downward spiral and contributes to what it intends to prevent. This is the serious consequence of the paradox of banking regulation: Basel II fails exactly in those situations where it is needed most.

The second argument has a different quality. It is about the perception of risk from the perspective of the market participants and risk management. How is risk perceived when using risk metrics, when trying to predict future changes, when hedging against a risk? Risk is seen as something happening out there. The market is external. Risk is seen as an almost objective fact which can be calculated and then acted upon the results. Danielsson *et al.* (2001) compare forecasting credit risk to forecasting weather. Just like forecasting weather does not influence the weather tomorrow, the assumption is that actions taken from a forecasting of volatility does not influence the market. This is a completely wrong assumption. It is the behaviour of the market participants, their constant decisions on buying and selling positions that creates the volatility. Anyone shaping models, calculating risks, and acting upon them, is part of the market and influences its further development. Risk is endogenous rather than exogenous. A price movement, so Danielsson *et al.* (2009, 2010) develop their argument further, consists of two components. The first are the price movements themselves. They are the result of mostly exogenous information immediately priced in. The other component they call an endogenous feedback component by the market participants over and above the incorporation of news. This is endogenous risk. In times of crises market developments gain additional momentum from the increasingly similar responses of market participants. If they are not willing to accept further risk and reduce their risk exposure, market conditions worsen and because market conditions worsen, participants are even less willing to accept risks. Endogenous risk is therefore at the centre of systemic risk. It effects are system-wide and the result of how the system is designed. The use of similar risk systems as stipulated by the regulation, and mark-to-market accounting rules lead to a similar, very short-term behaviour. A regulation, so the consequence of their argument, which hardwires very similar or even the same risk models into risk management, installs a feedback loop with potent destabilizing forces in times of extreme market reaction, both in booms and busts, into the system. This represents the double negative quadrant of my *pharmakon* matrix. Poison meets poison. Regulation intensifies the reaction to bad news.

Despite their orientation to quantitative modelling, Danielsson and his colleagues came to sociologically flavoured conclusions. What was publicly coined as herding behaviour or the trail of lemmings, already got a disturbing image of inevitability with their reasoning. Emphasizing the sociological approach gives further insight into the functioning of the market. If risk is considered as an exogenous feature the underlying assumption is that risk management does not influence the prices in the market. This has proven to be wrong and led to the insight into 'second-order dangers'. These are the unintended by-products of systems of risk management and containment. As paradoxical side effects, second-order dangers bring about adverse events that the systems themselves cannot reconfigure as risks and therefore cannot manage (Holzer and Millo 2004: 6). Second-order dangers represent the risk of risk management. Risk management fails to see the effect of its own decisions to the risk it intends to manage.

Especially helpful for an explanation of the otherwise strange occurrences in the financial markets is the work of Donald MacKenzie. His interpretations of the force of performativity (2003a, 2004, 2008) and imitation creating a global microstructure (2003b, 2008) are an empirically founded research as the basis for a solid theoretical reflection. In 1998 the hedge fund Long-Term Capital Management (LTCM) almost collapsed. His discussion of the events is an alternative reading of what led to this crisis. It is a bit provocative, though, as he brushes other arguments against the grain. The failure was researched from several perspectives as the case had several spectacular ingredients. Concerning the personnel, LTCM combined both, the best of finance theory and the best of practice. It consisted of two Nobel laureates, Merton and Scholes, winning the prize for calculating instruments of financial markets, the famous Black-Scholes-Merton option price model (BSM) and a team around John Meriwether, a most successful bond trader. It is obvious that this collection of excellence is in danger of organizational narcissism (Stein 2003), especially in an environment where success is attributed to individual actors rather than the whole organization. Also a generation of groupthink, overconfidence can lead to complacency and myopia (Toft 2001). The interesting question is: How could a fund, fully equipped with all the experience and mathematical knowledge available at the time, fail? For an explanation Donald MacKenzie (2003b) shifted the focus from immediate popular explanations on the personal level of actors, greed, gambling and blind faith in mathematical models to a sociological approach. He acknowledged, but did not accept, as a full explanation, the results of the government working group that too large levering, i.e. the level of own capital to borrowing was too low, caused the problem. The most common explanation, the devaluation of the rouble which triggered a flight-to-quality in the market, can be seen as an immediate trigger for LTCM's troubles, but not as the cause. The fund was, due to the reputation of the personnel and the success of the first years, under close scrutiny of market participants. Despite the fact that others did not necessarily understand why LTCM was acting like they did, they were imitated in a way that a superportfolio of overlapping portfolios emerged in the market. The fact that copies existed and tried to react at the same time in the same direction created adverse price movements which rendered the assumptions of the model incorrect in a changed environment. A basic, though not explicit assumption, was proven wrong: methods of using price discrepancies (as in this example) are themselves neutral, are not themselves part of the market, do not influence the rules of the market itself. Of course the market can hit the originator of the trades and prove his assumptions wrong, resulting in the loss of the stakes. A fund is not unconnected to the market in which it trades. But what MacKenzie brings to light, is a much more fundamental involvement of the actors. Their activities can change the rules, and it is, at the given point of time, almost impossible to understand the shift itself and its consequences. Despite the fact that LTCM's strategy could be considered correct,[4] an event changed the environment and made it impossible to act. 'The "nature of the world had changed", says Meriwether, "and we hadn't recognized it"', MacKenzie (2003b: 374) quotes from an interview he had with Meriwether. The microstructure of the globalized market of investors in arbitrage[5] had changed and no one foresaw the consequences of this change.

Risk is endogenous and any action on the markets reacting to events in the market influences the situation the actor bases her assumption on in a way that is not necessarily predictable. Any calculation, as well as it may cover the variables in the market, can only cover them at a certain point in time. It rests on assumptions that are only valid at a certain point of time, and it is by no means clear how long these assumptions prevail. Models represent an in-built blindness to changes, rendering its assumptions incorrect. Phrasing it in Derridean terminology, models cannot cover an event, the im-possible of what rests beyond the horizon of the model's assumptions. This insight does not necessarily need to be informed by a philosopher. It can also come from the experience of a trader, especially when the trader, like Nassim Taleb, retreats from the job and acquires an external perspective, commenting on what he did for a considerable time. Taleb, later the author of the bestseller *The Black Swan* (2007), and nowadays celebrated for his prediction of the crisis in 2008, already made it perfectly clear a decade earlier where the deficiencies of a mathematical-oriented risk management lay. He was extremely suspicious of the introduction of VaR:

> VAR has made us replace about 2,500 years of market experience with a co-variance matrix that is still in its infancy. We made a tabula rasa of years of market lore that was picked up from trader to trader and crammed everything into a co-variance matrix.... To me, VAR is charlatanism because it tries to estimate something that is not scientifically possible to estimate, namely the risks of rare events. It gives people misleading precision that could lead to the buildup of positions by hedgers. It lulls people to sleep.
>
> (Kolman 1997)

It is the fat tails of the VaR distribution curve which are interesting, the rare events. Even acknowledging that Taleb did not think of a Derridean understanding of the event, this is exactly the dimension of the event that is needed to be considered.

Risk – the order disseminates

Dissemination can be well observed in the banking industry of the past years. A few examples shall demonstrate how its logic, infusing the *pharmakon*'s effect can be observed and how it sheds light on the nature of changes in the financial markets. The examples are arbitrage, shadow banking, the originate-to-distribute model. Although everything can be explained once it had happened, hindsight has to be emphasized to prevent the triumphant attitude of those who know afterwards. Knowing all the ingredients, it is possible to reconstruct the way that has led to this result. During the development, on the way to the result, it is enormously difficult, if not impossible, that is, im-possible in Derrida's term, to foresee what will have happened. The complexity of the three examples, and their interconnectedness, nicely demonstrate this insight.

Arbitrage seems to be the prototype for active attempts to disseminate. Arbitrage is the means to make use of price discrepancies. Once invented to make profit of the different prices at different trading places, it is now a much more complex business to identify dependencies of assets in different markets (Beunza and Stark 2005). The effect, and from the perspective of market transparency an intended effect, is that the price discrepancies disappear. Arbitrage can be interpreted as a price regulating mechanism. In a market where arbitrage belongs to the core competency of actors, however, it cannot be of surprise that they use the logic of their business wherever and whenever they perceive the chance to profit from it. This is the case with regulation, or: 'regulatory arbitrage considerations' (Danielsson *et al.* 2010: 27; Das 2010; Stiglitz 2008). If the actors see differences between the regulated and the non-regulated parts of the financial markets, they seek to profit by developing a business pattern that makes use of the advantages from both sides. The peculiar mixture of legal entities creating, transferring and holding products in regulated and non-regulated parts of the market was one reason for the lack of transparency in the sub-prime mortgage crisis. Special purpose vehicles (SPV), especially founded for the processing of one asset and the administration of cash flows, were placed outside the regulated sector. They did not need to be included in banks' balance sheets. The whole potential *value at risk* could only become clear once the sector collapsed.[6] The risk did not have to be covered by regulatory capital according to Basel II.

This is not only undesirable from the perspective of regulation and the prevention of systemic risk. It has a dangerous side effect. The regulated part of the financial markets, i.e. the banking sector, becomes adapted to the non-regulated sector. The well-intended regulation of the banking sector aiming at a stable market with sound and resilient banks is undermined by maintaining the opportunity to trade the differences to unregulated parts of the markets. Arbitrage works and makes the difference to unregulated parts of the markets disappear. It does not vanish formally, but in everyday trading and risk management.

The result of this kind of arbitrage is a phenomenon that has come to be known as shadow banking. The term is used for at least two developments. The first came along with the mortgage-based securitization for regulatory arbitrage considerations, as explained above. Independent of whether the reasons for this kind of organization were only due to motives like tax or regulation arbitrage, the result is that the risk contained in the business disappears from the balance sheet of the originator. After all, this is the purpose of securitization. In the shadow they are, because they are not covered by any banking regulation and the effect of a volatile development of the whole of the SPVs in a direct feedback loop on the originating bank and the banking system as a whole is opaque.

However disastrous they proved to be in 2008, SPVs are only part of the whole topic of shadow banking. What is known as OTC, over the counter market, is the sum of all trades outside exchanges and clearing houses. OTC is the term for all bilateral trades between buyer and seller with both not necessarily being banks. These activities do not require a banking permit. Therefore this market remains essentially unregulated. There is no disclosure requirement. OTC markets are opaque, and this has obviously been the choice of the market participants. A lack of transparency offers the potential of competitive advantages by the use of superior information. Any involvement of a third party, such as clearing houses or exchanges, would have made the markets more transparent and, with an enforcement of margin requirements, more stable. To call this part of the financial markets shadow banking is almost a euphemism. To be in the shadow, one would assume that a larger part spends the shadow in which the hidden parts exist. This BIS statistics, however, reveal that the contrary is correct. OTC represents more than 88 per cent of the financial markets (BIS 2011: 12).[7] Emphasizing the impact of shadow banking, Christopher Cox, the chairman of the Securities and Exchange Commission (SEC), can be quoted from his testimony to the US Senate, on the danger of the lack of regulation:

> The Division of Enforcement has undertaken a sweeping investigation into market manipulation of financial institutions, focussed on broker-dealers and institutional investors with significant trading activity in financial issuers and with positions in credit default swaps. The reason for this aggressive enforcement investigation is the significant opportunities that exist for manipulation in the $58 trillion CDS market, which is completely lacking in transparency and completely unregulated.
>
> (Cox 2008)

US$58 trillion in 2008 represent a doubling to 2006 (ibid.). With CDS being at the centre of the global financial crisis in 2008, and the fact that they are only one part of the OTC business, the disastrous potential of this 'hidden world' (Tett and Davies 2007, as quoted by Weitzner and Darroch 2009: 11) becomes obvious. The crucial change is the growth of financial markets and the changes of credit facilities and risk transfer which made the markets the primary source of debt for firms (Weitzner and Darroch 2009). The markets are open for firms to finance their growth. Shadow banking represents banking activities supplemented to the traditional banking business in order to grow with well-known and newly developed instruments, but circumvent limits. The rules of banking and its regulation are used to pass them. Banking disseminates.

Asset Backed Securities (ABS) have proven to be a valuable method to clear off banks' balance sheets after the dot com bubble. Banks were able to securitize a bundle of credits they had in their portfolio with very different value and sell them as a new security to interested investors. The process was accompanied by a careful due diligence of the buyers and a very limited number of participants in the process, both on the selling and the buying side. The intended effect was to regain the scope of the normal credit business by disencumbering the regulatory capital. With the advent of a mass market the emphasis shifted from an originate *and* distribute to an originate-*to*-distribute model. The credits were no longer originated to keep them on the bank's balance sheet and make the business with the risk calculation of a healthy – that is small and predictable – risk according to the experience of the credit manager and statistical data, and only distribute them as a more or less exceptional case. In the case of mortgage-backed securities, the mortgages were no longer seen as the primary business for the originator. The main business became to collect mortgages, combine them and sell them – in other words, to get rid of the risk as fast as possible. Although the structure of the process and product remains very similar, there is a massive change in the parties involved and their incentive structure. The product, market and the participants were supplemented. ABS were adapted for any kind of credit business, the size of the market grew exponentially, and new participants were introduced. Innovation in products, where no standard channelled the innovation, added to the complexity of the market and led to an opacity in which even events like bubbles, which are not really surprising as such, turn out to become an im-possible event. In a report, the European Central Bank (ECB) commented on the sub-prime mortgage segment with fine understatement: '... coupled with the opacity of information on complex structured finance products, [this] posed challenges for appropriate risk assessment and valuation by investors, thus raising financial stability concerns' (ECB 2008: 5). Too late, could be added with the advantage of hindsight, and a challenge impossible to meet for many. In their analysis, ECB also addressed the incentive structures of the parties in the originate and distribute model.[8] Four main types of participants are identified: originators, intermediaries, third parties, investors. The authors nicely demonstrate that the mix of different interests among these groups showed adverse consequences:

> [O]riginators may reduce their efforts in screening and/or monitoring borrowers and select originated assets in the event of their being sold to intermediaries; intermediaries' interests may conflict with investors' objectives of balancing the risk/return trade-off; credit rating agencies (CRAs) may be less willing to effect timely downgrades; and servicers may not be inclined

> to adopt the most efficient measures with respect to problem loans. Moreover, investors may not have the proper incentives to conduct their own risk assessment of structured finance products, thus relying excessively on external ratings and failing to play an effective disciplining role with respect to the other actors in the 'originate and distribute' model. Finally, different types of investors (i.e. senior, mezzanine and equity investors) may have different incentives depending on the priority in the payment 'waterfall' of the structured finance products.
>
> (ECB 2008: 5)

The effect of dissemination is described almost in a nutshell. The original (but what is the original here? It could be better said: the previous version of the model) incrementally yet profoundly changed its character when set out to the different interests of changing parties and new parties not involved before. Though there is just one main incentive for all participants, i.e. to maximize their revenues, and the main idea of the product in question remained the same, a fundamental shift took place by implicitly neglecting the second part of the transaction. ABS are securities that can be traded, but they are also a construct to transfer risk from one party to another. The price is set according to the value of the assets in the security. Their value depends on the default risk and the regularity of payments of interest. The risk/return trade-off estimation is destabilized with the development of a mass market for the MBS, the special form of ABS, which were at the centre of the crisis.

In fact, the development represents a shift from traditional banking business to investment banking. The business idea changed completely from debt in the retail market to an instrument in the financial market. It is not the granting of a credit as the source of profits for the bank, it is the immediate distribution of the credit in the form of a security, which has become the core of the business. The credit itself, the mortgage, is just an intermediate product needed to create the real profit. As it was intended for immediate distribution, any motivation for investing in thorough screening of the borrowers is removed from the system. There is also an effect on the idea of regulatory capital. Purnanandam (forthcoming) showed that the effect on poor mortgage quality is stronger for capital-constrained banks. On the one hand the management of capital proves to be an incentive for distribution. Removing the credits from the balance sheet raises potential for new business. On the other, there is no loss to be calculated any more if the risk is handed over to investors as part of the same process. The capital is not affected any more. Therefore the distribution shows adverse systemic effects. The quality of at least the mortgages became poorer and poorer. The primary motivation was to get a constant flow of new mortgages to be securitized.

The meaning of the instrument changed from a defensive strategy to correct negative credit decisions or the effect of market turbulences to an instrument of gaining profits. The amazing *pharmakon*, which seemingly helped to produce gold out of dirt, again proved its double-edgedness. Remedy and poison at the same time: source of profit, and well of disaster.

9 Containing risk

Towards a regulation to come

> There is no such thing as a harmless remedy. The *pharmakon* can never be simply beneficial
>
> (Derrida 2004c: 102)

Risk and regulation in the financial industry are so closely connected that their connection seems to be natural, rather than imposed or the result of a longer development. Looking back into history, regulation can be seen as a reaction when crises led to the consequences of risks, resulting in losses that could no longer be contained by the investors. There always were, and there are still, spillover effects from the banking sector to other parts of the economy. Indeed, now, more than ever, as the global financial crisis of 2008 clearly demonstrated, financial investments added a peculiar dimension.

Interpreting the development of risk as supplementary in the Derridean (1983) sense offers an intriguing perspective on the relationship between risk and regulation. The effect is to emphasize the growing complexity of the supplementary logic of risk taking and risk management. From simply going to sea as a self-evident part of daily life to considering the trip as a risky investment in manning a ship; from the individual voyage to an organization of investment detached from the individual ship; from transferring a concrete risk from one party to another to trading these risks at exchanges and 'over the counter'[1] between interested parties; from trading the concrete risk of a business to standardizing concrete risks into risk management products; from using these products as tradable, but still with a connection to a concrete business, to a trading of risk products completely detached from any business except the trading of the products themselves; from the domination of risk management aspects to the taking of risk with products formerly linked to the risk management of a concrete business; from fate to the ordering of the future by trading risk ... is a long and by no means complete list of the supplementary changes since the introduction of 'risk'. Taking risk required a management of risk. From the beginning [*sic*!], risk taking was accompanied by calculation, by statistics and mathematics. Interestingly enough, risk calculation developed as a tool to predict the chances in gambling (Bernstein 1996, Hacking 1975), an 'odour' the financial industry is still tainted with. Strange (1986) and Sinn (2009) refer to the financial markets as *Casino Capitalism*. Banking regulation started out with the attempt to make risk management, in the form of risk calculation, mandatory for the whole sector of internationally operating banks, instead of merely relying on best practices being disseminated out of the insight of their superior quality. Regulation, as is the intention, should serve the task of containing the risk of the banking sector, to avoid systemic effects, i.e. spillover effects to other parts of the economy, threatening globalized industries with bankruptcy for reasons out of their control.

In the following, regulation will be examined from several perspectives developed in the theory section. The Basel accords will first be discussed from the perspective of *différance* and supplementarity to prepare the introduction of a *coming regulation*, based on the insight of the effect of the *pharmakon* on risk, risk management and regulation. The first part looks at regulatory requirements, as laid down in the Basel accords as an excess of data collection, in answer to the excesses of the markets. The regulators show an open mistrust in the validity of an exclusive reliance on calculation. Instead, they introduce a kind of qualitative supervision and try to strengthen internal risk management to a more or less holistic view, and include market participants as enforcers of regulation. The conclusion will be that rules and rule following are even more complex than the complexified concept assumed by the regulators. What dimensions this may have will be discussed by introducing the idea of a regulation to come.

The futility of excess, or the displaced world of rules and regulations[2]

Life in the time after the orgy: the attempt to tame excess by regulation

When talking about excess in economic terms the phenomenon of 'bubbles' easily comes to mind. To remind people who took part in or just watched the dot.com hype that these kinds of bubbles are by no means recent developments, commentators often referred to the Tulip Mania in the early seventeenth century in Holland (Mackay 1995). First, a fashion among the wealthy people in Amsterdam collecting rare varieties of tulips became a matter of speculation. It had a very slow beginning as long as it was restricted to the collectors. However, the demand grew and soon exceeded supply. The market expanded further when the popularity of the flower expanded into the middle class. The explosive growth that ensued made tulip bulbs an item of professional exchanges, where market participants were only interested in trading and not in the beauty of the flowers. The prices increased steadily and created a confidence in this development as natural. More people of every class were attracted and traded bulbs, entering the market by selling most of their property assets. This resulted in ridiculously high prices at the climax of the speculation. In 1636 tulip bulbs were officially quoted on the Amsterdam Stock Exchange, but only a year later the bubble burst. The market collapsed as soon as the conviction spread that this price inflation could not go on forever. Those who had borrowed money and sold their property for taking part in the speculation went bankrupt when the prices fell to ten percent of the climax.

Tulip Mania is an early example of what can go wrong when trading becomes an end in itself. The logic of buying goods for use was broken in favour of immediate, or later, re-selling. In the world of exchanges, traders talk about exchange value rather than use value or, in the case of tulip bulbs, the beauty of the grown flower. In the logic of the exchanges, buying a bulb to plant it in the garden means to waste an opportunity to earn money by re-selling at a higher price. Financial markets are not concerned with production and distribution to clients, but with trade of currencies and financial instruments not designed for consumption. Financial market transactions are second-order trading arrangements related to the first-order economy only very indirectly by the profits generated (Knorr Cetina and Bruegger, 2002b: 913).

Looking back over the last thirty years, the increase in value of business in the global financial markets is breathtaking. One of the most important markets today, financial derivatives,[3] were so unimportant – and, in fact, most of them illegal in the early 1970s – that no reliable figures about their volumes exist (MacKenzie and Millo 2003: 109). According to the Triennial Central Bank Survey on foreign exchange market activity (BIS 2010) the global daily turnover rose to US$4 trillion, marking a 20 per cent increase compared to 2007. The amounts outstanding of all positions in notional amounts rose to US$63.3 trillion, i.e. US$63,313,000,000,000. This increase by 9 per cent to 2007 is considered as moderate by the authors of the survey, compared with an increase of 83 per cent in the triennial survey for the period of 2004 to 2007.

While this is already a really impressive figure,[4] the more interesting one is the gross market value, representing the cost of replacing all open contracts at the prevailing market prices. In absence of a comprehensive measure of risk the gross market value can be considered the most useful indication. This measure increased at a considerably higher rate (96 per cent) than notional amounts during the reporting period, to US$3.2 trillion at the end of June 2010. The foreign exchange market is the largest, but not the only derivatives market (all figures taken from BIS 2010). The underlying of these deals is always a concrete commodity or security. The markets, however, soon discovered that these instruments can also be used to speculate on the future prices of the underlyings without possessing them or intending to buy or sell them. It is possible to settle them without delivery of the underlying. Profit or loss is made with the changes in prices of the instrument. The value of all the financial instruments – such as futures, forwards, options, swaps, etc., which were once created as a form of risk management in volatile commodity and exchange markets – nowadays exceeds the physical deliveries of the underlyings many times over. The market works, one may conclude, devoid of its original meaning. It works while its idea has been lost. A crucial boundary has been transgressed here. To characterize the current state of development, Baudrillard describes it as the state after the orgy. The orgy is the explosive moment of modernity in which everything, politically, sexually, economically, is liberated. Everything, women, children, the unconscious, the destructive forces, the arts, etc. has been liberated. We have moved along all ways of production and virtual over-production, of objects, of signs, messages, ideologies and entertainments. When everything is liberated, we have to face the question: What to do after the orgy? (Baudrillard 1992: 9). For derivative instruments there was only a short step to transgress the boundary, to liberate them from their original meaning. No longer bound directly to the availability of the underlying, they are freed to be used on their own market. They have become hyperreal, to use Baudrillard's term (Baudrillard 1992: 10). The figures may serve as an illustration of how well things go on working while their original idea has been lost.

McGoun (1997) uses Baudrillardian terminology to describe financial markets. Commodities have a use value, a real value which is the basis for a price, or a symbolic value, as the good represents something for which it can be exchanged. In contrast to this

> hyperreal money is exchange value without use value or even symbolic value. It doesn't stand for any *thing*. It is a pure sign. The hyperreal economy is an economy of signs, detached from real things, but nonetheless having the ability to affect real things. It need not be electronically mediated, although that certainly adds to the effect.
>
> (McGoun 1997: 108, emphasis in the original)

Despite the fact that this is trading for the sake of trading, the actors in these markets may be affected by the failures of trading. Basel II can also be interpreted as the attempt to prevent the spillover of the negative consequences of losses in the hyperreal markets to the real markets via the collapse of banks involved in both.

As early as the 1980s, Susan Strange coined the development of the international financial markets as *Casino Capitalism* (Strange 1986). She analysed the transformation of the markets after the Bretton Woods agreement when stable currencies had been abolished. Within not much more than a decade the volumes in the financial markets had already risen to an amount hard to imagine for the observer: 'Every day games are played in this casino that involve sums of money so large that they cannot be imagined' (Strange 1986: 1). Since then, the average *daily* turnover in foreign exchange markets amounted to US$3.9 trillion, i.e. US$3,981,000,000,000, in April 2010 (BIS 2010). In contrast to derivatives, the foreign exchange markets were already substantial in the 1960s. It was in this market where the failure of a bank initiated the first attempts to regulate the financial markets on an international level. In 1974 German supervisors withdrew the banking licence for Herstatt Bank. This signalled the largest bankruptcy in the banking industry in Germany since the Second World War. The reason for the bank's failure lay in uncontrolled, and almost unlimited, engagement in huge deals in international foreign exchange markets. The owner and CEO of the Bank was proud of the enormous profits for several years, did not set adequate limits and did not employ adequate risk management. In the end, there was an attempt to cover up the foreseeable losses with balance sheet manipulation (Brors and Knüwer 2004). As a consequence of this bankruptcy the first Basel accord was agreed upon in 1975, which attempted to regulate the responsibilities for the foreign operations of international banks. This did not turn out to be sufficient, as there were too many grey areas where national authorities relied on each other, so that, in practice, no thorough supervision was achieved. This was replaced by an agreement on common rules that banks should apply. The basic idea of this regulation, known as Basel I, was the capital adequacy, i.e. that each bank must have sufficient capital for their assets in case these lose value or are lost completely (Strange 1998).

Basel, with the Roman numbers indicating the edition, now serves as a synonym for an international framework of regulating the financial markets. The Swiss town of Basel is the seat of the Bank for International Settlements (BIS), an international organization which fosters cooperation among central banks and other agencies in pursuit of monetary and financial stability. It hosts the central secretariat of the Committee on banking supervisions, called the Basel Committee. The Committee has no legislative power and no supervisory authority, but its recommendations are followed by national legislation and regulation on financial markets almost worldwide.

The development of the markets picked up speed and became excessive, as expressed in the figures quoted above. There is more of everything, and not just the volume of deals. Strange lists the points at the end of the 1990s:

> The sheer size of these markets, the volumes traded, the variety of possible deals to be done, the number of new financial centres, the men and women employed directly or indirectly in the business of international finance, including the victims, the involuntary gamblers in the casino.
>
> (Strange 1998: 9)

She also includes enormous and very fast innovations in operations, i.e. the ability of banks to process ever more business on a globalized scale.

In 1995 Barings Bank collapsed. It was an individual trader who was able to hide his increasing portfolio imbalances, and tried to balance them with ever higher deals. The market did not develop according to the dealer's expectation and the level of exposure became too high to be fulfilled by the bank. Basically, Barings, like Herstatt, failed because of a lack of effective risk management (Azarmi 2005; Drummond 2002). Ruinous excesses could not be prevented. Barings was an example of the effects of market risks, which were insufficiently covered by Basel I. Despite the fact that these risks were included, it turned out that the rules were not sufficient (Crockett 1997). In 1999 the first consultation paper for Basel II, the *International Convergence of Capital Measurement and Capital Standards*, was published, heavily discussed, revised and finally passed in June 2004 (BIS 2004).

The Basel II accord contains three major chapters, called pillars. Pillar 1 fixes the generally accepted outcomes of the attempts of capturing a bank's risk situation in a quantitative way as minimum requirements on the one hand, and the conditions of use for more advanced models on the other. Pillar 1 is about the calculation of minimum capital requirements for meeting the financial consequences of realized risks. This sounds mathematical and it is, to a very large extent. Pillar 1 is dominant in the document. The explanations of mathematical models and different approaches for risk assessment, evaluation and reporting take up about 90 per cent of the official document's length. This symbolizes the already long history of mathematical models in risk management, and that the first pillar is a development and inclusion of models already introduced by banks. The models include evaluations for credit and market risk, with several aspects under these more general designations, such as counterparty, liquidity, foreign exchange, commodity, share and interest risk, and operational risk as the risk of loss resulting from inadequate or failed internal processes, people and systems or from external events. These include internal and external fraud, workplace safety, business disruption, system failures, damage to physical assets, etc. All of these are quantified by mathematical models. The other two pillars share the rest of the document's space. With the supervisory review process and market discipline Pillars 2 and 3 describe new dimensions of regulations. They were not part of Basel I.

Basically, Pillar 1 intends to give an answer to the questions of how valid indicators can be extracted to judge the risks inherent in the banking business, and how the risk for the bank resulting from losses can be controlled. The answer to the first question is massive data collection and quantification of each business involved. As to be expected in an environment which is based on figures, the initial solution of dealing with the complexity of factors lay in the creation of figures indicating the risk level. It is a combination of several instruments – for example, setting limits for types of business or the volume of exposure with single counterparts; simulations to give an overview of the bank's overall exposure day by day and the possible development of the credit and trading book; stress tests to answer the 'What-If' question: what is the effect on the profit and loss situation of the bank, if the prices of the underlyings or collaterals rise/fall by x per cent?

Several figures developed, such as Value at Risk (VaR) or the Monte Carlo Simulation.[5] These figures soon gained broad recognition and were established as a market standard. However, there has always been consensus among banks that these standardized figures and models were insufficient to capture the peculiarities of individual banks or national markets (Crockett 1997). Therefore, the banks, especially those acting globally and in diverse markets, went on adapting these models to their special situation and, at the same time, tried to achieve more sophisticated models. The result is a heterogeneous landscape of risk management, built on a commonly accepted basis of de facto standard approaches.

The Basel II accord acknowledges this fact. Its intention is not to prevent further developments by binding the industry to a fixed number of methods. Instead, it defines minimum requirements which can be refined and adapted to special markets. A difference between standard and advanced approaches has been made to acknowledge the different ambitions and states of development.

The standard approach is set as a minimum requirement for every bank, and an individual approach which operates with advanced methods can be used. Adaptation and further development usually mean the move from generalized assumptions and evaluations about a market segment or a group of products to an individualized, customer- or counterpart-based approach. It is the move to a rating-based approach. Each counterpart will be evaluated according to the special risks involved. One consequence will, of course, be a risk-adequate pricing, i.e. the higher the risk, the higher the interest or collateral; or, it is to strive for ever more data.

The answer to the question about controlling the effects of realized risks also leads to an increase in data and calculation. It is now international standard that banks are required to hold a total capital equivalent of at least 8 per cent of the risk-weighted assets. This means that their business is restricted by their base capital. To capture the individual situation of a bank due to its market and its business structure, these assets are weighted and subject to questions of netting (e.g. the potential results of several contracts with the same counterpart, which have buyer and seller positions for both sides, can be netted) and what is counted as capital in the bank's balance sheet is subject to complicated rules as well.

The detailed collection of the adequate data and the development and maintenance of the systems needed for these tasks require a very high level of effort. Banks, which invest in more advanced risk management as defined in the framework, should, therefore, be rewarded with a reduced capital adequacy. The risk management procedure, systems and mathematical models have to be accepted by the national supervisory authorities. Rules and time frames for the preceding data collection are given in the Basel II accord. When accepted, the capital adequacy can be reduced down to 80 per cent of the basic value stipulated for the respective risk. In other words: once accepted, the bank can make more business with the same amount of capital. The struggle for ever more data is rewarded.

The crucial factor becomes data collection and data processing. Even if we consider that the individualization does not cover the complete business – e.g. consumer credits can well be standardized – but corporate business and securities of any kind, the amount of data required of markets, balance sheet figures, or performance in the past, is enormous. The result of all these figures is a complex internal and external reporting. The daily internal reporting should give management the possibility to control the business keeping to the limits, but also provide them with adequate data to perceive potential threats in the future. The external reporting to the national bank and the national regulatory authority is, depending on the topic, on a daily, monthly, quarterly or annual basis. It includes data for capital adequacy in a very detailed form, as well as every single security business. All these data are processed into new results: daily balance sheets, P&Ls, risk reports, exposures, external reporting, etc., which again increase the amount of available information.

As a result of the enormous and fast-moving innovations in banking operations, there is enough IT power to handle incredible masses of data, not only to store them but also to process them through complex models. The potential excess of the markets is met by an excess of controlling. In Baudrillardian terms it can be claimed that risk management is in danger of entering the realm of simulation. We face an excess of almost unlimited collection of data to prevent the risks of the orgy, the unlimited expansion of financial markets and the number and size of the market participants, the still growing speed of development of products in almost every combination conceivable. Poor supervisors, then, always coming late and only capable of recording the damage and perhaps identifying the guilty? Basel II provides an interesting attempt to deal with this problem. The following will therefore be an interpretation of the supervisors' reaction. The description of the Pillars 2 and 3 is included in this discussion.

Basel II – a supervisor's interpretation

Now the excessive amount of data waits to be handled and the reaction of the Basel Committee demonstrates that there is a clear consciousness about the dimension of risks in the international banking industry, and also the conviction that controlling and excessive data collection alone do not solve the problem. Therefore Pillars 2, the supervisory review process, and 3, market discipline, are introduced. Both add a very interesting perspective to the models. They are a first step to broaden the regulator's burden. The supervisors intend to integrate the bank's internal auditors and the market via the obligation of a wider disclosure of information regarding the risk management approach taken by the banks. Helmut Bauer, first director of BaFin, the German financial markets supervisory authority, and, within BaFin, responsible for the supervision of more than 2,000 banks and the decision on basic questions of banking supervision, described his view of the role of Pillars 2 and 3 and his expectations publicly at the internal auditors' annual meeting (Bauer 2004). His characterization of Pillar 1 supports the critical view of the belief in quantities: 'Here the authorities mainly act in the mode of quantities. It rests on the – unfortunately only seemingly – reliable ground of definite risk measurement' (Bauer 2004: 7).[6] What follows is an open attack on the blind belief in figures and a vote for the importance of the qualitative factors.

The extensive discussion around the measurements and their profoundly increased sophistication has made one point very clear: the increased need to *interpret* the data. This represents the acknowledgement of the futility of data collection for its own sake on a new level. Bauer makes the paradigm shift astonishingly clear: 'In view of this the meticulous pushing through of complex regulations in each and every detail comes second. This has become even more true since Basel II' (Bauer 2004: 11).

This scepticism against the pure reliance of quantification results in the acceptance of the fact that advanced internal risk measurement is a necessary but by no means sufficient element of risk management (Bauer 2004: 8). Therefore Pillar 2 draws on the internal management and steering processes, the internal control processes and the risk management. Pillar 2 expresses the conviction that only these qualitative 'soft factors' decide the effectiveness of the risk measurements in Pillar 1. Thus Bauer's statement: 'Pillar 2 is placed in the middle. And that's exactly where it belongs' (Bauer 2004: 7). Supervision has to become a qualitative supervision, with a focus on the quality of these processes. This approach is not completely new. Parallel to the efforts of refining the risk models by banks in the time before Basel II, qualitative measures, which were only briefly mentioned in laws concerning the soundness of the banking business, were already detailed and set into practice via regulations by national regulatory authorities. These so-called 'minimum requirements' are rules for the organization, such as the segregation of duties, rules for checks in processes, or rules for internal auditing. These rules set standards which have to be fulfilled by a bank within the departments credit business, trading and internal auditing.[7]

The Basel II Framework is another step in this direction. It is part of the *Audit Explosion* (Power 1994). It describes bureaucratic procedures which can be used for internal and external verification. The point is not that risks are discovered and met with adequate action, but that there are procedures which describe the necessary action. An audit will check if these procedures are in place and if they are documented in a way that externals can understand, but the audit will not judge the success or failure of the procedures, i.e. if the bank's judgements about the risk situation are correct or not. This remains the bank's sole responsibility. 'A pervasive feature of audits is that they work not on primary activities but rather on other systems of control' (Power 1994: 6). Without using the terminology, Power describes the creation of another hyperreal activity. Auditing can operate completely detached from primary activities. For risk management, it can be claimed that Pillar 2, placed in the middle, 'exactly where it belongs', as Bauer (2004: 7) states, liberated the audit from risk management's original idea. The auditing of risk management processes aims less at real dangers, the original risks in the banking business, but more at good organization. The banks are obliged to show how they organize risk management, and this is evaluated.

Market discipline will complement the minimum capital requirements and the supervisory process. It tries to give the answer to the question of how the heterogeneous landscape of risk management, which will emerge from the regulation, and the obvious imbalance to the controlling abilities of the authorities, can be matched. The Committee's answer is market discipline. With a set of disclosure requirements, market participants will be able to assess key pieces of information on the scope of application, capital, risk exposures, risk assessment processes, and hence the capital adequacy, of the institution. The pressure to behave according to standards in risk management is transferred to the market participants in the conviction that they have the deepest interest in the stability of their counterparts. 'The Committee believes that providing disclosures that are based on this common framework is an effective means of informing the market about a bank's exposure to those risks and provides a consistent and understandable disclosure framework that enhances comparability' (BIS 2004: No. 810).

Pillar 3 rests on the assumption that market participants evaluate their deals with counterparts in the financial markets by the same risk management preferences as with other counterparts or customers. Counterparts are rated and the conditions of the deals are dependent on the rating. Disclosure of information on risk handling then means the possibility for counterparts to judge each other according to sound risk management. A bad rating makes business more expensive, and the bank will be less competitive. This, according to the logic of disclosure, will be avoided by market participants.

The supervisor is the gamekeeper who looks after the disclosure of the banks, but he does not judge the information published. Market discipline will help the supervisor, via the counterpart's reaction to the information published regarding the conditions of deals made between the market's participants. Bauer admits that the complexity of the markets becomes too much for the national supervisors. The supervisor may answer with accordingly complex regulations, but is immediately faced with enormous difficulties of enforcement. His answer is: 'Create a team-mate. Pillar three is about the external team-mate, the market. It is armed by the disclosure of information demanded by the regulations to punish high risks, unconvincing business models, or bad management by the means of the market' (Bauer 2004: 10).

The supervisor's discomfort can clearly be seen. Afraid of the risks from the excesses in business, perfectly aware of their own limitations in meeting these excesses with control on the same level, they look for limits which work. To paraphrase Baudrillard (1992), Basel II can be interpreted as the attempt to find new limits in the life after the orgy, while accepting the euphoria of ever increasing business. Basel II avoids the prohibition which only ever creates a black market. It is more the tentative attempt of orientation in a self-created environment which continuously develops and may show unpredicted effects, like new bubbles. Looking from the outside into the ever faster developing financial markets, the message could be understood as: 'If you want to go on making business as you are used to, you have to create and maintain the conditions of the possibility of the market's existence yourself.' This is no longer possible through a heroic act of legislation by a supervisory authority. A law would be overtaken before it is passed. Basel II recalls and simulates the economic logic of the system. It is, to put it into an excessive wording, the feedback of the liver function reading into binge-drinking to encourage the mates to turn the tap if one of them can't get enough.

The displaced world of risk and rules

Another interpretation rests on less obvious considerations, at least when judged from the claim which laws, rules and regulations have: namely, that they should be followed or obeyed and if not, there will be serious consequences in the form of prosecution and punishment, or what is called 'appropriate supervisory action' (BIS 2004: 162) in the Basel II terminology. That this is an ideal belongs to our common knowledge: before prosecution somebody has to notice the rule's violation, the one who notices has to be concerned about it and to report it to the authorities and the authorities must be able to prove the violation. We also know perfectly well that rules are being broken, either because of ignorance about their existence, insufficient training to perceive their implications, or consciously, because it is the easiest way in a certain situation and probably no one will notice, or for gaining a personal advantage. Rules may contradict each other, so that the person who should follow them has to decide which one to break to fulfil the task. Rules need exceptions, but what is counted as an acceptable exception can only be decided in the concrete case. As the rule usually has to be used in diverse contexts and changing environments, it is impossible to define the actual use and the exceptions beforehand.

These few remarks already indicate that the realm of rules and regulations is not as easy to conquer as an idea of order would like to have it. 'Paradoxes of social order' is the telling subtitle of Günther Ortmann's book *Rule and Exception* (*Regel und Ausnahme* 2003b) where he looks intensively at the role of rules in an organizational context. He explores the very different modes in which the relationship between rule and exception can be interpreted to develop a more adequate understanding for the complexities involved in rule following.

Ortmann uses Derrida's concept of *différance* (Derrida 1990) to argue that a rule can, at the same time, be followed and violated, that validity is, at the same time, assumed, but, in its application, finally defined and changed or deferred (Ortmann 2003b: 25). Applying the rule always changes its meaning. The supervisor cannot finally determine the rule's use. It is always dependent on how the user understands the rule, how s/he is able to use it and how the context has to be interpreted when the rule is applied. The rule will always be supplemented in Derrida's sense of *supplément*. Any use of the rule supplements the user's interpretation qua applying the rule. Applying the rule means slightly altering its contents. Let it be to keep the rule's original intention in a changed environment, let it be a faulty application, there will be a mediation between the rule and the situation and each application will supplement the rule in a slightly different way; or, a violation of the rule is inherently part of every use of that rule. What we consider to be rule conformity in everyday practice is a practice of repealing plus preserving, in which the repealing is the tacit acceptance of the alterations necessary to achieve the intention of the issue on which the rule is to be applied (Ortmann 2003b). The supplements give meaning to what they displace. This is the solution to the fact that there is no such thing as the original situation, or, in other words, an origin. There is no immediate presence, no original perception. All immediacy is derivative. Everything starts with the mediated (Derrida 1983: 272). A rule starts in the middle, is an intervention in an ever changing environment.

Ortmann notices the paradoxes involved here: 'Laws, institutions, rules contain imperatives which shall orient our actions, but what they explicitly mean will in a strange way only be decided during these actions, by these actions which the rules shall guide' (Ortmann 2004: 42). Rules follow actors. Ortmann calls this reversal of the usual view – that actors follow rules, to the retrospective view that rules also follow actors – upsetting, almost Kafkaesque, but nevertheless an inevitable ambiguity. Accepting this, the basic fictionality of organizational rules and rule following comes into view, the paradox goes on.

Organizational rules do not help because they work, but because they do not work, but we, deceived or deceiving ourselves, believe in their effectiveness and make them work; or, if we do not believe in the effectiveness of the rules, we deceive others with pretending that we believe in their effectiveness and make them work in this way, performatively; or, we take refuge in informal, subversive means to achieve the intended goals (Ortmann 2003b: 127).

Ortmann's view about rules mirrors the enormous uncertainty in the social world. In his recent books (Ortmann 2003a, 2003b, 2004) this uncertainty, fluidity, multi-perspective, is not only acknowledged and taken as a topic of research to achieve a better understanding and with this achieve more order conquered from an overpowering disorder, but understood as the basic condition, which will remain as the point of departure for all attempts to organize or to set rules. It is the unavoidable acceptance that order and disorder are mutually dependent, that order defines itself by drawing a boundary to disorder and in this way is determined by disorder (Cooper 1990), that a rule defines a territory in which it claims validity and the validity has always to be enforced. Order and rules are not objective facts but processes which, in absence of an objective, stable foundation, reproduce themselves. Nevertheless, the result of these processes is a sufficiently reliable environment.

Replacing the term 'deceit' mentioned earlier in the context of rule following with 'as if' points in the direction Ortmann moves. He is working with the metaphor of 'bootstrapping' to illustrate his view on organizations. Bootstrapping is the fiction that we can walk over shaky ground and leave dangerous situations, pulling oneself up by one's own bootstraps and lifting our feet over the critical ground. When organizing or writing rules, we do something similar. We have an idea in mind how to proceed, how to solve a problem. However, before actually acting, we do not know if what we plan will lead effectively to the intended target. We can only judge if it was successful with hindsight. In other words: we have to act as if we are certain that we act correctly and, with this fiction, we are able to start to interpret the rule according to the difficulties and opportunities that emerge during our actions. We create the ground on which we stay ourselves, with no foundation beyond the belief that this ground will carry us.

The consequence: hyperreal rule following?

Macintosh *et al.* reflect on the hyperreal quality of accounting figures. For many of today's pressing accounting issues there is no underlying reality to which accounting signs refer (Macintosh *et al.* 2000: 16). They are arbitrary, but that does not render them meaningless. Financial hyperrealities should be considered as results of extensive institutionalizations regulating the use of financial numbers in social situations. Accounting numbers are observable and verifiable *ex post* (Macintosh *et al.* 2000). Once figures such as VaR are accepted in a community and, above that, also find acceptance in official contexts like a worldwide regulation, their definition provides a basis for using and understanding the overall risk situation without further reality testing. Numbers become social resources through their self-referential significance in institutionalized standards; they are signs within an institutionalized system of their circulation and, within the system, trigger specified activities. VaR is reliable not because it represents the reality, but because everybody using this figure in the context of banking can be expected to use it according to the expectations of other participants. Stability of and by simulacra is achieved in hyperreality: 'People who understand this see institutional information as an arbitrary but essential feature of a hyperreal world' (Macintosh *et al.* 2000: 42). Rules and regulations may be arbitrary. Nevertheless they provide a degree of reliability on which market participants can act.

Basel II provides such reliability, despite the paradox involved in its construction. There is a telling ambiguity in Basel II's dealing with quantification. On the one hand, Bauer (2004) warned of the blind belief in figures and insisted on a judgement of the whole risk management process, instead of checking each and every detail. This is a refusal to fight an excess of unlimited markets with an excess of controlling on the same level. On the other hand, the supervisors produce exactly that excess which goes along with the development from standardized to individualized approaches. The amount of data increases on two sides. Each bank is faced with rising amounts of data due to a look at the individual customer. The landscape of different risk management approaches in the banks becomes heterogeneous. The regulation co-produces the situation about which a leading supervisor warns.

With Baudrillard the financial markets can be analysed as being in a state of crisis shortly before the end which does not occur – this is how he defines paroxysm (Baudrillard 2002). The Framework reproduces the excesses of what it intends to frame. Seen in this light, it is an instrument which prevents the end from taking place and therefore an instrument of simulation which keeps the financial markets in hyperreality. It guarantees the stagnation of ever faster orbital moves without meaning. The authors of the Framework, of course, will not accept this interpretation. Ensuring stability offers the chance of development which they want to enable but not to determine. The zest in taking the very serious world of international banking supervision as an example for the slightly frivolous statement of the French philosopher, lies in the collapse of imagined and taken-for-granted boundaries between them. Both are aware of the fact that excesses have taken place. While Baudrillard does not see a solution, except one that countenances the ever faster circulation of simulation, the supervisors believe in the possibility of creating new boundaries while the system, the globalized financial market, is in orbital move.

Looking at this situation through Ortmann's view of rules, the precarious foundation of the regulation becomes apparent and the supervisors' attempt to alter their way of supervision is justified. Bauer's comment makes clear that the authors of the Basel II Framework realized that a traditional understanding of supervision is no longer capable of meeting the increased requirements of the markets on both sides – neither on the supervisors' side nor on the banks' side. The increased requirements of the capital markets regarding complexity, speed, volume, development of new segments and the risk deriving from these factors, can no longer be met by individuals. They can only be fulfilled by procedures which are inevitably carried out by multiple actors. Any regulation, which does not consider the flexibility and quick changes of the markets and tries to cope with the risks with rigid rules, will inevitably fail due to massive ignorance of these rules – either overtly, by publicly fighting their inadequacy or covertly, by reinterpreting them in the process of applying the rules. However, the challenge reaches further. The necessary complexity of the regulation has reached a degree where no strict rule following can be expected, even if the insights of *différance* and *supplément* do not belong to the background of supervisors. Considering the situation of the Basel II Framework on the background of the remarks on rule following and the somewhat swampy ground on which they are built, we can notice that the regulators' situation is even more treacherous. The national supervisors have power, as they have the ultimate means to enforce their interpretation – the withdrawal of the banking licence – and they are ready to take action: 'Supervisors should take appropriate supervisory action if they are not satisfied with the result of the process' (BIS 2004: 162). However, with the definition of Pillar 3 and the judgements of competitors on the disclosed information, another rather diverse interpreter appears. The supervisors will find it difficult to enforce an interpretation against the will of the market, expressed by the acceptance of the risk management of the bank in question. The Framework's rules will also be developed, i.e. repealed and preserved, by the generally accepted behaviour of market participants.

A more traditional view would interpret this understanding as an additional source of uncertainty, perhaps even as an invitation to moral hazard. In a world where rules are seen as a fixed set of actions or behaviour, instructions as outside of the scope of the actors, and clear criteria can be established to test if the rule has been followed or not, this understanding of rule following must be a nightmare. Understanding rules as dependent on their application and subject to repealing plus preserving opens the view for another handling of unstable environments: the coexistence of a further development of methods in the regulated world and a Framework acknowledging that it cannot cover these developments adequately in due time, but providing room for future enhancements, a supervisor judging the whole procedure of risk management instead of every detail of the rules, and participants judging each other.

The ongoing ambivalence can be demonstrated by the fact that, despite the authors' consciousness of the necessary limits of regulation, as described above, the striving after completeness is still expressed in the regulation's expansive mode. The number of risks to be quantified and controlled has been greatly expanded. To beat that, the second pillar explicitly asks for the treatment of risks not fully, or not at all, included in the first pillar (BIS 2004: No 724). This is a striving for completeness and perfection which can well be seen as a final excess itself. Seel (2004) suggests a deconstruction in Derrida's sense as a chance to overcome the neurosis of transparency, completeness and perfection. 'Neurosis' will indicate that we might be driven to achieve waterproof theories and, I would add, waterproof regulations, but that this is in vain facing an ever changing, uncertain environment. Deconstruction made us aware that all our notions, definitions and theories are bound to time and the immense variety of human practices, and therefore we can only achieve more or less satisfying and ever newly-to-be-acquired explications of our actions. Connecting this with the metaphor of bootstrapping again, we can state that the supervisors create a fiction of how to achieve the intended target of stability despite the uncertainties and intransparencies. We can only judge if the approach taken is successful *ex post*, with hindsight after the rules have been used for some time, and should not be surprised by the differences to the written text. The supervisors have to act as *if* they are certain that their proceeding is correct. Bootstrapping as an exit for excesses in hyperreality: the supervisors have gone further than they probably had imagined.

Towards a regulation to come

The major part of this chapter so far was written before the global financial crisis of 2008. Reading it closely now, it becomes clear that it contains an underlying bias: beyond all the theoretical considerations and the critique implied with this, there is an acceptance that regulation in the form of Basel II is necessary and that it can work if the paradoxes involved in any rule following are considered. Bauer's arguments were introduced as the proof that there is unease on the side of the regulators, regarding the concentration of risk management on calculation. The unease should have gone much further. It is a bit worrying that major points of criticism had already been raised by academic commentators and even published on the homepage of the Basel Committee (Danielsson *et al.* 2001) before Basel II was finally passed, that is, long before it became clear that it could not cope with a crisis.

'After the current crisis, it is clear that Basel II is dead' announced Joseph Stiglitz (2008: 21). The answer could be, Long live Basel III! By the time of writing this, several parts of the new instruments are still in discussion, while some changes to existing rules are agreed upon and wait to become effective in national legislation. Instead of discussing the details of the new initiatives, which would suffer immensely from the time lag between writing and publication, I will further follow the potential of Derrida's concept of 'to come'. Financial risk needs to be repoliticized (Goede 2004, Langley 2008), as it is not something 'out there'. It affects everyday life of everyone. The argument will be based on an analysis of a dynamic which challenges the current scope of regulation. A concentration on the smooth functioning of banks, if that is at all possible without systemic crises, is not sufficient in a world in which risk has become a central issue of planning for everyone. Starting from a sketch of the ingredients of a general theory of regulation by Stiglitz, the need for regulation will be confronted with insights into the 'world risk society' (Beck 2008) and into the use of financial markets' logic of risk calculation in everyday life. This prepares the ground for the discussion of Derrida's elaborations on the relationship between law and its use. Quite surprisingly, but necessarily, this involves the inclusion of justice into the discussion. This prepares the ground for considerations about a regulation to come.

Principles of regulation according to Stiglitz

In 2008 Joseph Stiglitz gave a presentation on principles of regulation, a subject he claims has been 'one of the most contentious' (2008: 1). He discusses advantages and disadvantages of regulation in the controversial setting of government failure versus market failure, but remains convinced that regulation is absolutely necessary. His arguments are not a blueprint for a special theory of the regulation of financial markets, but, because of the time of the presentation, also address financial sector regulation as one of the areas of application.

The need for government intervention rests on three reasons. First, markets are not pareto efficient. With noticeable sarcasm, he points out that the basis for the arguments of market efficiency and keeping government out of the regulation of markets has a basic flaw: 'whenever information is imperfect or markets incomplete – *that is, always* – there is a presumption that markets are not (constrained) pareto efficient' (Stiglitz 2008: 2, emphasis added). Market mechanisms are insufficient, as proven, among other cases, with accounting in the case of Enron, or the rating agencies as one of the causes of the global financial crisis. The second reason calling for regulation is market irrationality. The individual is not necessarily rational.[8] The deviation from rationality may work in systemic ways. So individuals and societies have to be saved from themselves, Stiglitz claims (2008). The third category deals with a crucial shortcoming of efficiency: even if the outcomes are efficient, this does not mean that they can be viewed as socially just. Regulation can be an instrument to achieve distributive justice.

Instruments of regulation can take the form of information requirements, proscriptions, or mandates. They can include the disclosure of certain qualified information; restrictions on behaviours; mandates to make connections between investments to generate profits and inclusion of groups or tasks as an exchange for governmental acceptance; restrictions on ownership. The best known example of the latter in the financial industry is the Glass–Steagall Act which forbade commercial banks to own investment banks. The mistrust in the market-driven function of Chinese Walls inside banks to prevent conflicts of interest instead of a regulation proved justified, again with Enron and WorldCom as examples.

Regulation always has efficiency and distribution consequences – that is what they are designed for. They affect property values – that is what makes them so controversial. This complexity is enhanced by the way regulation is enforced. Once a regulation has passed into legislation, control of keeping to the regulatory requirements is passed over to a supervising authority with the relevant technical expertise. Stiglitz's concern about democratic accountability, 'particularly given the frequency with which regulatory agencies are captured by special interests' (2008: 14), mirrors Hellwig's (2009) remarks on the incorporation of regulation by the expertise of the regulated. Writing about the regulatory failure of preventing fraud, Fooks (2003) saw one reason in a corporate colonization in US Government and financial regulation. Reading the situation with Agamben, (as in Chapter 3), this is a sign of the state of exception. Democratic control is rendered impossible, because the development of instruments and the tools for risk management and regulation, as well as the actual financial supervision, are performed outside parliamentary responsibility.

Government failure (and there is no discussion that it exists and will occur again), cannot be used as an argument against regulation. Stiglitz is optimistic about the potential of corrective processes created by sufficient transparency and competition. Governments, for example, will be replaced when they lose their credibility. The consequence of his high regard for democratic processes is that those regulatory processes, which are more subject to failure, should face larger disclosure requirements and multiple oversights. If one supervisory authority fails to correct flaws or violations of regulation, another authority may step in. Here he refers to possibilities which US legislation allows with multiple agencies. When the US Securities and Exchange Commission (SEC) failed to react to abuses, New York State did so. His optimism is in some contrast to the aforementioned concern about the possibilities of democratic accountability, but a clear hint to the difficulties of enforcing the intention of any regulation.

In the case of financial sector regulation Stiglitz addresses five reasons for government intervention in the financial markets in general:

- ensuring competition between banks
- protecting consumers
- ensuring safety and soundness of financial institutions and the financial system (Basel failed disastrously here)
- ensuring access for disadvantaged groups or neglected markets with lending mandates against discrimination
- promoting macroeconomic stability and growth.

Regulatory interventions, however, may have unintended consequences regarding cyclical implications, and face contradictions, i.e. policies for one bank in trouble may make sense, but if all are in trouble, the same actions can contribute to a downturn.

Financialization: the colonization of the lifeworld

These five points give an indication why the current discussion on improvements of banking regulation falls short of the necessary. They deal with only two points, leaving aside the discussion about whether they do this efficiently or not: the safety and soundness of financial institutions, and macroeconomic stability with the keyword of systemic risk. Defining rules about the size of a bank beyond 'it is too big to fail', or naming rules for additional regulatory capital, are a clear interference with the topic of the first reason, that of ensuring competition. This aims at making very large banks more sound and stable to prevent a public bailout in the next crisis. At the same time, it is cementing market structures in favour of the very large banks. I can see no consumer protection in the Basel accords, but this is a matter of other regulatory initiatives.[9] Lending mandates are also not a matter of current banking regulation. Stiglitz's reasons for government intervention, however, indicate that regulation must go beyond a technical regulation of the business itself to prevent crises such as those we have witnessed. Furthermore, it is obvious that the introduction of regulation needs an idea and a public consensus on what should be achieved. Helmut Schmidt expressed it like this:

> There is a global financial crisis. Governments in the whole world have to understand that banks and financial institutions have the purpose to serve the producing economy and the working and saving society. By no means can it be allowed that they degenerate to an end in itself – and even less for the sole purpose of making their managers rich. No bank should be too big to fail. Banks are for the citizens, not the taxpayers for the banks.
>
> (Schmidt 2011: 22, author's translation)

This is the clear opinion of a politician, a former German chancellor. The demand is old, as Vogl (2010) tells us, pointing to Aristotle, who strictly subordinated economy to politics. But Vogl argues that the situation has changed in a dimension that Schmidt fails to see. The dimension that needs to be discussed only becomes clear when a crucial spillover effect is taken into consideration. Risk, as a method to deal with the future, to render decisions in an uncertain environment possible today, as a means just to think about the future, has become so self-evident that it has almost gone unnoticed that this represents *a takeover of civilized thinking by the rationale of financial markets*. What was once coined as the *colonization of the life world* in the 1960s, by authors like Marcuse (1967/1979) and Habermas (1968/1981), reappears today as financialization (Martin 2002).[10] The logic, however, remains the same. Critical Theory described Weber's process of rationalization as a covert form of political power. Instrumental rationality, as the choice between strategies, use of technologies and effective construction of systems within set objectives and given situations, isolates this process from the societal context in which strategies are chosen, technologies used and systems constructed, and renders any reflection and reasonable reconstruction impossible. Any rationality only covers relations of technical availability, which asks for a certain type of action-based on a certain type of ruling, of nature or of society and excludes others. A rationalization of life worlds under the guiding principles of this rationality is equivalent to the institutionalization of a power of which the political implications become unrecognizable. Legitimization is replaced. It is not necessary any more to provide an external legitimization, it becomes self-referential. The form of production is the technically necessary form of a rational society. It proves itself by its efficiency. Interpreted like this, rationalization is not just a process of long-term changes in society – it is a Freudian rationalization as well: technical imperatives hide the fact that the power in rule, judged objectively, cannot be sustained (Habermas 1968/1981).

The ingredients of financialization were quickly found: increased shareholder value; bank-based mechanisms dominated by capital market systems; the ascent of a rentier class; increased volume of financial trading and instruments; increasing profit shares through financial channels, instead of through trade and production (Krippner 2003, in Martin *et al.* 2008). Together, these signs can be taken to indicate 'the increasing role of financial motives, financial markets, financial actors and financial institutions in the operation of the domestic and international economies' (Epstein 2005: 3). These alone are interesting observations from an economic perspective. It is a shift from value creation, or at least wealth creation, from production and trade, to the financial markets. What renders it a move of central significance for society and individuals is indicated in the inclusion of biographical risks in the discussion about the 'world risk society' (Beck 2008), or Bauman's discussion of *liquid modernity* (2000). The individual is directly concerned by developments on the financial markets, independent of whether she is involved in buying financial instruments or not. Financial markets influence daily life by judging the value of the workplace independent of individual performance, leaving whole economies dependent on the markets' judgement as in Greece; leaving pensioners without their pension when the pension fund of the company runs bankrupt after the company ran into troubles, when private equity funds reorganize a company in order to resell it within a short period and make the company take the cost of this operation; the partial replacement by public pension schemes to private provision for the future – to name just a few examples. What becomes clear is that the boundaries in which we judge have changed. The temporal structure of financial contracts dictates the measure of contracting, and social contacts. The reproduction of financial capital becomes the model for all economic, social and cultural reproduction (Vogl 2010).

The logic of financial markets has colonized the life world. Independent of whether one thinks this is a necessary step in the development of an increasingly complex civilization or a threat to the well-being of citizens, it is clear that the process needs to be a conscious one,[11] and one which needs to be considered carefully. The reference to colonization was not intended to refuse risk's logic upfront. The term helps to understand how financialization could succeed in a similar way to rationalization. It is not necessarily a conscious drive of a clearly identifiable part of society looking exclusively for its own advantage – this is only part of the development. Financialization can serve as an example of a – preliminary – result of emerging processes which cannot be foreseen at the beginning. What can now be seen as a situation which can be analysed along the terms used by Krippner 2003 in Martin *et al.* 2008, were themselves emerging, or just intended as a slogan, one or two decades ago. How they are received, how they interact with the other ingredients, who has which ideas to support or to counteract, and what will be the result, can only be seen with hindsight. Financialization, however, points at the dynamics which need to be considered when regulating.

Dissemination of risk: the world risk society

The analyses of the global financial crisis made one point very clear. The hope that focussing on risk, asset by asset, and ignorance of correlations between risks, would be healed by incorporating banks' own risk management systems and credit rating agencies, as Basel II did, proved to be an illusion. Neither correlations nor fat-tailed distributions were systematically included. This does not mean that they were ignored intentionally. 'Systematically' should describe the fact that the systems were not designed to take them into account. Without doubt Stiglitz's principles of regulation are carefully put together and offer valuable insight. What gets a bit lost from sight is the context in which regulation faces demands for changes, or, to be more precise, the changes in the context of what it is that regulation aims at. What is it exactly that should be regulated? The Basel accords are only one example of the incorporation of risk into regulation. In fact, they can serve as an excellent example, because banking regulation must deal with risk, since risk is at the core of banks' business. Risk, as Hutter (2005) observes, has become the new lens through which to view the world and has taken over regulation in many areas. Power's analysis of the audit society (1999) and new forms of risk, like organizational risk and the attempts to quantify them, as well as the restructuring of organizations to meet regulatory or legislative requirements for risk management (2005), demonstrates how deeply the thinking of risk and the attempts to manage it pervade life in organization nowadays by *Designing a World of Risk Management* (2007). The consciousness of risks, or the anticipation of potential risks in the future, leads to a need for control in the form of risk management which does not lead to certainty. As Power points out: 'If ERM[12] is an illusion of control, it is also somehow one of a number of necessary illusions which constitute management practice' (Power 2005: 264).

In 2008 Ulrich Beck updated his well-known book about 'risk society' (1986) as 'world risk society'. Risk seems to be ubiquitous. More than ever, he claims, it is necessary to acknowledge the fundamental changes which an ordering of the future by risk have brought along. His book is only in passing about financial risk – it was published before the financial crisis gained global attention – in acknowledging that it forms one of four logics of global risks, with the others being ecological, terrorist and biographical risks (Beck 2008: 37), but is still relevant here.

Beck's thrust is that we are suffering from the side effects of successful modernization. Risks and dangers are increasingly less directly manageable and cannot be insured adequately any more. The effects of this are, among others: a globalization of dangers; the undermining of the credibility of experts; a feeling of uncertainty, even angst, ruling attitudes to life. This vague feeling of uncertainty can be used, or misused, as the basis for politics or business. Since the publication of his first analysis, he observes two fundamental developments. World risk is the *staging* of the reality of the world risk. He does not intend to blame public discussion for an intended forging of reality. Without naming it, he uses the logic of financial markets to describe his observation. Only by making the catastrophe present, by staging the world risk, the future of the catastrophe becomes present, with the aim of finding means to prevent it by influencing decisions today: 'the staged anticipation of devastations and catastrophes commits to preventive action' (Beck 2008: 32). Because we are informed about climate change, because of the media coverage of 9/11, politicians are forced to do something, even if this something is as staged as the anticipation of future catastrophes is. Risks are always future events which we may have to face, which threaten us. This permanent threat, however, more and more rules our expectations and becomes a political force which changes the world. The difference between risk and the cultural perception of risk becomes blurred. What is accepted as risk can best be described as a social construction.[13]

Yes, we may nod approvingly and accept that we live in the world risk society. A financial disaster and a nuclear catastrophe[14] later, within just three years after the publication of Beck's book, the general line of his argument does seem convincing. Without naming it a colonization, he draws a similar conclusion: 'Risk calculation allows for a kind of technical moralization without any need for ethical imperatives.... In this way, risk calculation symbolizes the mathematical ethics of the technical era' (Beck 2008: 59). With regard to the logic of the financial markets, however, Beck does not cover the whole dynamics. As alarming as his analysis may sound and as well as it is argued, Beck nevertheless does not get the crucial point in the effect of an understanding of risk as a means to order the relationship between the present and the future. He fails to see that the difference between the future present – the catastrophe which may take place in the future – and the present future – the anticipation of what might take place in the future – is exactly the way financial markets price volatility. This kind of anticipation enables investment decisions. The logic of the financial market permeates everyday thinking of risk.

Regulation is needed, but an approach concentrating on regulation itself fails to consider important aspects of the context. Financialization adds to this a decisive part, but only in combining these arguments with the effects of the rising awareness of risk and the significance of risk and risk management for everyone in daily life, does the effect of its combination come into view, and Schmidt's intervention finally becomes justified. Risk returns to everyday life as a comprehensive term for managing the future, with a crucial difference though. Risk, once supplemented to Nis Randers' life, now returns to his successors as financial calculation, e.g. as the need to make private provisions for old age – for one's personal future, that is – to accept responsibility for it, but with a different logic attached, as a staged anticipation of tomorrow's world as a disaster. Risk used not to be part of the individual's life, but now it is. Vogl concludes that modern precautionary societies organized themselves around the change from dangers to risks and the taming of the chance, but, by doing that, chance, danger and an untamed storm of events return to the centre of society in an archaic shape: irregular, amorphous and surrounded by unknowns. The unknowns have become arcane and make decisions which, in their detachment, in their lawlessness, appear fateful. This is the opaque and wild space of surprises into which our societies have financed themselves (Vogl 2010: 178). Vogl phrased it extremely well: our societies have financed themselves into a situation where what they once financed now opposes them with the appearance of sovereignty. As overwhelming as global financial crises appear, rolling over humans irresistibly like tsunamis, wiping out the savings of many, they seem to look strangely familiar: sublime, as if fate had returned. It had not. Vogl addresses the problem very effectively in describing his book as the attempt to understand how modern economics of finance tries to understand a world created by economics itself. He called his book *The Spectre of Capital* (Vogl 2010), a clear reference to Derrida's book *Spectres of Marx* (1994). Vogl would not have done this if he did not share Derrida's final farewell to any kind of teleology. Indeed, this is what both authors emphasize: the world we live in is the result of human decisions. But that does not render the outcomes of decisions predictable or calculable. They remain a source of profound unknowing; or, they allow for the insight into the 'eventness' of historicity.

Regulation needs an idea of how to manage future

Risk expresses an attitude to the future. It is a relation to time and the relationship of times[15]: future, present and past. In risk management, risk tends to become order, following the mathematical ethics of the technical era. Here lies the basic paradox of risk. Risk is about the future, but it is entirely rooted in the present. Risk and risk management are order, but the future is unwritten. The order is necessary to substantiate a decision which inevitably aims at the future. Risk is an illusion of control enabling us to decide and to act upon the decisions. Derrida, however, reminds us of the requirements of a decision. It is a paradoxical statement, of course. The condition of the decision is the undecidable (Derrida 2004b). A decision cannot be derived from knowledge. There is no safe ground on which to base a decision. There must be something new, an unknown which needs to be decided, despite the fact that it is unknown and therefore undecidable. The coming risk is undecidable – therefore it is subject to decision. Applying this logic to risk as order shows that its enabling to act leads us astray. Risk as order is only the execution of a program, a continuation of the past represented in the calculation about the present future. Risk as order cannot cope with the future present. It is designed for the present future. If risk is calculated, the resulting decision, no matter if it is a decision or a program, will be subject to change immediately after the decision. The context of the decision is changed by the decision. It does not rest as a potential, it turns out to be a matter of fact and is set out to other decisions and programs reacting to it. Any risk calculation has at its basis a huge 'if-clause': the decision will have the intended result, *if* the assumptions made in the risk calculation turn out to have shaped the decision in a way which will be still fitting after the future present turns into the present and becomes the past present, which can be interpreted. Risk is a means to manage the future. Risk calculation is a tool which supports management. It can always only be a part of risk management. If a regulation leads to an acceptance of calculation as risk management, as Pillar 1 of Basel II did, this is a reduction of the scope, which inevitably leads to the kind of defuturization, as suggested by Esposito (2007). Risk has at least two sides: the safeguarding of the future, so that future events have no destructive effect, that we are prepared for potential events and can meet the consequences; it is also a present-ation of the future, with the effect that financial logic leads to a consumption of the future today. This has always been the basic idea of credit. By a credit an investment which would only be possible with the profits made in the future is made possible today. The arrow of time is compressed, future pre-sented. Both the creditor and the debtor enjoy possibilities today, but without cutting the link to the future: the credit has to be paid back and will be financed by the profits generated with the credit. There is a profound change in the application of this logic with the introduction of provision into a mass market. Risk returns to the individual's life as financial calculation for meeting the needs of the future, creating a special new risk: the risk of individual risk management. If the mathematical logic of risk calculation becomes the tool for planning individualized provision according to financial market's products, the huge danger is twofold. The obvious one is that provision becomes extremely vulnerable to the bankruptcy of actors on the financial markets. What is more disturbing is that the defuturization of those markets which deal with the instrument to manage the future – i.e. risk – results in an absurd consequence: by buying products which transfer risk in the future to others who are willing to bear them to make a profit now, future profits are present-ed, made present in the same act. It is a consumption of the future on both sides, but only one side does so consciously. Risk as product traded follows a different logic to taking the risk itself. The buyers of risk products consume their future with others enjoying the fruits. The different time frames of the actors can be exploited by one side.

The most impressive example of the fundamental change in the old logic is the recent mortgage bubble. A home owner pays for a mortgage to enjoy the house today. A bank finances the house and receives interest. The payment of the debt is transferred to the future for the owner, the interest a constant flow for the bank. Securitization meant a decisive change in this logic. Immediately after financing the mortgage, the bank bundled mortgages and sold the bundles as securities. The risk for the bank was transferred to the investors, and the bank set free regulatory capital for new business. The idea was that the profit could be booked immediately with no risk left. Besides its role as trigger for a global financial crisis and the important insights to be drawn from that, the mortgage crisis can serve as an illustration for two more developments. The first one is linked to speed, the speed of change in almost anything that comes into contact with financial markets. Neither securitization as such nor the securitization of mortgages was a new phenomenon. Securitization, the bundling of assets into a new security (Asset Backed Securities, ABS), is a risk management tool to remove an amount of credits from the bank's balance sheet. Special kinds of ABS served as problem-solvers during the dot.com bubble. This was a controlled removal of assets of a bank's portfolio inside a narrow market. Both sides were professional financial market actors. The ABS went through a due diligence by potential investors and a price was negotiated. During the 1980s securitization of mortgages was developed.[16]

During the mortgage bubble, securitization changed from a defensive move to save the balance sheet to an aggressive tool to increase business. Due to the massive rise of the amount of securities created by banks more buyers were needed. The size of the market increased from a narrow circle of investors to a mass market within a short time, to the extent that new mortgage applications with no fundamental possibility of ever paying back the sum borrowed, plus interest, was not only encouraged but actively promoted. The character of the market changed completely, with nobody planning this development and only a few noticing the potential consequences.

The second change is in the risk distribution. The home owners are left with the risk of losing the house if they cannot meet the obligations of the mortgages. The banks were able to remove the risk from their balance sheet. When they realized that the hedging did not work as anticipated, when the im-possible event took place, they were able to rely on the *pharmakos*, the taxpayer. This change deals with the ability of the actors to change their attitude to the future, or with the existence of different time perspectives within the same business. Again this is nothing new. Different time perspectives enable the sharing of risk. The home owners take a credit and invest traditionally. Banks used a well-known method of risk management in a new way: the volumes now in orders of magnitude larger than before. The result was a different market, leaving the actors on both sides in different roles. The principle originate-to-distribute released the banks from their responsibility of checking creditworthiness. It was not their risk any more, and they did not have to look into the quality of the new mortgages (ECB 2008). These examples demonstrate the incredible rate and speed of change in the financial markets and the different dealings with the future. They represent a change in the shares of risk. Defuturized risk can be traded away, though it will return in a different form, as the crises of the past decades also proved. Regulation must consider the unpredictable moves of actors on the markets creating impossible events.

Regulation must also have an idea of how to manage the future. This is the main task of financial markets, though with completely different abilities and opportunities on the part of the actors of the financial markets, and on the part of the clients relying on their advisors.[17] If risk is the means to get an idea about the future, regulation must reflect what may be a desirable way of coming to these ideas. It must make clear that beyond the present future of financial markets and future present other actors aim at, there is a future future, i.e. the future present of the future present which the present future attempts to frame. This may be called systemic risk, but I can see no link to such an elaboration in present regulation. It would be a speculation on what is 'to come'.

Regulation as a rational fallacy of writing?

Derrida's work on dissemination (1994), as already discussed in the previous chapter, provides a thorough discussion of the relationship of speaking and writing in occidental thinking. Plato's main interest in *Phaidros* was to demonstrate that writing is added to speaking with language being the superior medium. Derrida (2004c) deconstructed this relationship, not to install something more important, but to unveil the derivative nature of speaking itself. Not only the signifier but also the signified, the living, knowing memory is supplemented to what it actually remembers. It is already an interpretation and not the original. The original does not exist (any more). We can only deal with the supplements – by supplementing them. Any meaning disseminates. The roles of risk and regulation can be interpreted accordingly. Regulation is writing, a writing supplemented to risk taking. If risk is treated as order, regulation takes a form like the Basel accords and the underlying [*sic*!] tools of banks for risk management. Regulation in this form is a rational fallacy: it assumes a stable hierarchical relationship between regulation, as superior, and risk and risk management, following the rules. Regulation in this form adds to dissemination, instead of understanding it and accompanying the changes of context. As writing is always supplementary, this is a necessary consequence – which is the insight gained from applying the arguments of Derrida.

Nis Randers was introduced to prepare a Derridean deconstruction. Risk is a supplement, too. Or, to express it in the language of the sector, it needs an underlying – that is, life itself. It is the struggle between the life world living in uncertainty, but not in need of the concept of risk, and the supplements that claim to help and rule. The conceited sovereign risk forgets that he was supplemented for clearly defined purposes. The look into the future, beyond the horizon, should have rendered complex action possible and predictable. That worked very well, in a way. But risk cannot deny its close relationship to gambling. From the beginning, the calculation of risk was the calculation both of the die and of the economic consequences of acting in the future (Bernstein 1996; Hacking 1975). Of course, clearly defined purposes also fall prey to dissemination. Once risk became derivative, the closer definition of dissemination from medicine gains meaning for financial risk: the dispersal of germs in the body, the proliferation of a plague. Risk is a *pharmakon*, as a derivative instrument it can cause catastrophe.[18]

Considering how the Basel accord came into being, it is of no surprise that this regulation is less a model to enhance banks' services for producing companies and society, as Schmidt aims at, than a self-referential confirmation of its own logic. The regulators did not feel they had enough competence to regulate the banking sector, so they invited banks to provide *their* experience in risk management. The Basel accords incorporate models developed by banks and set them as a worldwide standard. Apart from that, Basel II encouraged the ongoing development of more sophisticated mathematical models by the possibility of reducing regulatory capital. In the case of the Basel accords, a nice irony is added: the supplementary interpretation came first, before the introduction of the regulation. Hellwig comments: 'The model-based approach of bank capital regulation originates from a process of annexation of regulation by the expertise of the regulated during the 1990s. The system of banking regulation itself has contributed to the downwards spiral' (Hellwig 2009: 15, author's translation). This can be phrased in the sector's language as a friendly takeover. It is the best of all worlds, facing the pressure of a regulation which might reduce profit opportunities. Hellwig's interpretation can also be seen as a reversed supplement. The supplementary interpretation took place before the text to be supplemented was written. The regulation is already a result of that kind of interpretation which usually comes after publishing the final version. It can be interpreted as an open invitation for dissemination without setting crash barriers. Of course, any crash barriers set in language will also be disseminated, but they would, at least, serve as a reference point. Without such a reference – the clear (political) expression of the role of regulation, of its function beyond an interest in an unrestricted functioning of financial markets – the field is open for any development in the interest of those who formulated the regulation for the regulators. I cannot imagine a more effective invitation for moral hazard.

Investment bankers consider risk to be the original, with themselves as the keepers of the holy grail of profits. In their view, risk management is uncalled-for, a hindrance to more profits, and regulation just an external obstacle which needs to be traded away, i.e. arbitraged.[19] Risk management and regulation are inferior writing, adding nothing to their business, but subtracting profit opportunities. Even in a detail, the traders' actions make them like Thamus, the god of gods in *Phaidros*. Thamus is sovereignly independent. He speaks, his word is enough. Traded risk is the language in which traders speak. Any documentation following the rules of writing is most unwelcome when the trade is done. The ticket can be just a Post-it with cryptic remarks. The back office has to guess what that means and to execute what was agreed on the phone or online by the trader. Things have changed, technology-wise. The systems document what is traded and send messages to the back office. But the principle of action retains the hierarchy. Those who trade the risk do not need writing; it may harm the position of the original. Writing is the prototypical *pharmakon*. Risk management and regulation are writing.

Writing is added to what is added to life; the relationship between economy, financialized life world, risk and regulation must be rethought and brought to a new balance. If regulation is seen as a solution to prevent crises by setting fixed calculations, by imposing a stable order, this expectation will remain a rational fallacy. In other words: regulation must take the disseminating logic of the markets, the ambiguity of the pharmakon, into account. Arbitrage may be no more than a special expression for a certain type of dissemination in the financial markets.

The reduction of uncertainty, setting prices for the present future rendering the present tradable (and, with that, manageable) is a prime motivation for risk calculation. The present is organized by keeping an order. If a management of the present is confused with the assumption that it is possible to manage the future into the intended direction by trading financial instruments, this is a rational fallacy. Financial instruments are about future, the present future that is, but they are part of decisions of the present. They do not prescribe the future, but organize expectations of the present.

Addressing the blind spot: justice

There is a roaring silence inside the topic of regulation, or a huge blind spot. It is a topic self-evidently broadly discussed in combination with law, yet absent from discussions about regulation. Although there is an intense discussion about the similarities and differences between law and regulation (Black 2002), the topic of *justice* seems to be neglected vis-à-vis regulation. Staying within the frame of Derrida's arguments, however, it becomes unavoidable. From the 1990s on, Derrida increasingly dealt with prerequisites which cannot be deconstructed, which are the foundation of deconstruction itself. These are discussed under the topics of the gift, the other, the event, hospitability and justice. It is because this can be interpreted as a move from working through the metaphysical heritage of the past to a sketch of a future, a philosophy to come and a democracy to come (Lüdemann 2011) that makes it such a good exercise for rethinking risk and regulation. The topic of justice is inextricably linked to law and the decisions of a judge. Following Derrida's intensive discussion on the paradox of law and justice, the impossibility of their coexistence and the necessity of any legal decision to be just at the same time,[20] opens to view the difficulties of a just regulation.

Adair Turner, chair of the Financial Services Authority (FSA) in the UK, coined the distinction 'socially useless transactions' (Turner 2010b: 33) for large parts of financial transactions nowadays. From the perspective that financial transactions are justified if they add economic value, he asks which value is added by complex securitization and derivatives. The complexity of the financial markets, as well as that of the innovations in products, according to the consensus before the crisis, gave investors the chance to pick exactly that combination of risk, return and liquidity that best met their preferences for risk management. With refined understatement Turner commented: 'We are now more aware of the instability risks which might offset the benefits of such innovation' (ibid.) and went on to outline what he considers to be socially useless:

> ...to the extent that complex structuring was driven by either tax or capital arbitrage, reducing tax payments or reducing capital requirements without reducing inherent risk, then it clearly falls in the category of the 'socially useless' (i.e. delivering no economic value at the collective social level) even if it generated private return. And a non-trivial proportion of complex securitization was indeed driven by tax and capital arbitrage.
>
> (Ibid.)

Instability risks are not among the risks Basel II tried to regulate. They belong to the risks to come. Turner's critique is a normative statement. While his arguments are rooted in economic theory, the implications of what he says go beyond a purely economic discussion and point into a similar direction to Schmidt's remark on the role of the financial sector as part of economy and society, with the attendant need to clearly define its tasks.

Stiglitz (2008) focussed on distributive justice to grant an equal access to credits. This is an important aspect, but does not take the broader view of a necessity for a just financial system. The implications of accepting justice as a topic of financial regulation are huge and stress the boundaries of banking regulation. But as the discussion of the included excluded has shown, these are topics that cannot be completely excluded. Intentionally or unintentionally excluded, they tend to haunt everyday practice. They form an additional risk. They are part of the systemic risk in that they endanger the stability of the financial system as soon as trust in the positive contribution of its services vanishes. I can give only a few hints here:

- If we live in a world risk society, if risk is the model to manage the future, if risk is a tool measured in financial terms, if life is financialized, if we assume that the taxpayer does not want to play the role of the *pharmakos* again, then regulation needs an idea of what it regulates beyond the stability of the system. It needs an idea of the role of the financial industry in a globalized economy. The contribution of the financial sector to the distribution of wealth globally and locally must come into focus.
- Banks perform an important role in the smooth functioning of markets. They have to function, they have to be innovative, they also have to develop new instruments for the management of risk, to help to manage new patterns on global markets. The key questions are: What are socially and economically useful financial transactions? How much volume is needed to make the financial markets work, i.e. how much volume can be accepted beyond the amount driven by concrete business outside the financial sector?
- Is the concentration on banks in the regulation justified? Do we not need a regulation of the financial markets that includes other actors such as pension funds, government funds, hedge funds, private equity funds, insurance companies like AIM, rating agencies? The relationship between banks and other financial institutions as actors in the international financial markets must be discussed.
- How can it be ensured that actors in the financial markets do not dominate those parts of economy and society for which they provide services? How can a just relationship be shaped?
- Who has to account for the crises generated by the financial system? Chapter 5 presented a few problems regarding the responsibility of the actors. Regulation that includes the responsibility for defining responsibilities complexifies the problem, especially regarding the actors in the regulation process:

regulators relying on the expertise of those who are regulated face a legitimization problem.

- Is it just or justified to restrict the size of institutions to avoid the 'too big to fail' issue? And, if the answer is yes, what is the preferable size of a bank operating globally? If no, are special rules needed for these institutions?[21]
- Justice between times – the delicate relationship between past, present and future, complicated by the expectations connected to the times, and when the expectations materialize, as shown with the help of the terms present future, future present and future future. When is which investment decision connected to which relationship in time, and who profits from it, and whose interests may be violated?
- Who performs the role of the judge? In the relationship between law and justice, it is clear that the judge has the task of making a fresh judgement every time she decides, with all the pitfalls of applying a law to a concrete case. A banking regulation under the roof of the Basel Committee faces challenges. An international regulation, negotiated by supervisors and banking associations of different, but not all, countries who are expected to follow the regulation, may have an agreement as a result, but is not legitimized by national parliaments. The regulation has to be transformed into national laws or regulation with national supervisors overlooking to see if the rules are kept. How can a unity in performing the international agreement be achieved? Not at all, when considering dissemination. The Basel Committee is very conscious about the importance of enforcement (Caruana 2010b), but does not have appropriate means, beyond the reminder of the otherwise bad experience of past crises.

Several of the topics addressed are already on the agenda of regulation. The list, however, is far from being complete. It should give an idea of the variety of topics necessary to be considered if such a thing as a regulation to come is aimed at. Including justice adds relevance and renders the paradoxes involved in the relationship between law, regulation and justice open to discussion. Regulation must ask what can be accounted for.

An option: towards a regulation to come

> I don't think that the best compliance is 'Press button'. I believe the best compliance has a brain.
>
> (Pierre-André Berchtolt)[22]

Regulation as writing has to acknowledge that it is a paradox: supplemented to risk to prevent bankruptcy and systemic risk, it does not just provide its own means for arbitrage and new ways for systemic risk, it is the instrument for arbitrage and a systemic risk *itself.* This is the consequence of writing as supplement. As long as regulation mirrors risk management, crises are reproduced systemically. Regulation is entirely the playground of the regulated and these will use the rules they already know perfectly for an interpretation in their favour. Of course, they cannot be blamed for that. It is a central assumption on the side of regulation that has to be changed. Incorporating risk models of banks into their regulation, the assumption is that the models are how they are, because it is in the self-interest of banks to manage the risk in a way that does not result in their destruction. However, the banking industry, as can be concluded from the frequent crises, may have risk management, but that has not prevented huge losses. Partly, this was due to internal power games between traders and risk managers. Partly, it leads to the insight that even the strict following of internal models does not prevent losses, because every actor in the markets follows the same logic and almost no one recognizes the pattern. The discussion so far in this book has shown that there are more than enough contradictions and paradoxes involved when reflecting on the possibilities of a regulation that works in the financial industry. Risk and regulation seen as *pharmakon* reveals the pitfalls. The topics mentioned lead to the insight that risk and regulation can only be had with both potentials, remedy and poison, ready to strike at any moment. In this book the potential of the *perhaps*, that which is *to come*, is proposed as a way to open up thinking for a more coherent thinking about risk, risk management and regulation. How must a regulation be shaped in such a situation? After the arguments in favour of a risk to come, a consideration of a regulation to come will come as no surprise.

The expression 'to come' is a moving target. It is the image of an ideal, but not of a teleological quality with a clear idea in mind what this ideal is, fixed and ready to be achieved in the future. It is not a regulative idea (Derrida 1999) – Derrida refuses any last idea, one that cannot be developed further and that leads the argument without being changed itself. That which is to come is an aim, set and missed again and again, because it changes while moving towards it. While trying to reach it, new insights about the aim are gained. The move towards the aim provides new aspects which change the view of the aim. But also reactions and decisions, the everyday overlapping and meshing of actions following the different interpretations of rules, result in a complex web which does not obey strict rules. On the contrary, by interpreting rules according to new situations, they are also changed. This is the supplementary use of rules by applying them, as Ortmann (2003b) interpreted Derrida.

A regulation to come must enable the inclusion of the risk to come. It must be able to keep and observe the difference between present future and future present. This irreconcilable difference already opens up more horizons. The real challenge, however, is to get an idea about the future present of the future present. Risk society, as the result of the move from fate to risk, is already quite a reflected way of understanding, as it acknowledges that the state of the world as it is, is the result of decisions of the past. What is not contained in this insight is the consideration of the effect of dissemination: the paradoxical result of disseminating order, the production of the event by setting up an artificial horizon – which then cannot be perceived as a horizon any more – with all the paradoxes acknowledged that such complex thinking brings along. Derrida, in all of his writings, invited this kind of thinking, to have us haunted by necessities of the future, by the consequences of today's decisions, by considering the im-possible event. It becomes really interesting, however, if the consequence is drawn: time is out of joint, the projectile of the arrow of time goes astray, time loses its normal orientation from past over present to the future. Being haunted by an origin from the future is puzzling, but exactly the demand for regulation. And, this must be clear, for responsibility:

> Without this *non-contemporaneity with itself of the living present*, without that which secretly unhinges it, without this responsibility and this respect for justice concerning those who *are not there*, of those who are no longer or who are not yet *present and living*, what sense would there be to ask the question 'where?' 'where tomorrow?' 'whither?'
>
> (Derrida 1994: xix, emphasis in original)

Regulation needs the reintroduction of responsibility. This has not been left completely unnoticed. In Pillar 2 of the Basel accord it was explicitly stated: 'Bank management is responsible for understanding the nature and level of risk being taken by the bank and how this risk relates to adequate capital levels' (BIS 2004, No. 728). I find it somewhat disturbing that an international framework has to remind bank management of its most basic responsibilities.[23] And this has to be emphasized, the problem is still on the agenda: 'The crisis revealed a number of shortcomings related to governance, risk management, due diligence, etc. that the private sector itself needs to address.' (Caruana 2010c: 1). In their report to the G20 meeting, the Basel Committee mentioned as the first point the need to rework Pillar 2 of the Basel accord, that several notable weaknesses within the risk management processes of banks have to be mended: 'firm-wide governance[24] and risk management' (Basel Committee on Banking Supervision 2010: 7). Responsibility is a huge topic for the financial industry, and given the result of Chapter 5 and the brief discussion of justice above, a topic that needs to be discussed in a much broader way than is shaped in these regulatory remarks.

If risk is 'to come', a regulation must be able to change its shape according to what it intends to regulate. Risk, as the expression of the present's thinking about the future, changes its shape according to the changes the future is presenting to the form in which the present future brings the future present – that is, risk. Risk is guided or misguided by data from the past, haunted by expectations about the future, and what is to come. It might go wrong in an unanticipated way. It *will* go wrong; at least it will have a very different shape, in an unanticipated way, based on the experience of financial history and the anticipation of economic historians (Chancellor 2000; Plumpe 2010). It is not clear how it will go wrong or be different the next time. This is the work of the event. Living in the radical today, as was analysed for investment banking, multiplies the opportunities for im-possible events. Concentrated on today, the im-possible is not just that which is beyond the horizon, the radical new, it is everything that is not priced in today, everything that an informed observer would include as the possibility of the force of the *perhaps*. Any news shatters the building of expectations, shatters the structure of risk. Financialized risk is in a much more intense way to come than risk would have it. The actors here are not blind or dumb, they are not ignorant. They draw conclusions from their observation of the market, i.e. their observation of other observers. If they want to take advantage of the situation on the market, if they want to make profits, they conclude from their observations that they have to act as if there is no future. This kind of second-order observation, as Luhmann named it (1991), only takes into account what the observers mutually perceive as relevant. It denies any influence of the outside, if the outside does not press the system to acknowledge its influence. Enforcement of regulation is a primary problem, as Nout Wellink, chairman of the Basel Committee and president of the Dutch Central Bank, acknowledges. He is convinced that the regulator's answer to the crisis will be adequate, but that a lot is left to be done. '[T]he crucial second step of the policy making process has yet to take place. I refer here to implementation and rigorous supervisory follow up' (Wellink 2010: 5). With the very next sentence he formulates some reservation from past experience: 'We must remember that memories fade quickly' (ibid.).

The thinking of 'to come' is not as alien to present banking regulation as it might seem. The ingredients of a regulation to come, and the challenges it poses to thinking in this dimension, can be taken from presentations and articles of leading regulators. In the same paragraph of the speech quoted above, Wellink addresses the obvious: 'Moreover, our standards need to keep pace with financial innovation' (Wellink 2010: 5). Any innovation sets new rules in the market and offers opportunities to interpret regulation differently. Or, of course, the motivation of the innovation is an interpretation of the regulation in a way that is contrary to its intention. The 'moreover' introducing the quote, however, is telling. It adds to the reservation of his remark on effective implementation and enforcement. Fading memories of the past and potential ignorance of the future, so it can be read, threaten regulation's capability to become efficient.

Jaime Caruana, general director of the BIS, put it much more bluntly:

> The more we convince ourselves that we have mastered risk and uncertainty and the more confident we are that we have learned the lessons of the past, the more vulnerable we become to lethal overconfidence and the probability that things will again go unimaginably wrong.
>
> (Caruana 2010a: 7)

There is a consciousness of the im-possible event in this remark. Caruana acknowledges that vigilance is needed for new developments. This also confirms another paradox in risk taking. Including the experience of the event does not mean that the consequences of the next event can be adequately met. Nonetheless this remark is a bit ambiguous. Read differently, it means that the only requirement to prevent the consequences of the event is to be suspicious of complacency, to rest on what has been achieved. If it were to be interpreted like this, the character of the im-possble event is missed completely. This is not what

Caruana aims at: 'In short, we need risk management that can deal with both the known unknowns and the unknown unknowns' (Caruana 2010a: 2). Unknown unknowns point in the direction beyond the horizon. But what would happen, if a chief risk officer (CRO) acted accordingly? Is there really a change in attitude on the side of banks? Otto Steinmetz, the CRO quoted in Chapter 7 as an introduction to the risk to come, imagined exactly such an incident. What would have happened, if he had wanted to build in the bankruptcy of a major American investment bank into his model? (Pfeil 2010: 27). He concluded that this would offer the perfect role model of an outcast left with no influence, or the need to leave. As Goodhart (2008: 16) comments on the unresolvable shortcomings of regulation facing the unknowable: 'Lack of foresight, lack of information, and human error can overwhelm any administrative design, however excellent.' The list could be extended with 'opportunities to increase profits'. What will the position of a CRO be if she considers restricting business opportunities?

Caruana, however, also provides us with the best definition for the basic characteristics of a regulation to come: 'We know the right direction even if we have not worked out the precise destination' (Caruana 2010a: 3). If he is still convinced that, after a very hard period of negotiation and intense discussion, the precise destination can be formulated, he would be wrong. It is not that the precise destination has not been worked out yet, the task will never have an end. Stefan Walter, the secretary general of the Basel Committee on Banking Supervision, expresses a bit of the needed dynamics: 'This is one of the key lessons of the crisis and we must do a much better job ensuring that we understand these system-wide developments and that regulation keeps up' (Walter 2010: 4). Regulation needs to keep up, this is the understanding of a never-ending approach a regulation to come requires. If this is seen as an optimistic outlook for a change in regulators' attitude to regulation, then a damper is put on it in a recent presentation of Caruana: 'we need to complete the reform agenda and finish the job' (Caruana 2011: 8), is how he concludes his overview of remaining challenges of the regulatory reform.

This is a pity, as the discussion stops before it starts to become interesting. Within the framework and the terms used in this book, it would start with a deconstruction. What are the core assumptions of the present thinking of banking regulation and what consequences are owed to these basic assumptions now inadequately discussed? This is less academic than one might assume, as Adair Turner, chair of FSA, remarks:

> Yes, the fact is that intellectual systems – the whole efficient market theory, Washington consensus, free market deregulation system – can become like a religion. You do need some sort of framework but it must be eclectic, and always subject to challenge.
>
> (Turner 2009)

Both sides are contained in this quote: there are preconditions of regulation which need to be openly discussed, and a framework is needed, but it must be *always subject to challenge*. There is no way to finish the job. Regulation must include the responsibility of the regulators. Their responsibility is not just making rules to create efficient financial markets and preventing systemic risk. Their activity is at the interface of financialized societies and the financial sector which should provide services for them. Taking the job of regulation seriously may include going beyond structural considerations to a tough discussion on content level. Regulation should not avoid the 'whither': 'Financial innovation has produced some products of very dubious social value and then there are other products that on paper you would have thought would be useful that have not happened' (Turner 2009). Financial markets do not offer those products common sense would like to have. Rephrasing Turner's comments, how can products answering to the needs of consumers be introduced even if the potential selling side is reluctant to offer them? Once alert to topics challenging the boundaries of banking regulation as set down in the Basel accords, it becomes self-evident how to broaden the discussion. Expressing doubt about the volumes in the financial markets and coining the term 'socially useless transactions' (Turner 2010b) is a first step. Turner is ready to drive the discussion much further:

> I think the fact that the financial services sector can grow to be larger than is socially optimal is a key insight. There clearly are bits of the financial system, and particularly the bits that relate to fixed income securities, trading, derivatives, hedging, but possibly also aspects of the asset management industry and equity trading, which have grown beyond a socially reasonable size.
>
> (Turner 2009)

It almost suggests itself to limit the excesses of the markets to a size which may serve a function, to reduce transactions to those which are socially useful. But who will decide where the boundary is to be drawn? Sovereign states have allowed the financial sector to grow and gain such a dominant position, as they allowed the rating agencies their role by asking ratings for public funding. The refusal of actively supporting the stability of the system, by endlessly continuing in the pre-crisis mode that generates their profits, seems to show a tendency towards suicide. This attitude mirrors the behaviour during the crisis: to act as if there is no tomorrow, to keep the present as long as possible to avoid missing the last cent of the profit. The suspicion of a regulator is that this attitude has not changed: 'Despite the severity of the crisis, we are already seeing signs that its lessons are beginning to fade' (Walter 2011: 1).

There is a power issue to be solved here. As long as the free market is defended almost like a religion, and the implementation of regulation is seen as a violation of the self-healing powers of the markets, such views tend to be marginalized or actively fought against, even if they are supported by a source to be taken seriously, such as the chair of an authority of one of the financial centres of the world. The *Prospect* interview panel to which Turner was invited agreed that a crude 'market is always right' philosophy has lost all its credentials. Turner emphasized:

> I think we are still trying to work that out after a fairly complete train wreck of a predominant theory of economics and finance. For the regulators of the world, once you've accepted that you don't have an intellectual framework of 'more market is always better,' you're in a much more worrying space, because you don't have an intellectual system to refer each of your decisions, and that requires more judgement and therefore confidence.
>
> (Turner 2009)

In a nutshell, many of the issues addressed in this book are contained in this quote. The global financial crisis proved, amongst other points, the danger of acting according to a fixed theory or ideology. While it is very reassuring, it will inevitably lead into the wrong direction once the world dealing with this theory develops in a different direction, which is – as not just Derrida made clear[25] – unavoidable. Relying on such an intellectual framework leaves one confident about owning the truth, but helpless facing emerging problems. Having no such framework, I agree with Turner, leaves the decider in a much more worrying space. Here the introductory quote of Berchtolt demonstrates its significance. He stated that the best compliance has a brain, insisting that human judgement cannot be replaced by buttons, as he phrased it. It is impossible to delegate a decision to a machine. What he insisted on for compliance, the reintroduction of judgement, also holds true for risk management. Regulation must enable decisions, judgements instead of performing programs. Taking up Derrida's missives[26] (1984) here places regulation and the regulators in a very interesting position.

Where is a decision in the Derridean version involved? Decision, as the opposite of performing programs, taking the absolute risk as the venture beyond knowledge and certainty (Derrida 1995), containing something completely undetermined (Derrida 2004b), is not that everyday action under time pressure often described as decision making. The latter needs a competence that is in some opposition to a decision. Competence is embedded in the known. Experience in the field, knowledge of systems and processes and how to carry them out, to know exactly the sequence of steps to be taken to achieve certain targets, all of these, according to the logic of Derrida's argument, are candidates for inclusion into an industrial logic, a Taylorist thinking, that knowledge is better included in the systems supporting the worker. Be it a machine, or an organization, the manuals, exact definitions of how to proceed in which situation, all of these follow the logic of the known from the past. There is no long hesitation before deciding and acting, because for the competent the situation is obvious. When time frames are extremely short, it is good to have someone around who is able to analyse, conclude from his/her knowledge and act immediately. A decision cannot be derived from certain knowledge, from a truth. A calculator can do this job, a program; however sophisticated, it remains a program acting within the limits of the known.

This is no argument for postponing competence. Trading and risk management need to be competent. Everyday practice relies heavily on people with experience who know what to do in all the situations which can occur under normal circumstances. Exploiting the opportunities of the markets and calculating the risk involved with a set of calculations to avoid unhealthy exposures is the minimum requirement for risk management. But no systemic risk, not even correlations of risks in the same bank, necessarily comes into sight under the ruling regulation, not to mention any event beyond the horizon. The necessary interruption of the programs' logic for breaking the fatal trajectory, having the im-possible in mind to interrupt the system for a decision, is effectively excluded. It needs intervention from outside of the closed circle of the competent to prevent the fatal logic from unfolding, or at least from unfolding its whole potential of destruction. Therefore, Turner's remarks on the regulators' role promise a much better understanding of what is missing today. Regulators need to take a very special risk, that which Nietzsche (1993) named as the dangerous *perhaps*. It is the risk of those who refuse to see the coming as the continuation of the already-expected. That which he analysed for the new philosophers, who are able to deal with the coming, is a reversed taste and character than known so far. It needs excellent nerves to withstand new insights that might shatter the hitherto certain knowledge. A regulation to come – including considerations about the consequences of financialization in a world risk society, the relationship between the financial sector and society, the reintroduction of judgement to add a crucial dimension to risk calculation, the contribution of regulation to justice, different time frames in the present – is nevertheless what is needed if risk should remain manageable. '[W]hat sense would there be to ask the question "where?" "where tomorrow?" "whither?"' (Derrida 1994: xix).

Paradoxically, the best regulator is the one who does not know what she is regulating before it is regulated. She knows what she is regulating only by observing the consequences, i.e. how the rules are applied and passed by, what kind of event emerges from the new rules. But she continues to judge how the regulation must be changed to keep its direction, and to reflect intensively on the destination (to rephrase Caruana's (2010a) comment). She knows that the destination will never be reached, there is no destiny, no fate to be fulfilled.

The risk to come framed by a regulation to come, filled with life by responsible humans with judgement – what an exciting prospect!

10 (This will not have been a) conclusion

'Extratext – Bookend'[1]

'This (therefore) will not have been a book', Derrida (2004c: 3) started his book about dissemination. He provided an introduction which absolutely refused to be an introduction out of the insight of its complete impossibility. An introduction is a contradiction in itself. It pretends to be the beginning of a book while every author knows that it is usually only written once the book has been written. Only then the author knows what he was writing about. It is at the same time both a path into the book, for the reader, and out of the book, for the author. The preface belongs to the book, but looks at the book itself, the parts following from outside. It seems to be neither inside nor outside. The same is even more reasonable for the conclusion, the final chapter of a book, trying to wrap up the lines of thought followed during the chapters. It leads out of the book, trying to link the arguments presented to their future of being used, hopefully much to the advantage of what the book was written about. The book, however, can only be a snapshot of moving thoughts about the topic. Any conclusion, pretending to have found a solution, is almost ridiculous. Maybe it is an offer from the view of the author, taking into consideration every available source published so far,[2] placing the text and the sources used into context, and concluding a strategy of how to go on, here of how to achieve a better understanding of risk and an image of a better regulation. Of course it remains the partial view of one author at a specific point in time. Even when accepting this, and claiming to try to open up a discussion on the topic, which will inevitably change the consequences (and of course, there is the slightly arrogant assumption that there are readers interested enough not just to read it, but also to start a discussion, to use the book as a stimulation for themselves), Derrida's argument is about the subtle work of dissemination. If we – you, the reader, and me, the author – start a discussion about my arguments presented here next month, we will talk about something different. Nothing is fixed, stability is challenged by learning, by contexts changing from decisions, even decisions which are not directly aimed at what is written in this book, by events taking place, by the subtle work of the *perhaps* having its effects. A conclusion about risk is as futile as the intention of a fixed, written regulation intended to order financial markets. Yes, this is a paradox. It sounds like a conclusion. Meeting the requirement Derrida indicates with dissemination, means withstanding the paradox and its demands. Despite the impossibility of a conclusion the argument presented in the previous chapters has consequences. The work of dissemination requires a certain openness, a readiness to re-evaluate and let go of things one had come to love, to question the order contained in risk, for example. That kind of openness is not in acknowledgement that there are still questions open, problems to be solved on the way to a solution. Questions remain open, that is, there is no solution solving a problem once and forever. On the contrary, dissemination and supplementation require a readiness to ever giving new, different answers to slightly changing demands posed by almost the same kind of problem. The answer must *remain* open (Pelzer 1995). Following one more of Derrida's vertiginous theoretical moves in a slightly changed mode prepares the ground for the introduction of a way of thinking which accepts tentativeness, a hesitating move forward into what will have been the present.

Risk is out of joint

Haunting is a surprising description of an aspect of future. Surprising, despite the fact that it can be seen as one of the most common features contained in the thinking of risk. Future determines thinking by its uncertainty, the not-known, the threat to violate assumptions on which decisions are based with the consequence of a loss – perhaps. This can be casually interpreted as the dark side of risk taking, the threat of being confronted by a future event smashing one's positions. This view emphasizes the aspect of fear. Derrida's peculiar take on the dissolution of the arrow of time, the taken-for-granted progression from past over present into the future, however, provides future with even more influence than risk usually assumes. Viewed from this perspective even the complexity of risk in the financial markets can be described as a mode of reducing complexity, resulting in an ignorance of an otherwise unquestionable responsibility.

What will have been the result of present decisions and resulting actions and supplements in the future presence will have consequences for the past of both, present future and future present. The past will be interpreted differently. The phrasing of decisions will have been judged differently knowing about the event which might have taken place in the meantime. Future has become tradable on the financial markets. With all their expectations, observations of other observers and the reaction of trades on the expectations, more levels of perceiving future are added. Time is out of joint, so the message can be understood, but one shouldn't forget that this was already possible to know in an era before risk made the judgement of time more complex by trying to reduce complexity by calculable forecasts. It was Shakespeare who had Hamlet say that time is out of joint. Derrida joined the game and drove it further. Time is not linear any more – if it ever was. The arrow of time seems to run mad, time becomes anticipative, anticipates its other, becomes recursive, haunted by itself. Haunted – Derrida plays with this expression to elucidate the not-at-all-clear sequence of times and makes them dance with each other. Past, presence and future do not exist out of themselves separately. They permanently influence each other in more ways than one. This is how it needs to be understood instead of the linearity.

> If there is something like spectrality, there are reasons to doubt this reassuring order of presents and, especially, the border between the present, the actual or present reality of the present, and everything that can be opposed to it: absence, non-presence, non-effectivity, inactuality, virtuality, or even the simulacrum in general, and so forth. There is first of all the doubtful contemporaneity of the present to itself. Before knowing whether one can differentiate between the spectre of the past and the spectre of the future, of the past present and the future present,[3] one must perhaps ask oneself whether the *spectrality effect* does not consist in undoing this opposition, or even this dialectic, between actual, effective presence and its other.
>
> (Derrida 1994: 39–40, emphasis in original)

Both, Hamlet and Derrida, consider the potential influence of spectres. Derrida took the occasion of a conference titled *Whither Marxism* as stimulation to reflect about Marx' famous remark that Europe is haunted by the spectre of communism. What may the effect of eeriness be, what may haunting mean? Time gets out of joint is his conclusion, but it can only get out of joint if it was seen as linear. Hamlet is the hint that this establishing of linearity is artificial, more due to economic need for planning than everyday experience. Time has always been out of joint, so the reasoning must be. The linear time arrow is just a special case trying to achieve planning and a reliable outlook into the future. Planning, however, is supplemented. Instead of reducing complexity, it adds a dimension interacting with the complex mix of pasts, presents and futures and itself creates events which are not contained in the planning. The contemporaneity of the present to itself has to be doubted, Derrida wrote in the quote above. Presence has always been haunted by the past. Freud made us aware of the eternal recurrence of the repressed. More unusual is the perspective of being haunted by the future. As already noted during the discussion on regulation, Derrida links two more terms to haunting from the future which help to understand why this wild dance of terms is necessary as a basis for thinking about risk and regulation. His question after the tomorrow indicates the direction:

> Without this *non-contemporaneity with itself of the living present*, without that which secretly unhinges it, without this responsibility and this respect for justice concerning those who *are not there*, of those who are no longer or who are not yet *present and living*, what sense would there be to ask the question 'where?' 'Where tomorrow?' 'whither?'
>
> (Derrida 1994: xix, emphasis in original)

This sentence contains the whole force of the demand. It is about taking responsibility to do justice to the one who cannot be present, because she is already dead or not yet born. Derrida works with the term inheritance, although in the broadest frame possible. Resulting from the fact that we are not born into nothing, that there is always already something on which we build our lives, we are heirs. 'Inheritance is never a *given*', Derrida put it, 'it is always a task' (1994: 54, emphasis in original). Hamlet, immortal for his question about being, provided the frame in which to ask inheritance. He was haunted by inheritance, by his father's spectre who made him act and in this way responsible for what happened at court before and after the spectre's appearance. 'All the questions on the subject of being or of what is to be (or not to be) are questions of inheritance' (ibid.). The connection of being and inheriting is extremely close. It goes beyond receiving something by testament and gaining advantage from its use, from the wealth a close relative has earned. The simple fact of being, already makes us heirs. We inherit what we are.

> And that, as Hölderlin said so well, we can only *bear witness* to it. To bear witness would be to bear witness to what we *are* insofar as we *inherit*, and that – here is the circle, here is the chance, or the finitude – we inherit the very thing that allows us to bear witness to it. As for Hölderlin, he calls this language, 'the most dangerous of goods,' given to man 'so that he bears witness to having inherited/what he is [*damit er zeuge, was er sei/geerbt zu haben*].
>
> (Derrida 1994: 54, emphasis in original)

Here, in the unavoidability of inheritance, which is so much more than inheriting grandma's little house, keeping a portrait as a remembrance and honour somewhere in the corner, lies the connection to spectres: 'An inheritance which is not accepted, of which no one bears witness as it is not assumed in a responsible way, so is one of the main assumptions of the book, will recur in the form of spectres' (Lüdemann 2011: 135). Even more: it is not just about the responsibility to come into the inheritance, it is also about the responsibility for the changes of the inheritance, how the inheritance will have been inherited in the future. How will those who have to inherit us, be able to come into the inheritance?

Actually this is an almost banal insight: fear of the future is fed by uncertainty which is repressed by risk as order. Repressed, the fear leads a lonely existence as spectre and haunts the present. Simplifying risk as order represses too many options of the future. Additionally to those events that might wait beyond the horizon, events are also produced by reducing the range of possible, i.e. observable consequences in relying on a defined set of methods: produced impossibilities.

Derrida builds up an interesting circularity into the argument about the relationship between past, present and future. If what planning, or just the intention of a decision in the present is aiming at, is in the future, and it necessarily is, then this aim proceeds from the future: 'Now, if this question, from the moment it comes to us, can clearly come only from the future..., what stands *in front of it*, must also precede it like its origin: *before* it' (Derrida 1994: xix, emphasis in original). The question of the 'whither?', the 'where will we go tomorrow?' as an orientation for decisions and actions in the present must be, like any providence, absolutely and irreversibly past. Here philosophy is extremely close to the financial markets, or vice versa. It represents a pluralization of futures, a thought which is very familiar to every trader. There are uncountably many futures – as products and futures in everyday acting – to trade.[4] Risk is directed to the future. That what risk aims at is an assumed outcome calculated in its probability, independent if it is agreeable or not, if it is a threatening loss or a tempting profit. Risk management reacts by buying or selling instruments. The models used for deciding on the strategy share a basic assumption. Buying and selling the instruments secures the transaction, but does not influence the development of the underlying. This turned out to be the blind spot of risk management and the business models based on it (MacKenzie 2008). The future which shall be produced with these instruments is always already passed, because the use of the instruments will have already changed it. Even more radical, as it was the fundament of the assumption for using the instruments, it was at exactly the moment when it was analysed, already provenance, and as any provenance irreversibly past. What is to come cannot be covered.

Derrida's analysis sheds light on the inability of risk management and regulation to cope with the demands, or, that it is at least understood what is at stake. Risk as order and regulation conceptualized as linear, projective control only cope with the known. The continuation of what has always been there covers only one aspect. Risk enables action in the present, it provides an idea of how the future might look and what the consequences may be. Risk management therefore delivers information about the probability of what has already taken place and is able to incorporate events once they have taken place. But we will have lived in the future present. Moving towards it the im-possible event materializes, might materialize, what is not and cannot be calculated. The coming risk is not in focus of risk management, no banking regulation so far fosters an idea to deal with it.

The crucial point is that the aim of regulation is in the future and deals with the instrument invented to make future manageable in the present – risk. Regulation must haunt risk from the future. This is quite self-evident. Risk is future oriented. Staged anticipation is a form of being haunted by the future outcomes of present decisions. But staged anticipation runs into danger of taking the form of an older pattern. It is staged as fate, and it is possible to prepare for the fate by divination. As long as the image that financial crises come over us like natural disasters is kept, as long as locusts are (mis-)used as metaphor, it remains impossible to discuss the ingredients of a regulation to come on a mature level. Reading ethnographies like that of Ho (2009) or Honegger *et al.* (2010) about actors in the financial industry, a paradoxical attitude to the future can be observed. Risk enables trade as if there is no tomorrow, as was argued above about the risk to come. Investment banks defuturize future, they are 'institutionally unable to peer into the future', as Ho (2009: 279) described these banks' dealing [*sic*] with the future. The daily contact with the instrument for achieving some kind of control over the volatilities of future developments in an environment which leaves almost no time for reaction to changing conditions of the trades, leads to an exclusion of what the trades are about. Trading, however, includes by exclusion, it is an invitation of the Red Death. Future is in a complex mode excluded, but with the exclusion we are at the mercy of the future, at the mercy of that which is triggered by the trades today and at the same time give away the means to deal with the future.

Time is out of joint. Derrida knew that without especially researching the financial sector and its catastrophes of the past years. Risk, as a very special consideration of the relation of times, cannot remain detached when time is haunted, when the present faces its own non-contemporaneity with itself: *risk, introduced as order, is profoundly out of joint.* If something like a conclusion could be drawn from the clash of Derridean arguments with the financial markets, this might become the starting point for future research of risk, risk management and regulation in a very different mode.

On the gradual development of risk in the process of taking and managing it: against competent bearers of responsibility

In 1821, in a letter to a friend, Heinrich von Kleist developed a strange thought: '*Über die Allmähliche Verfertigung der Gedanken beim Reden – On the Gradual Development of Thoughts in the Process of Speaking*' (Kleist 1984: 340ff.). He anticipated the bewilderment of the reader. He imagines his friend answering him that the advice from his education was to speak only about what he already understands. It seems to be more than considering good or bad manners, preventing the listener from chaotic arguments, leading nowhere. Arguing from the safe ground of authority, of what is thought through, a report of the result of the process of thorough thinking, is highly valued and grants the speaker recognition. Developing the thoughts in the act of speaking fundamentally challenges this conviction. Kleist claims that this is, at least sometimes, necessary to speak to others in 'the sensible intention of instructing yourself' (Kleist 1984: 340). He considers working at his desk during his normal occupation of reading legal documents of a complicated case when he is not able to get the point. Talking to his sister then results in understanding what he is thinking about. He doesn't need comments or questions to provide him with hints. For him it is the process of clarifying the, at first sight, contradicting thoughts. Her reactions, the expression on her face or movements as if to interrupt him, enhance the concentration needed for getting to a conclusion. The process of speaking enables the expression of coherence. Moving beyond his own experience he gives another example which demonstrates the potentially performative character of this kind of speaking.

It is Mirabeau's answer to the royal master of ceremonies if he had heard the king's order to end the estates' meeting. 'Yes', was the beginning of the answer, 'we heard the king's order', and after a while confirming it: 'yes, my lord, we heard it', which clearly gives the impression that Mirabeau didn't have a prepared answer, but only developed it in the process of speaking. Hesitatingly, he still didn't know what he wanted to express: 'But what gives you the right', he continued, all of a sudden realizing what is at stake, 'to indicate orders to us? We are the representatives of the nation.' That was the argument he needed, 'the nation orders and does not receive orders'. He went on: 'And to make it perfectly clear', he expressed his newly formulated resistance, 'tell your king that we only leave our places by force of bayonet.' After the master of ceremonies had left the room, Mirabeau immediately proposed they should constitute as National Assembly and as such inviolable (Kleist 1984: 342f.). This process of speaking started to fundamentally change not just the situation; Kleist wanted to indicate that, at this concrete point in history, even an event like the French Revolution could be started by a gradual development of thoughts in the process of speaking.

With this idea Kleist was well ahead of his time. In complex environments, there is no easy or obvious solution. There is no lasting answer to a problem. Once developed, any solution needs to be carefully scrutinized and rejudged in the light of new developments. Any situational change needs to be considered and checked if a different, or a completely new answer is possible or even necessary. At that point when the king's representative returned in a moment of the assembly's hesitation to reinforce the king's authority, Mirabeau realized the danger as well as the opportunity of the situation and took a little time to develop his answer out of a different interpretation. The answer developed gradually, but once it was given, it changed the situation completely. This incident happened right in the middle of a struggle for power in France. The delicate stability between estates and the monarchy was already challenged and the constitution of the National Assembly can well be interpreted as the logical consequence at this point in history. But which logic is it that we apply? No matter which explanation we as readers of Kleist's text apply, it is an interpretation after the fact. We create the knowledge of the incident with hindsight. Only after it happened do we know what happened. Kleist's description is a vivid demonstration of a decision under pressure at the moment of new insight.

His short essay, however, can serve as an introduction to a changed attitude of thinking about risk, risk management and regulation. Such thinking requires a highly developed understanding of what can be known in the relationship of past, present and future and of how change materializes. By interpreting Kleist, Ortmann (1997) illustrates the need for some kind of a circular recursiveness in judging and acting. Recursive loops lead from a provisional thinking to a cautious acting and back and so forth. Five arguments can be derived from Kleist's essay. First, recursiveness needs time. This is not an argument for slowness, rather than for a gradual approach. Second, there is some kind of embodiment in understanding. The situation needs to create an inner meaning in the person judging it. Judging is by no means just a rational process, it involves emotion, recurrence to experience and the relationship to the other (Haidt 2001; Pelzer 2005). Third, there is some kind of a path dependency. The steps to proceed into the future are not determined, but once the first step is taken, the next ones need a connection to the first one. Any next step needs to orientate in the slightly new context which a step involves. Fourth, and this is very Derridean in its paradoxical phrasing, it understands the solution of a problem as a constitutive part of the problem definition. Only when solving a problem is it possible to understand what the problem is about. It is necessary, Ortmann insists, referring to Hirschman, to act with an ignorance of our ignorance of what the final result will be. Humans don't know what they don't know, and exactly this enables us to act instead of resigning, facing all the uncertainties related to the future. Fifth, is the importance of small events which trigger new developments. It cannot be said what exactly triggered Mirabeau's reaction, a glimpse of a sneer of the master, or an ambivalent play on the cuffs, it is a small event which otherwise would have been left unnoticed as normal behaviour. The result however, and this is the exciting insight for organization theory, was the constitution of the National Assembly as an inviolable institution. Organization and institutionalization as a means of caution and security against the power of the court is a remarkably far reaching reaction and result of this incident. The most important point in the 'gradual development of thoughts in the process of speaking', however, is the scepticism expressed against prognosis and fixed planning. Instead it offers the insight into the surprising human capabilities to do without their certainty and assurance (Ortmann 1997).

If a lesson is contained, and a suggestion can be derived from dissemination and the im-possible event, of what is to come: the insights into the limits of calculation and planning, the paradoxes of decision taking; the traps of competency; the supplementary character of risk and regulation; and if we allow ourselves to put it into the words of a romantic poet, it could be – on the gradual development of risk in the process of taking and managing it – against competent bearers of responsibility. The world should not be left to the competent bearers of responsibility. Regulation must ask what is accountable, what can be answered for. Risk and regulation cannot pretend to operate in a neutral space, as if what is traded is just money and not the future. Traded future is always also the future of others.

This text meanders between the world of financial markets and philosophers' arguments to provide alternative interpretations. Concerning the sophisticated market of risk taking and distributing, it could be held against these lines that they openly introduce interpretations of the ignorant. But of course: 'We are the specialists in discourse and texts, all sorts of texts', claims the philosopher (Derrida 1984: 22). Any discussion, any text of regulation, any minimum requirement is open for deconstruction. Seven missiles sent as a message in the form of seven missives, as the title of Derrida's paper suggests, take up the topic in their own way, but like the missiles on a trajectory, they aim at the blind spots of the competent arguments. I tried to follow the trajectories on their highly sensible and always disturbing way to find a different language to talk about risk in the financial industry. It was an exciting journey, but there can be no doubt about one issue: I desperately failed to do justice to the incredible richness of Derrida's arguments, the result (but, what is a result?) of the whole life of a philosopher. Nevertheless it immensely enriched my thinking about risk. I hope this will lead to further discussion enriching the academic, public and specialist discussion within the financial industry and legislative and regulatory bodies. Not very likely, but – *perhaps*.

Notes

1 What is to come?

1 XXIII. International SCOS conference, 8–10 July 2005, Royal Institute of Technology, Stockholm, Sweden. Parts of the article (Pelzer 2007) are included in the argument of Chapter 9.
2 Cooper can be considered as a forerunner in explaining the contribution of poststructural philosophy and using it himself in his research (for his consideration of the early work of Derrida (Cooper 1989), an introduction into Cooper's work is provided by Spoelstra (2005)). However, the list is by no means exhaustive. Journals like *Philosophy of Management* or *Culture and Organization* are further examples whose editors are explicitly interested in publishing this kind of research.
3 All the references given here are only indicative of a huge body of literature about risk. Many more could have been taken as examples, as other overviews show (e.g. Lupton 1999).
4 Again just a very small selection of the publications. Meanwhile the research, from academic as well as institutional sources, can be considered well developed and provide ample information about the reasons which led into the crisis.
5 The unusual use of hyphen in 'im-possible' is a conscious violation of orthography by Jacques Derrida, which will be explained in the following chapter.
6 I am very aware of the fact that the introduction of Agamben in a book, which mainly relies on arguments by Derrida, is not without tension. Derrida was quite sceptical about several theoretical moves of Agamben (Derrida 2006; 2009). The concept of the state of exception, however, and the figure of the inclusion of the excluded, is very powerful in Agamben's theorizing and provides deep insight into what is at stake.

2 Thinking about the im-possible risk in the financial industry

1 Starting this book with 'perhaps' is an indirect quote of Derrida whose thinking provides the line of argument for this book (Derrida 1976: 422): his chapter starts with 'perhaps' soon followed by the event, gathering two terms of utmost importance for what will be argued in the following.
2 Translation provided by the ebook available at planetbook.com (Nietzsche, without year: 7).
3 Risk and regulation interpreted in the light of its dissemination and Derrida's (2004a) introduction into the world of the 'pharmakon' is the topic of Chapter 8.
4 Already the title of this German translation of a presentation gives an impression of what is at stake here: 'A certain impossible possibility to speak of the event (*Eine gewisse unmögliche Möglichkeit, vom Ereignis zu sprechen*)' (Derrida 2003).
5 The double meaning of 'execution' is striking. There is some finiteness, fatal consequence included here.

6 Building on Derrida's arguments, Günther Ortmann wrote an excellent book about rules and their unavoidable paradoxes: *Regel und Ausnahme* (rule and exception) (Ortmann 2003b).

7 This is an indirect reference to one of his other texts: '*The Gift of Death*' (Derrida 1995) where it is the headline of Chapter 3.

8 Dattel, Leeson, Kerviel and Adoboli are the names of the traders who were blamed for the massive losses of these banks in trading. However guilty they were in trading beyond limits and hiding losses, their public naming as 'rogue traders' (Greener 2006) hides the systemic failing of risk management and serious shortcomings in the responsibility of management.

9 This interview had a strange fate. Originally it was done by Thomas Assheuer (Assheuer and Derrida 1998). The text went back and forth as Derrida was unhappy with the formulations. The text finally printed was shorter than the whole interview. Peter Krapp translated the complete text into English and made it available in *Culture Machine*.

10 Elsewhere (Pelzer 2011) I followed arguments of Hörisch (1996) and Deutschmann (1999) that a precondition for the equivalence of time and money is a crucial change taking place during the transition to a secular world: money, so they argue, replaced God in the relationship to time and eternity.

> Both resources, time and money, are scarce and are attributed the highest value. Eternity which was discontinued [*sic*!] with the negation of a god, is revitalized by money as the means to keep time liquid and infinite. Scarce money can counteract scarce time at several levels. In favour of meta-temporal money we invest time; gaining money motivates the loss of time; money accumulates past and passing time; money is virtually eternal; wealth survives the mortal who owns it. Money cannot die. In short, time is money because the meta-temporal medium money makes it possible to rule time.
>
> (Pelzer 2011)

11 Parts of the argument appeared in a similar way in Pelzer (2011) and Pelzer (2009).

12 It is an invention also in Derrida's (2003) strict definition. It is not a development of something existing, adding a few new aspects. It is the radical new, something which has not been considered before.

13 Or to 1974, the year Portugal left its remaining colonies, as Sloterdijk (2006) makes the strict time boundary a bit more flexible.

14 Bayatrizi (2008) researched the quantification of mortality in early modern statistics to follow the track from fate to risk. If even death becomes a matter of calculation with probabilities attached, it underlines humans' demand for their own organization of life by a denial of fate.

15 I'm following Sloterdijk's (2006) argument here. The point is, irrespective if he is correct in each detail of his argument regarding the process of globalization, especially from an economic historic perspective, that Columbus can serve as an example of the necessary changes of thinking required at this stage of development. First examples may well have occurred before on a smaller scale and less lasting public attention.

16 The following was already developed in 'Risk as present futures' (Pelzer 2011).

17 To paraphrase Weick's own suspicion of his use of an argument by Stinchcombe (Weick 1995: 96).

18 The geographical horizon is the principal meaning here; in the context of risk it is also the possible horizon of understanding as Derrida understands it.

19 This is the title of a film about the life of Joe Strummer, singer and songwriter of The Clash, director: Julian Temple (2007).

20 Parts of this argument were already included in Pelzer (2011).

21 Of course such a straightforward construction of derivatives dates back to the times

when the close link between the 'real' economy and the financial markets was still dominating in terms of organizing risk in deliveries for goods and services. How much the financial markets and the products traded within them have changed in the stunningly short period from the 1980s on, provides the context of books such as of Lewis (1990, 2011) or Das (2010).

22 The abstractness is of a different kind as the virtuality of the business of derivative trading referred to in Chapters 4 and 6. Arnoldi insists that 'derivatives use uncertainty by virtualising it' (Arnoldi 2004: 23). Derivatives as a technology do not merely create risk, but use uncertainty as a resource. MacKenzie (2007) insists that this kind of virtuality is materially produced. The link of the virtual world on screens and its underlying is never completely broken. This is the nature of systemic risk.

23 Haunting, of course, is also inspired by one of Derrida's books: *Spectres of Marx* (1994).

3 Risk – the sovereign exception

1 Despite the main person's name, Prospero, the similarities to Shakespeare's *The Tempest* are not easy to track. Given Poe's wide reading, 'Prospero' must have been a conscious reference. Caliban's curse 'The red plague rid you,/for learning me your language' (Shakespeare, as quoted by Vanderbilt 1968: 383) might have inspired Poe with the name for the Red Death. Vanderbilt (1968) provides an excellent introduction into the parallels of the characters and the consequences for Poe's arabesque. However, they do not influence the interpretation here.

2 Sacer is a figure of the ancient Roman legal system. The reference to the sacrifice results either from the double exclusion from the polity and the divine order, or to the double meaning of holy and damned: a culprit dedicated to the gods of the underworld is holy, but cannot be touched without becoming unclean (Agamben 2002).

3 Agamben develops his definition of sovereignty and the state of exception largely from the discussion of the work of Carl Schmitt and Walter Benjamin. During this he refers to mutual direct or indirect referencing, the exchange of letters and Schmitt's appraisal of Benjamin's work in this regard. This kind of exchange keeps a strange flavour given the fact that Benjamin died on the flight from the representatives of the Nazi system Schmitt was working for as one of the major intellectual voices of legal theory.

4 This is not to say that a bank is choosing credits from its portfolio to securitize them and then sells and trades this security. The more liquidity is in the market, the more securities are created, the more opportunities there are for major players to act on both sides, even if any 'Chinese wall' is obtained and they don't act on the same issue on both sides.

5 This can be called regulation arbitrage. It is part of the argument in Chapters 8 and 9.

4 The displaced world of risk: risk management as alienated risk (perception?)

1 There is some redundancy here to the arguments developed in Chapter 2. It is retained in this chapter for the coherence of the argument.

2 Stephan Hessler made me aware of this interpretation, similarly in Hessler (2007).

3 It should be noted that immeasurability is a characteristic of the sublime. The sublime hints at that which is greater than mankind and able to rule humans: the reintroduction of religious, at least magical belief (Pelzer and Case 2008).

4 A derivative, e.g. a future or an option, is a financial instrument whose value depends on the price of another asset, the 'underlying'.

5 Talking of 'bonds' here is of special ambiguity. The bonds traded in financial markets indicate a depersonalized quality, the pooling effect.

5 From 'risk and responsibility' to the risk of responsibility

1 Stefanie Kratz, editor with Kiepenheuer & Witsch, about Christoph Schlingensief's proposal for the title of his autobiography on the occasion of his obituary (Interview by Ijoma Mangold, *Die Zeit*, 35, 26 August 2010, 44, author's translation).
2 Though only Luhmann directly refers to Knight and considers his definition as ossified into a dogma so that any further development of the term is confronted with the reproach of not having understood the term sufficiently (Luhmann 1991: 9).
3 No matter how disputable this difference is, it may help to describe how events that are not covered by the reality, created by risk management enter the scene. The world manifests itself in the event, which is an event for reality precisely because it is excluded.
4 Daston's arguments mirror the relationship between state and banking industry in the quarrels about regulation. Risk and regulation will be discussed in more detail in Chapter 9.
5 Any direct quote of Honegger *et al.* (2010) was translated by the author.
6 In these examples I refer to organization instead of banks, because the transfer of risk does not necessarily require a banking permit and therefore can be traded by other organizations like funds as well.
7 This figure is widespread, but difficult to track down to official statistical sources like those of the BIS. Sources which quote the figure are educational websites for trading like Dawson (2011), who claims that 'only 2 per cent of all Commodity Futures contracts are actually delivered', or futurestradingpedia.com (2011) stating: 'In fact, less than 5 per cent of futures contracts in the US market are ultimately delivered'.
8 According to the BIS report on 'OTC derivatives market activity in the first half of 2011' (BIS 2011) the notional amount of exchange traded derivatives is less than 12 per cent.
9 The point of regulations defining what a bank is and what kind of business is exclusively reserved for organizations with a banking permit, is not followed here. It makes no difference for the argument of the changing power relation of the markets, if the participants of the financial markets other than banks can act independently or have to use banks as an interface to the financial markets.
10 It should be mentioned that the transfer of the creditor to another organization as a bank also has consequences for the credit takers involved in the package. It increases the pressure if the rates fail.
11 This is the attempt to translate a German phrase which has no exact equivalent in the English language. '*Die Kuh geht aufs Eis*' says the original quote. In nature cows do not go on ice, and especially not on an icy lake, as it is much too dangerous for them. They could slip, or even break in. To get the cow off the ice means solving a tricky, dangerous situation in the German context. The banker here makes additional sense of the phrase in indicating that the banks needed to use the cow on the ice. It is the market.

6 'Who's afraid of red, yellow and blue' – towards an aesthetics of risk

1 *Who's afraid of red, yellow and blue* is the title of a painting by Barnett Newman. A discussion of the painting and Newman's intention will be part of the discussion in this chapter.
2 This may sound self-evident nowadays after many publications and several conferences on this topic during the past fifteen years or so. To name just a few: the journal *Aesthesis*, newly founded in 2007; Consumption, Markets and Culture (2002); Guillet de Monthoux (2004); special issues of Human Relations (2002); Linstead and Höpfl (2000); Organization (1996); and Strati (1999). It must be noted, however, that

Cooper presented this paper before the topic became fashionable and easy to publish. He provided a framework to reflect on the necessity of the aesthetic view in organization theory with the required breadth and depth that this topic deserves. Strangely enough it seems that this groundbreaking paper has never been published.

3 The boundaries are not as sharp as formulated here. These kinds of trades do not necessarily require a banking permit and, therefore, this kind of trading is not restricted to investment banking. It can also take place in Funds.

4 I'd like to thank Geoff Lightfoot and Simon Lilley for sharing this fascinating source with me on occasion of writing Lightfoot *et al.* (2009). The quotes contained in this chapter are taken from this article.

5 Spelled 'robuster' in original transcript.

6 According to the BIS report on 'OTC derivatives market activity in the first half of 2011' (BIS 2011) the notional amount of exchange traded derivatives is less than 12 per cent.

7 The painting is in the collection of Stedelijk Museum, Amsterdam, the Netherlands. An image can be found at: www.ieku.nl/wp-content/uploads/2009/10/ortland09–26–06–211.jpg.

8 Interestingly Stranger never makes clear what the level of risk actually is, i.e. how many accidents are reported and what the injuries or fatalities are.

9 It may be coincidental, or not – the name Thompson turns up at several places in this chapter, and the name is always related with a certain type of risk taking: Hunter Thompson, the motorbike driver; Michael Thompson, the mountaineer and anthropologist; Valerie Thompson, the trader; and P. Thompson simply recording trader's life and risk taking.

10 Psychologists might argue differently. In their article 'risk as feelings' Loewenstein *et al.* (2001: 267) argue 'that emotional reactions to risky situations often diverge from cognitive assessments of those risks.' Similarily Slovic *et al.* (2004).The edge is a matter of perception and therefore also deeply aesthetic.

11 Motorbiking and the example of Hunter Thompson was already taken as an introduction to sublime aspects of trading in the banking industry during a participation of the author in Lightfoot *et al.* (2009).

12 For a more detailed argument following arguments by Sloterdijk (2006), Hörisch (1998), Bernstein (1996), see Chapter 2.

13 It has to be acknowledged that this figure is correct, but seems to be taken to emphasize the overwhelming relation, despite the fact that its informative value may be limited. While the figure is correct and rose to US$707,569 trillion (BIS 2011), this is the notional amount outstanding and as such a measure for the market size and market liquidity, but gives only a limited information of the risk involved. The better figure as a proxy for the potential risk transfer is the gross market value (King and Mallo 2010). In June 2011 this was US$19,518 trillion (BIS 2011). Despite the fact that deals between affiliates are netted out, positions between counterparts are still gross value, i.e. the net value of the position is lower. Lower, but significant, considering the size of the position. The relation of these figures is a very clear indication of the potential systemic risk and provides an ample justification for a more coherent regulation of financial markets.

14 It has to be reminded that the Basel accords are only relevant for banks, originally only for internationally operating banks. This excludes other market participants which do not need a banking permit, such as hedge funds and other funds, or insurance companies. Derivatives can be traded OTC by any of these market participants. The coverage of 8 per cent points at an ideal state: the inclusion of all participants into financial regulation.

7 The risk to come – a different way of thinking risk

1 Like, for example, the author of The Black Swan: The Impact of the Highly Improbable (Taleb 2007).
2 BaFin: Bundesanstalt für Finanzdienstleistungsaufsicht, the German regulatory body for banking, security trading and insurance.
3 Translation of the German original by Marcus Pfeil.
4 See Chapter 2.
5 Shackle (1988) Business, Time and Thought, selected papers, edited by Stephen F. Frown. The similarities with the im-possible, with what is behind the horizon of what can be perceived in the present time, is obvious. Shackle repudiates the possibility of a calculable history. Despite these similarities, however, one cannot oversee a major difference to Derrida. Shackle looks for an uncaused cause, what he would call a beginning. The author of the trace, of the différance, the haunting, Derrida, takes the characteristics of what is to come further and much sharper, and especially argues against any form of origin.
6 I consciously left out the term 'messianic' (Derrida 2006: 130) here, as it would be even more confusing to explain what messianic is in absence of any ontology and theology.
7 'Defuturized' is Esposito's expression for the effect of the confusion of the two types of future she analysed: present future and future present. The blind spot she points at is contained in this almost sarcastic statement: 'pretending that the probability of risk can be transformed into certainty by stochastic calculation is equivalent to a "defuturization of future"' (Esposito 2007: 84, see also Chapter 2 and 10). Reality of Wall Street drives this conclusion to the extreme.

8 Risk and regulation disseminate: the pharmakon

1 This insight goes beyond Rockett's remark that definitions are not what they seem (Rockett 1999) when he reflected about a definition of risk.
2 A matter of translation and adding to the argument developed here: the word 'Gift' in German means poison, not present. This dimension is reminiscent in the text as well: 'Isn't this *pharmakon* a criminal thing then, a poisoned present?' (Derrida 2004c: 82).
3 On initiative of the Trading Book Group of the Research Task Force of the Basel Committee on Banking Supervision an ad hoc working group reviewed the academic literature. The examples quoted here mirror the arguments of the underlying literature.
4 MacKenzie (2003b) notes that none of the banks who invested in LTCM and who had to reinvest to stabilize the portfolio, had to face a loss in the end.
5 A trading which seeks to profit from price discrepancies.
6 The time that went along before the estimations on the potential of losses stabilized, and the still remaining spread of the estimations demonstrate that a full transparency is almost impossible.
7 Table 1: the relation of the grand total of the amounts outstanding in the global OTC derivatives market of US$707.569 trillion in relation to the Memo: Exchange traded contracts US$82.972 trillion.
8 ECB refers to 'originate and distribute' model instead of 'originate-to-distribute' which other authors (e.g. Szegö 2010, Purnanandam forthcoming) prefer. I would prefer to insist on the significance of the change from *'and'* to *'to'*. It signifies the important shift of the whole model elaborated here.

9 Containing risk: towards a regulation to come

1 OTC – over the counter, those trades in the financial industry which are processed outside exchanges directly between two institutions. This is not restricted to trading between banks. Counterparts can be banks, funds, or other companies.

2 This part of the chapter is based on an article in *Culture and Organization* (Pelzer 2007). It is reproduced by kind permission of Taylor & Francis. The figures of the trading volumes have been updated and some language editing has taken place.
3 A derivative, e.g. a future or an option, is a financial instrument whose value depends on the price of another asset, the 'underlying'.
4 The figures become even more impressive when comparing them with the GDP of the countries in which the currencies are traded. The total foreign exchange turnover exceeds the GDP of the United States and Japan fourteen times. In other counties the ratio is even much higher, e.g. 200 times in the UK (King and Rime 2010).
5 Given the reference made to Strange's term 'Casino Capitalism' (Strange 1986), the naming, by professionals, of a simulation model after a city famous for its casinos hints at least to a solid sense of irony if not a clear consciousness of what they are actually doing: playing games on a global level. The origin of risk management and the calculation of probabilities in gambling is well researched (Hacking 1975).
6 All translations from German originals in this text have been done by the author.
7 In Germany the requirement of soundness is part of the German Banking Act (KWG – *Kreditwesengesetz*) and for trading of WpHG (*Wertpapierhandelsgesetz*) and is detailed in the minimum requirements.
8 Daniel Kahneman and Amos Tversky (e.g. 1984) did a lot of research on decision under risk. They argued that the interpretation of figures are very different, depending on how they were presented and lead to very different decisions; similarily Gigerenzer (2002).
9 The EU MiFID (Markets in Financial Instruments Directive) could be named as a prominent example inside. It sets rules for the trading of securities with retail customers.
10 Financialization is not just a topic of academics. In a lecture at the reserve bank of India Adair Turner observed an 'increased "financialisation" of the economy' (Turner 2010a: 2).
11 Or, it should involve a decision.
12 ERM: Enterprise Risk Management. According to Power (2005) ERM is a set of ideas for rethinking the organization of risk management. It has two main sources: shareholder value for its risk-return relation; internal control as the bedrock of the good organization as part of the corporate governance movement.
13 Dake (1992) emphasizes the importance of the social construction of risk against a myth of nature; Abolafia (1998) sees markets as socially constructed cultures.
14 I'm referring here to the meltdown of the reactors in Fukushima, Japan, after the earthquake and a tsunami in 2011.
15 See also Chapter 10 of this book.
16 For a vivid description of the development of this market and the mindset of the actors see Lewis (1990).
17 Emphasizing just the two sides, evil banks and financial advisors, and poor customers, is of course a very limited perspective. Greed is on both sides and seems to be an unavoidable part of the story (Neckel 2011; Sievers 2012). On the foreign exchange market, for example, the 'trading activity by small retail investors has made a significant contribution to growth' (King and Rime 2010: 31). However, it can also be interpreted as another massive change. Neckel (2011) analyses the logic of increasing speculative returns in banks as the sign that greed has become the structural principle of financial economic action. He represents the end of greed as calm passion with the function of binding decisions to long-term economic interests.
18 This insight as such is not new. Investor Warren Buffett named these kinds of instruments 'weapons of mass destruction' (as quoted by Das 2010).
19 This opinion is shaped by many personal experiences inside banks, but also fed by literature like Das (2010); Ho (2009); Honegger *et al.* (2010); Lewis (1990, 2011); Pfeil (2010).

20 See Chapter 2 for a more detailed discussion.
21 The work of the Basel Committee and other institutions working on the consequences of the 2008 crisis points into this direction. Banks which are considered to be of systemic relevance, i.e. too big to fail, shall be identified and obliged to hold more regulatory capital than others.
22 Former compliance manager of a bank Pierre-André Berchtolt during a discussion on compliance, on the occasion of a project introducing a new software package where I was one of the project members.
23 This conclusion was already drawn in a text with Peter Case (Pelzer and Case 2008).
24 Interestingly the German translation refers to '*Bankweite Führungsverantwortung*' which would translate as 'bank-wide responsibility of leading'. In my ears that addresses much more directly failures of management.
25 Instead of the philosophy of Jacques Derrida, the general thrust of this book could also be developed with Luhmann's systems theory (and parts of my argument here took up Elena Esposito's (2007, 2010) reading of Luhmann applied to the financial markets), or with complexity theory. Even the sociology of Norbert Elias (1976, 1983) was already argued in this direction decades ago.
26 Paraphrasing the title of his article in Diacritics: 'No apocalypse, not now (full speed.

10 (This will not have been a) conclusion

1 Two of the titles of the introduction to *Dissemination* (Derrida 1994: 1) indicating the ambivalence, even the impossibility of any introduction.
2 This is a cumulative strategy which couldn't be further away from Derrida's reading strategy, and above that, impossible for the topic discussed here, considering the overwhelming amount of literature published.
3 Past present and future present are terms that have appeared frequently throughout this book. So far I used Esposito's (2007, 2010) elaboration on this more complex relationship between present and future. It is interesting to note that these terms are also used by Derrida. Luhmann on whom Esposito relies in her writings, however, acknowledged the closeness of second-order observation and deconstruction. Deconstruction, he wrote, is the most relevant description of the self-description of modern society (Luhmann 2001).
4 Refering once more to terms in the German language to illustrate a link: to act and to trade can be translated with the same word: *handeln*. It depends on the context meant. Trading is acting, of course, and faces reactions which influence the materialization of the trade's effects.

References

Aalbers, M.B. (2009) 'Wrong Assumptions in the Financial Crisis', *Critical Perspectives on International Business* 5(1/2): 94–97.

Abolafia, M. (1998) 'Markets as Cultures: an Ethnographic Approach', in M. Callon (ed.) *The Laws of the Market*, Oxford: Blackwell, 69–85.

Abolafia, M. (1996) 'Hyper-Rational Gaming', *Journal of Contemporary Ethnography* 25(2): 226–250.

Agamben, G. (2002) *Homo Sacer. Die Souveränität der Macht und das Nackte Leben [Homo Sacer. The Sovereignty of Power and Naked Life]*, Frankfurt: Suhrkamp.

Agamben, G. (2003) *Was von Auschwitz Bleibt [Remnants of Auschwitz]*, Frankfurt: Suhrkamp.

Agamben, G. (2004) *Ausnahmezustand [State of Exception]*, Frankfurt: Suhrkamp.

Armstrong, J.M. (2003) 'Danger: Derrida at work', *Interdisciplinary Science Research* 28(2): 1–12.

Armstrong, J.M. and Paynter, S.P. (2004) 'Safe Systems: Construction, Destruction, and Deconstruction', *Technical Reports Series CS-TR-830*, School of Computing Science, University of Newcastle upon Tyne.

Arnoldi, J. (2004) 'Derivatives. Virtual Values and Real Risks', *Theory, Culture & Society* 21(6): 23–42.

Assheuer, T. and Derrida, J. (1998) 'Ich Misstraue der Utopie, Ich Will das Un-Mögliche', *Die Zeit*, 11.

Azarmi, T. (2005) *The Collapse of Barings Bank: Nikkei Stock Average Futures Trading on SIMEX*, available: www.csulb.edu/~tazarmi/BARINGS.html (accessed 19 April 2005).

Baecker, D. (1991) *Womit Handeln Banken? Eine Untersuchung zur Risikoverarbeitung in der Wirtschaft*, Frankfurt: Suhrkamp.

Bartels, K. (1989) 'Über das Technisch-Erhabene', in C. Pries (ed.) *Das Erhabene – Zwischen Grenzerfahrung und Größenwahn*, Weinheim: VCH Acta Humaniora, 295–316.

Basel Committee on Banking Supervision (2010) *The Basel Committee's Response to the Financial Crisis: Report to the G20*, Basel: Bank for International Settlements, available: www.bis.org/publ/bcbs179.pdf (accessed 12 August 2011).

Basel Committee on Banking Supervision 2011) *Messages from the Academic Literature on Risk Measurement for the Trading Book*, available: www.bis.org/publ/bcbs_wp19.pdf (accessed 4 May 2011).

Baudrillard, J. (1983) *Simulations*, New York: Semiotext(e).

Baudrillard, J. (1992) *Transparenz des Bösen*, Berlin: Merve.

Baudrillard, J. (2002) *Paroxysmus*, Vienna: Passagen.

Baudrillard, J. (2002) *The Gulf War Did Not Take Place*, Bloomington, IL: Indiana University Press.

Bauer, H. (2004) *Die Interne Revision als Gesprächspartner der Bankenaufsicht*, Referat zur 1. Plenarsitzung des IIR (Deutsches Institut für interne Revision e.V.) – Forums Kreditinstitute, Würzburg, available: http://iir-ev.de/deutsch/veranstaltungen/Grossveranstaltungen/PL1_Bauer.pdf (accessed 7 March 2005).

Bauman, Z. (2000) *Liquid Modernity*, Cambridge: Polity Press.

Bauman, Z. (2008) *The Art of Life*, Cambridge: Polity Press.

Bayatrizi, Z. (2008) 'From Fate to Risk. The Quantification of Mortality in Early Modern Statistics', *Theory, Culture & Society* 25(1): 121–143.

Beck, U. (1986) *Risikogesellschaft. Auf dem Weg in eine Andere Moderne*, Frankfurt: Suhrkamp; English: (1992) *Risk Society: Towards a New Modernity*, London: Sage.

Beck, U. (1988) *Gegengifte*, Frankfurt: Suhrkamp.

Beck, U. (2008) *Weltrisikogesellschaft*, Frankfurt: Suhrkamp; English: (2009) *World at Risk*, New York: John Wiley.

Beckert, J. (2009) 'Die Anspruchsinflation des Wirtschaftssystems. Zur Theorie des Spätkapitalismus im Licht der Finanzmarktkrise', *WestEnd. Neue Zeitschrift für Sozialforschung* 6/2, 135–149.

Berger, J. (1972) *Ways of Seeing*, London: Penguin.

Berger, J. (1992) 'Eine Andere Art zu Sehen', *ZEIT Magazin* 14, 40–44.

Bernstein, P.L. (1996) *Against the Gods, the Remarkable Story of Risk*, New York: John Wiley.

Beunza, D. and Stark D. (2005) 'How to Recognize Opportunities: Heterarchical Search in a Trading Room', in K. Knorr Cetina and A. Preda (eds) *The Sociology Of Financial Markets*, Oxford: Oxford University Press.

Bible (1985) *Einheitsübersetzung der Heiligen Schrift*, 3rd edition, Stuttgart: Katholische Bibelanstalt; English quotes from Exodus: available: www.worldwideschool.org/library/books/relg/bible/KingJamesBible02-Exodus/Chap1.html (accessed 15 March 2007); Book of Joel: www.gcfweb.org/institute/prophet/joel.html (accessed 15 March 2007); Book of Revelation: http://biblia.com/bible/rev9.htm (accessed 15 March 2007).

Biegler, M. (2010) 'Finanzskandale. Produkte Strukturierter Verantwortungslosigkeit', in C. Honegger, S. Neckel and C. Magnin (eds) *Strukturierte Verantwortungslosigkeit, Berichte aus der Bankenwelt*, Berlin: Suhrkamp, 245–258.

BIS (2004) *Basel Committee on Banking Supervision: International Convergence of Capital Measurement and Capital Standards*, Basel: Bank for International Settlements.

BIS (2010) *Triennial Central Bank Survey, Report on Global Foreign Exchange Market Activity in 2010*, Basel: Bank for International Settlements, available: www.bis.org/publ/rpfxf10t.pdf (accessed 7 November 2011).

BIS (2011) *OTC Derivatives Market Activity in the First Half of 2011*, Basel: Bank for International Settlements, available: www.bis.org/publ/otc_hy1111.pdf (accessed 28 November 2011).

Black, J. (2002) *Critical Reflections on Regulation*, CARR Discussion Paper 4, London School of Economics and Political Science.

Böhme, G. (2003) 'Contribution to the Critique of the Aesthetic Economy', *Thesis Eleven* 73, 71–82.

Böhme, H. (1989) 'Das Steinerne', in C. Pries (ed.) *Das Erhabene – Zwischen Grenzerfahrung und Größenwahn*, Weinheim: VCH Acta Humaniora, 119–142.

Boltanski, L. (2008) 'Individualismus ohne Freiheit. Ein Pragmatischer Zugang zur Herrschaft', *WestEnd, Neue Zeitschrift für Sozialforschung* 2, 133–149.

Boltanski, L. (2010) *Soziologie und Sozialkritik*, Berlin: Suhrkamp.

Boltanski, L. and Chiapello, È. (2003) *Der Neue Geist des Kapitalismus*, Konstanz: UVK Verlagsgesellschaft.

Boltanski, L. and Thévenot, L. (2007) *Über die Rechtfertigung. Eine Soziologie der Kritischen Urteilskraft*, Hamburg: Hamburger Edition.

Brors, P. and Knüwer, T. (2004) 'Der Fall der Goldjungen', *Handelsblatt*, available: www.handelsblatt.de/pshb/fn/relhbi/sfn/cn_artikel_drucken/strucid/PAGE_200012/pageid/PAGE_200039/docid/739882/SH/0/depot/0/ (accessed 19 April 2005).

Burke, E. (1998 [1757]) *A Philosophical Enquiry into the Sublime and Beautiful*, London: Penguin Classics.

Carroll, R. (ed.) (2009) *Risk Management Handbook for Health Care Organizations*, 5th edition, Wiley.

Carter, P. and Jackson, N. (1997) *Risk 'Analysis' as Discourse*, Working paper series no. HUSM/PC/32, School of Management, The University of Hull.

Caruana, J. (2010a) *Financial Stability: 10 Questions and About Seven Answers*, speech at the 50th Anniversary Symposium of the Reserve Bank of Australia, Sydney, 9 February, available: http://bis.org/speeches/sp100209.htm (accessed 4 May 2011).

Caruana, J. (2010b) *Systemic Risk: How to Deal With It?*, paper 12 February, available: http://bis.org/publ/othp08.htm, (accessed 4 May 2011).

Caruana, J. (2010c) *Basel III: Towards a Safer Financial System*, 3. Santander International Banking Conference, Madrid, 15 September, available: http://bis.org/speeches/sp100921.htm (accessed 4 May 2011).

Caruana, J. (2011) 'Regulatory Reform: Remaining Challenges', Speech at the annual Pierre Werner Lecture, Luxembourg, 7 July 2011, available: www.bis.org/speeches/sp110711.htm (accessed 11 August 2011).

Chancellor. E. (2000) *Devil Take the Hindmost. A History of Financial Speculation*, New York: Plume.

Cloke, J. (2009) 'An Economic Wonderland: Derivative Castles Built on Sand', *Critical Perspectives on International Business* 5(1/2): 2009, 107–119.

Cooper, R. (1987) 'Information, Communication and Organization: A Post-Structural Revision', *Journal of Mind and Behavior* 8(3): 395–416.

Cooper, R. (1989) 'Modernism, Post Modernism and Organizational Analysis 3: The Contribution of Jacques Derrida', in *Organization Studies* 10/4, 479–502.

Cooper, R. (1990) 'Organization/disorganization', in J. Hassard and D. Pym (eds) *The Theory and Philosophy of Organizations*, London: Routledge, 167–197.

Cooper, R. (1991) *Institutional Aesthetics: The Case of Contestation*, paper presented at Utrecht University, The Netherlands, January.

Courtney, C. and Thompson, P. (1996) *City Lives: The Changing Voices of British Finance*, London: Methuen.

Cox, C. (2008) *Testimony Concerning Turmoil in U.S. Credit Markets: Recent Actions Regarding Government Sponsored Entities, Investment Banks and Other Financial Institutions*, Before the Committee on Banking, Housing, and Urban Affairs, United States Senate, 23 September, available: www.sec.gov/news/testimony/2008/ts092308cc.htm (accessed 30 November 2009).

Crockett, A. (1997): *The Theory and Practice of Financial Stability*, Princeton Essays in International Finance, No. 203.

Dake, K. (1992) 'Myths of Nature: Culture and the Social Construction of Risk', *Journal of Social Issues* 48(4): 21–37.
Danielsson, J. (2002) 'The Emperor Has No Clothes: Limits to Risk Modelling', *Journal of Banking and Finance* 26(7): 1273–1296.
Danielsson, J., Embrechts, P., Goodhart, C., Keating, C., Muennich, F., Renault, O. and Shin, H.S. (2001) *An Academic Response to Basel II*, LSE Financial Markets Group, special paper no. 130, available: www.bis.org/bcbs/ca/fmg.pdf (accessed 4 May 2011).
Danielsson, J., Shin, H.S. and Zigrand, J.-P. (2009) *Risk Appetite and Endogenous Risk*, AXA Working Paper series no. 2, Discussion Paper 647, London School of Economics and Political Science.
Danielsson, J., Shin, H.S. and Zigrand, J.-P. (2010) *Endogenous and Systemic Risk, Risk Research*, available: www.riskresearch.org/files/JD-HS-JZ-37.pdf (accessed 14 April 2011).
Das, S. (2010) *Traders, Guns & Money*, revised edition, Harlow: Prentice Hall.
Daston, L. (1992) 'Objectivity and the Escape from Perspective', *Social Studies of Science* 22, 597–618.
Dawson, D. (2011) 'Physical Delivery or Cash Settled?', *Online Trading Academy*, 23 February 2011, available: www.tradingacademy.com/lessons/20110223/commodities_article.htm, (accessed 28 November 2011).
DeLillo, D. (2003) *Cosmopolis*, New York: Scribner.
Derrida, J. (1976) *Die Schrift und die Differenz*, Frankfurt: Suhrkamp.
Derrida, J. (1983) *Grammatologie*, Frankfurt: Suhrkamp.
Derrida, J. (1984): 'No Apocalypse, not Now (Full Speed Ahead, Seven Missiles, Seven Missives)', *Diacritics* Summer, 20–31.
Derrida, J. (1990) 'Die différance', in P. Engelmann, (ed.) *Postmoderne und Dekonstruktion*, Stuttgart: Philipp Reclam jr., 76–113.
Derrida, J. (1992) 'Force of Law: The "Mystical Foundation of Authority"', in D. Cornell, M. Rosenfeld and D. Gray Carlson (eds) *Deconstruction and the Possibility of Justice*, New York, London: Routledge, 3–67.
Derrida, J. (1993) *Falschgeld: Zeit Geben I*, Munich: Fink.
Derrida, J. (1994) *Specters of Marx. The State of the Debt, the Work of Mourning, & The New International*, transl. Peggy Karmuf, New York, London: Routledge.
Derrida, J. (1995) *The Gift of Death*, Chicago: University of Chicago Press.
Derrida, J. (1999) *Préjugés, Vor dem Gesetz*, 2 Auflage, Vienna: Edition Passagen.
Derrida, J. (2001) *Die unbedingte Universität*, Frankfurt: Suhrkamp.
Derrida, J. (2002) *Politik der Freundschaft*, Frankfurt: Suhrkamp.
Derrida, J. (2003) *Eine Gewisse Unmögliche Möglichkeit, vom Ereignis zu Sprechen*, Berlin: Merve.
Derrida, J. (2004a) *Marx' Gespenster*, Frankfurt: Suhrkamp.
Derrida, J. (2004b) *Marx & Sons*, Frankfurt: Suhrkamp.
Derrida, J. (2004c) *Dissemination*, transl. by Barbara Johnson, London: Continuum.
Derrida, J. (2006) *Schurken, Zwei Essays über die Vernunft*, Frankfurt: Suhrkamp.
Derrida, J. (2009) *The Beast and the Sovereign*, Vol. I, Chicago: University of Chicago Press.
Derrida, J. and Ferraris, M. (2001) *A Taste for the Secret*, trans. Giacomo Donis, Giacomo Donis and David Webb (eds), Malden, MA: Blackwell.
Derrida, J. and Rottenberg, E. (2002) (eds) *Interventions and Interviews 1971–2001*, Stanford, CA: Stanford University Press.
Deutschmann, C. (1999) *Die Verheißung des Absoluten Reichtums. Zur Religiösen Natur des Kapitalismus*, Frankfurt/New York: Campus.

Deutschmann, C. (2008) 'Die Finanzmärkte und die Mittelschichten: der Kollektive Buddenbrooks-Effekt', in *Leviathan* 36(4): 501–517.

DiNoia, C. and Micossi, S. (2009) *Keep it simple: Policy Responses to the Financial Crisis*, Centre for European Policy Studies, Brussels, January.

Douglas, M. (2003a) *Risk Acceptability According to the Social Sciences*, Collected Works, Vol. XI, London: Routledge.

Douglas, M. (2003b) *Risk and Blame. Essays in Cultural Theory*, Collected Works, Vol. XII, London: Routledge.

Drummond, H. (2002) 'Living in a Fool's Paradise: The Collapse of Baring's Bank', *Management Decision* 40(3): 232–8.

ECB (2008) *The Incentive Structure of the 'Originate and Distribute' Model*, Frankfurt: European Central Bank, available: www.ecb.int/pub/pdf/other/incentivestructureoriginatedistributemodel200812en.pdf (accessed 23 October 2011).

Elias, N. (1976) *Über den Prozeß der Zivilisation*, Frankfurt: Suhrkamp.

Elias, N. (1983) *Engagement und Distanzierung*, Frankfurt: Suhrkamp.

Epstein, G. (2005) *Financialization and the World Economy*, Cheltenham, UK: Edward Elgar.

Ernst, O. (1907) 'Nis Randers', in *Siebzig Gedichte*, Leipzig: L. Staackmann, 118–119.

Esposito, E. (2007) *Die Fiktion der Wahrscheinlichen Realität*, Frankfurt: Suhrkamp.

Esposito, E. (2010) *Die Zeit des Geldes in Finanzwelt und Gesellschaft*, Heidelberg: Carl-Auer.

Fooks, G. (2003) 'Auditors and the Permissive Society: Market Failure, Globalization and Financial regulation in the US', *Risk Management: An International Journal*, 17–26.

Foucault, M. (1977) *Discipline and Punish*, Harmondsworth: Penguin.

Foucault, M. (1983) *Der Wille zum Wissen. Sexualität und Wahrheit I [The Will for Knowledge. Sexuality and Truth I]*, Frankfurt: Suhrkamp.

Freiberger, H. (2010) 'Mr. 25 Prozent, Bitte mehr Bescheidenheit', *Süddeutsche Zeitung*, 2 November, available: www.sueddeutsche.de/geld/josef-ackermann-mr-prozent-bitte-mehr-bescheidenheit-1.1018342, (accessed 28 November.2011.

futurestradingpedia.com (2011) 'Physical Delivery', futurestradingpedia.com, available: www.futurestradingpedia.com/physical_delivery.htm, (accessed 28 November 2011).

Gibson, W. (2003) *Pattern Recognition*, New York: C.P. Putnam's Sons.

Giddens, A. (1999) 'Risk and Responsibility', *The Modern Law Review* 62(1): 1–10.

Gigerenzer, G. (2002) *Calculated Risks: How to Know When Numbers Deceive You*, New York: Simon & Schuster.

Goede, M. de (2004) Repoliticizing Financial Risk, *Economy and Society* 33(2): 197–217.

Goodhart, C.A.E. (2008) *The Regulatory Response to the Financial Crisis*, LSE Financial Markets Group Paper Series, special paper 177, London School of Economics and Political Science.

Greener, I. (2006) 'Nick Leeson and the Collapse of Barings Bank: Socio-Technical Networks and the "Rogue Trader" ', *Organization* 13(3): 421–441.

Grimm, J. and Grimm, W. (1854/1960) *Deutsches Wörterbuch*, Leipzig: S. Hirzel, available: http://germazope.uni-trier.de/Projects/WBB/woerterbuecher/dwb/wbgui?lemmode=lemmasearch&mode=hierarchy&textsize=600&onlist=&word=vielleicht&lemid=GV06725&query_start=1&totalhits=0&textword=&locpattern=&textpattern=&lemmapattern=&verspattern, (accessed 28 September 2009).

Guillet de Monthoux, P. (2004) *The Art Firm: Aesthetic Management and Metaphysical Marketing*, Stanford, CA: Stanford University Press.

Günther, K. (2002) 'Zwischen Ermächtigung und Disziplinierung. Verantwortung im Gegenwärtigen Kapitalismus', in A. Honneth (ed.) *Befreiung aus der Mündigkeit. Paradoxien des Gegenwärtigen Kapitalismus*, Frankfurt/New York: Campus, 93–116.

Haas, D. (2008) 'The Crushing Potential of Financial Derivatives', available: www.marketoracle.co.uk/Article6756.html (accessed 25 January 2010).

Habermas, J. (1981/1968) *Technik und Wissenschaft als 'Ideologie'*, Frankfurt: Suhrkamp.

Hacking, I. (1975) *The Emergence of Probability, a Philosophical Study of Early Ideas About Probability, Induction and Statistical Inference*, Cambridge: Cambridge University Press.

Hacking, I. (1990) *The Taming of Chance*, Cambridge: Cambridge University Press.

Haidt, J. (2001) 'The Emotional Dog and Its Rational Tail: A Social Intuitionist Approach to Moral Judgement', *Psychological Review* 108(4): 814–834.

Hansson, Sven Ove (2005): 'Seven Myths of Risk', *Risk Management: An International Journal* 7(2): 7–17.

Hellwig, M. (2008) *Systemic Risk in the Financial Sector: An Analysis of the Subprime Mortgage Financial Crisis*, Bonn: Preprints of the Max Planck Institute for Research on Collective Goods.

Hellwig, M. (2009) *Brandbeschleuniger im Finanzsystem*, Max Planck Forschung 2/09, 10–15.

Hessler, S. (2007) 'Fressen und Gefressen Werden', *BIG Business Crime* 15(1): 21–25.

Ho, K. (2009) *Liquidated: An Ethnography of Wall Street*, Durham, NC: Duke University Press.

Holt, R. (2004) 'Risk Management: The Talking Cure', *Organization* 11(2): 251–270.

Holzer, B. and Millo, Y. (2004) *From Risks to Second-Order Dangers in Financial Markets: Unintended Consequences of Risk Management Systems*, CARR Discussion Paper 29, London School of Economics and Political Science.

Honegger, C., Neckel, S. and Magnin, C. (2010) *Strukturierte Verantwortungslosigkeit, Berichte aus der Bankenwelt*, Berlin: Suhrkamp.

Höpfl, H. (2000) 'On Being Moved', *Studies in Culture, Organizations and Societies* 6(1): 15–34.

Hörisch, J. (1996) *Kopf oder Zahl. Die Poesie des Geldes*, Frankfurt: Suhrkamp.

Horkheimer, M. and Adorno, T.W. (1971/1944) *Dialektik der Aufklärung*, Frankfurt: Fischer.

Hutter, B.M. (2005) *The Attractions of Risk-based Regulation: Accounting for the Emergence of Risk Ideas in Regulation*, CARR Discussion Paper 33, London School of Economics and Political Science.

Imdahl, M. (1989) 'Barnett Newman Who's Afraid of Red, Yellow and Blue III', in C. Pries (ed.) *Das Erhabene: Zwischen Grenzerfahrung und Grössenwahn*, Weinheim, VCH Acta Humaniora, 233–252.

Jain, A.K. (2009) 'Regulation and Subprime Turmoil', *Critical Perspectives on International Business* 5(1/2): 98–106.

Johnson, B. (2004) 'Translator's Introduction', in J. Derrida *Dissemination*, London: Continuum, VII–XXXV.

Jones, C. and Munroe, R. (2005) *Contemporary Organization Theory*, Oxford: Blackwell.

Kahneman, D. and Tversky, A. (1984) 'Choices, Values, and Frames', *American Psychologist* 39(4): 341–350.

Kant, I. (1974/1790) *Kritik der Urteilskraft*, Frankfurt: Suhrkamp.

Kayshap, A., Rajan, R. and Stein, J. (2008) *Rethinking Capital Regulation*, Federal Reserve Bank of Kansas City, Jackson Hole Symposium on 'Maintaining Stability in a Changing Financial System', 12–23 August.

King, M.R. and Mallo, C. (2010) 'A User's Guide to the Triennial Central Bank Survey of Foreign Exchange Market Activity', *BIS Quarterly Review* December, 71–83.

King, M.R. and Rime, D. (2010) 'The $4 Trillion Question: What Explains FX Growth Since The 2007 Survey?', *BIS Quarterly Review* December, 27–42.

Kleist, H. von (1984) 'Über die Allmähliche Verfertigung der Gedanken beim Reden', in H. von Kleist *Sämtliche Erzählungen und Andere Prosa*, Leipzig: Reclam, 340–6.

Klimecki, R. and Willmott, H. (2009) 'From Demutualisation to Meltdown: a Tale of Two Wannabe Banks', *Critical Perspectives on International Business* 5(1/2): 120–140.

Knight, F.H. (1921/1940) *Risk, Uncertainty and Profit*, London: London School of Economics, Series of reprints of scarce tracts in economic and political science 16, 5th impression, Boston, MA: Houghton Mifflin.

Knorr Cetina, K. and Bruegger, U. (2002a) 'Trader's Engagement with Markets, a Postsocial Relationship', *Theory, Culture & Society* 19: 161–185.

Knorr Cetina, K. and Bruegger, U. (2002b): 'Global Microstructures: The Virtual Societies of Financial Markets', *American Journal of Sociology* 107(4): 903–950.

Knorr Cetina, K. and Bruegger, U. (2002c) 'Inhabiting Technology: The Global Lifeform of Financial Markets', *Current Sociology* 50(3): 389–405.

Knorr Cetina, K. and Preda, A. (2007) 'The Temporalization of Financial Markets: From Network to Flow', *Theory, Culture & Society* 24(7/8): 116–138.

Kolman, J. (1997) 'The World According to Nassim Taleb', *Derivatives Strategy*, December/January, available: www.derivativesstrategy.com/magazine/archive/1997/1296qa.asp (accessed 8 July 2011).

Koslowski, P. (2009) 'Spekulation: Wette oder Glücksspiel?'; *Frankfurter Allgemeine Zeitung* 246, 23 October, 12.

Kostolany, A. (2004) *Der Große Kostolany: Börsenseminar. Börsenpsychologie. Die Besten Geldgeschichten*, Frankfurt/Berlin: Ullstein.

Krapp, P. (2000) 'Intellectual Courage: an Interview', *Cultural Machine 2*, available: http://culturemachine.tees.ac.uk/Cmach/Backissues/j002/Articles/art_derr.htm (accessed 3 October 2008).

Langley, P. (2008) 'Sub-prime Mortgage Lending: A Cultural Economy', *Economy and Society* 37(4): 469–494.

Lewis, M. (1990) *The Liar's Poker*, New York: Penguin.

Lewis, M. (2008) *The End*, available: www.portfolio.com/news-markets/national-news/portfolio/2008/11/11/The-End-of-Wall-Streets-Boom/ (accessed 29 November 2009).

Lewis, M. (2011) *The Big Short. Inside the Doomsday Machine*, New York/London: W.W. Norton.

Lightfoot, G., Lilley, S. and Pelzer, P. (2009) 'Motivating Risk? The Sublime Supplement of Market Exchange', *Society and Business Review* 4(2): 110–122.

Lilley, S. and Lightfoot, G. (2006) 'Trading Narratives', *Organization* 13: 369–91.

Linstead, S. and Höpfl, H. (2000) *The Aesthetics of Organisation*, London: Sage.

Linstead, S.A. (2003) *Organization Theory and Postmodern Thought*, London: Sage.

LiPuma, E. and Lee, B. (2004) 'Financial Derivatives and the Rise of Circulation', *Economy and Society* 34(3): 404–427.

Loewenstein, G.F., Weber, E.U., Hsee, C.K. and Welch, N. (2001) 'Risk as Feelings', *Psychological Bulletin* 127: 267–286.

Long, S. and Sievers, B. (eds) (2011): *Towards a Socioanalysis of Money, Finance and Capitalism: Beneath the Surface of the Financial Industry*, London: Routledge.
Lüdemann, S. (2011) *Jacques Derrida zur Einführung*, Hamburg: Junius.
Luhmann, N. (1991) *Soziologie des Risikos*, Berlin, New York: Walter de Gruyter; English: (2005) *Risk: A Sociological Theory*, Berlin: de Gruyter.
Luhmann, N. (2001) 'Dekonstruktion als Beobachtung Zweiter Ordnung', in N. Luhmann (ed. By Oliver Jahrus) *Aufsätze und Reden*, Stuttgart: Reclam.
Lupton, D. (1999) *Risk*, London: Routledge.
Lyng, S. (1990) 'Edgework: A Social Psychological Analysis of Voluntary Risk-Taking', *American Journal of Sociology* 95(4): 851–886.
Lyotard, J.-F. (1984) 'Das Erhabene und die Avantgarde', *Merkur* 38(2): 151–164.
Lyotard, J.-F. (1989) 'Das Interesse des Erhabenen', in C. Pries (ed.) *Das Erhabene – Zwischen Grenzerfahrung und Größenwahn*, Weinheim: VCH Acta Humaniora, 91–118.
Lyotard, J.-F. and Pries, C. (1989) 'Das Undarstellbare – Wider das Vergessen', in C. Pries (ed.) *Das Erhabene – Zwischen Grenzerfahrung und Größenwahn*, Weinheim: VCH Acta Humaniora, 319–348.
Macintosh, N., Shearer, T., Thornton, D.B. and Welker, M. (2000) 'Accounting as Simulacrum and Hyperreality: Perspectives on Income and Capital', *Accounting, Organizations and Society* 25: 13–50.
Mackay, C. (1995) *Extraordinary Popular Delusions and the Madness of Crowds*, Wordsworth Editions, originally published in 1841.
MacKenzie, D. (2003a) 'An Equation and its Worlds: Bricolage, Exemplars, Disunity and Performativity in Financial Economics', *Social Studies of Science* 33: 831–868.
MacKenzie, D. (2003b) 'Long-Term Capital Management and the Sociology of Arbitrage', *Economy and Society* 32(3): 349–380.
MacKenzie, D. (2004) 'The Big, Bad Wolf and the Rational Market: Portfolio Insurance, the 1987 Crash and the Performativity of Economics', *Economy and Society* 33: 303–334.
MacKenzie, D. (2007) 'The Material Production of Virtuality: Innovation, Cultural Geography and Facticity in Derivative Markets', *Economy and Society* 36(3): 335–376.
MacKenzie, D. (2008) 'An Engine, Not a Camera, How Financial Models Shape Markets', Cambridge, MA: MIT Press.
MacKenzie, D. and Millo, Y. (2003): 'Constructing a Market, Performing Theory: the Historical Sociology of a Financial Derivatives Exchange', *American Journal of Sociology* 109(1): 107–145.
Mandelbrot, B.B. and Hudson, R.L. (2004) *The (mis)Behaviour or Markets – A Fractal View of Risk, Ruin and Reward*, New York, Basic Books.
Mansfield, N. (2006): 'Refusing Defeatism: Derrida, Decision and Absolute Risk', *Social Semiotics* 16(3): 473–483.
Marcuse, H. (1979/1967) *Der Eindimensionale Mensch*, 12th edition, Darmstadt: Luchterhand.
Martin, R. (2002) *Financialization of Daily Life*, Philadelphia, PA: Temple University Press.
Martin, R., Rafferty, M. and Bryan, D. (2008) 'Financialization, Risk and Labour', *Competition & Change* 12(2): 120–132.
McGoun, E. (1997) 'Hyperreal Finance', *Critical Perspectives on Accounting* 8, 97–122.
Mian, A.R. and Sufi, A. (2008) 'The Consequences of Mortgage Credit Expansion: Evidence from the 2007 Mortgage Default Crisis', available: http://papers.ssrn.com/sol3/papers.cfm?abstract_id = 1072304 (retrieved 29 November 2009).

Miller, K.G. (2009) 'Organizational Risk after Modernism', *Organization Studies* 30(2/3): 157–180.

Müntefering, F. (2005): Interview, *Bild am Sonntag*, 17 April 2005, available: http://de.wikipedia.org/wiki/Heuschreckendebatte (accessed 15 March 2007).

Neckel, S. (2010) 'Refeudalisierung der Ökonomie: Zum Strukturwandel Kapitalistischer Wirtschaft', *MPIfG Working Paper* 10/6, Köln: Max-Planck-Institut für Gesellschaftsforschung.

Neckel, S. (2011) 'Der Gefühlskapitalismus der Banken: Vom Ende der Gier als "ruhiger Leidenschaft"', *Leviathan* 39(1): 39–53.

Neiman, S. (2004) *Das Böse Denken*, Frankfurt: Suhrkamp.

Newman, B. (1948) 'The Sublime is Now', *The Tiger's Eye*, December.

Nietzsche, F. (1993) *Jenseits von Gut und Böse*, KSA 5, 3rd edition, München: dtv/ Berlin, New York: de Gruyter.

Nietzsche, F. (without year) *Beyond Good and Evil*, planetbook.com, available: www.planetebook.com/ebooks/Beyond-Good-and-Evil.pdf, (accessed 2 December 2011).

Norris, C. (1991) *Deconstruction. Theory and Practice*, revised edition, London: Routledge.

Orford, A. (2004) *Trade, Human Rights and the Economy of Sacrifice*, New York: New York University School of Law, available: www.jeanmonnetprogram.org/papers/04/040301.rtf, (accessed 3 October 2008).

Ortmann, G. (1997) 'Das Kleist-Theorem. Über Ökologie, Organisation und Rekursivität', in M. Birke, C. Burschel and M. Schwarz (eds) *Handbuch Umweltschutz und Organisation, München*, Vienna: R. Oldenbourg, 23–91.

Ortmann, G. (2003a) *Organisation und Welterschliessung*, Wiesbaden: Westdeutscher Verlag.

Ortmann, G. (2003b) *Regel und Ausnahme, Paradoxien sozialer Ordnung*, Frankfurt: Suhrkamp.

Ortmann, G. (2004) *Als ob – Fiktionen und Organisationen*, Wiesbaden: VS Verlag für Sozialwissenschaften.

Oxford (1989) Oxford Advanced Learner's Dictionary of Current English, 4th edition, Oxford: Oxford University Press.

Panetta, F., Faeh, T., Grande, G., Ho, C., King, M., Ley, A., Signoretti, F.M., Taboga, M. and Zaghini, A. (2009) 'An Assessment of Financial Sector Rescue Programs', BIS papers No. 48, Basel: Bank for International Settlements, available: www.bis.org/publ/bppdf/bispap48.pdf (accessed 5 December 2011).

Pelzer, P. (1995) *Der Prozess der Organisation. Zur Postmodernen Ästhetik der Organisation und ihrer Rationalität*, Chur: G+B Verlag Facultas.

Pelzer, P. (2005) 'The Hostility Triad – The Contribution of Negative Emotions to Organizational (Un-)Wellness', *Culture and Organization* 11(2): 111–123.

Pelzer, P. (2007) 'The Futility of Excess, Or: The Displaced World of Rules and Regulations', *Culture and Organization* 13(2): 157–169.

Pelzer, P. (2009) 'The Displaced World of Risk: Risk Management as Alienated Risk (Perception?)', *Society and Business Review* 4(1): 26–36.

Pelzer, P. (2011) 'Risk as Present Futures – an Elaboration on Risk and Fear', in S. Long and B. Sievers (eds) *Towards a Socioanalysis of Money, Finance and Capitalism: Beneath the Surface of the Financial Industry*, London: Routledge: 149–162.

Pelzer, P. (2012) 'The Im-possible – Towards a Different Way of Thinking Risk', *Philosophy of Management*, special issue: philosophical lessons from the global financial crisis, forthcoming.

Pelzer, P. and Case, P. (2008) 'The Displaced World of Risk Management: Covert Enchantment in a Calculative World', in M. Kostera (ed.) *Mythical Inspirations and Storytelling for Organizational Realities*, Houndsville, NY: Palgrave, 100–111.
Perrow, C. (1984): *Normal Accidents. Living with High-Risk Technologies*, New York: Basic Books.
Pfeil, M. (2010) 'Too Much Time Has Gone By: interview with Otto Steinmetz', *Sonnemann Business Magazine*, Frankfurt School of Finance and Management, 5, 22–27.
Plumpe, W. (2010) *Wirtschaftskrisen. Geschichte und Gegenwart*, Munich: Beck.
Poe, E.A. (1842) 'The Masque of the Red Death', in *Graham's Magazine* 20(5): 257–259, available: www.eapoe.org/works/tales/masquea.htm (accessed 3 December 2009).
Poenicke, K. (1989) 'Eine Geschichte der Angst? Appropriationen des Erhabenen in der englischen Ästhetik des 18 Jahrhunderts', in C. Pries (ed.) *Das Erhabene – zwischen Grenzerfahrung und Größenwahn*, Weinheim: VCH Acta Humaniora, 76–91.
Power, M. (1994) *The Audit Explosion*, London: Demos.
Power, M. (1999) *The Audit Society: Rituals of Verification*, Oxford: Oxford University Press.
Power, M. (2005) 'Enterprise Risk Management and the Organization of Uncertainty in Financial Institutions', in K. Knorr Cetina and A. Preda (eds) *The Sociology of Financial Markets*, Oxford: Oxford University Press.
Power, M. (2007) *Organized Uncertainty. Designing a World of Risk Management*, Oxford: Oxford University Press.
Pries, C. (1989) 'Einleitung', in C. Pries (ed.) *Das Erhabene – Zwischen Grenzerfahrung und Größenwahn*, Weinheim: VCH Acta Humaniora, 1–32.
Purnanandam, A. (forthcoming) 'Originate-to-Distribute Model and the Subprime Mortgage Crisis', *Review of Financial Studies*, available: www.bus.wisc.edu/finance/workshops/documents/subprime_latestversion.pdf, (accessed 23 October 2011).
Rockett, J.P. (1999): 'Definitions Are Not What They Seem', *Risk Management: An International Journal* 37–47.
Rosa, H. (2005) *Beschleunigung. Die Veränderung der Zeitstruktur in der Moderne*, Frankfurt: Suhrkamp.
Schmidt, H. (2007) 'Beaufsichtigt die Neuen Großspekulanten!' *Die Zeit* 6(1): 21–23.
Schmidt, H. (2011) '…aber die Währung ist gut', *Die Zeit* 19: 21–22.
Seel, M. (2004) 'Der Geist des Dekonstruktivismus', *Neue Rundschau* 115(4): 177–183.
Shackle, G.L.S. (1967) *The Years of High Theory. Invention and Tradition in Economic Thought*, Cambridge: Cambridge University Press.
Shackle, G.L.S. (1988) *Business, Time and Thought, selected papers*, edited by Stephen F. Frown, Houndmills: MacMillan.
Shafer, A. (2001) *What is the Value of Money?* Seminar for the Australian Institute of Socio-Analysis' series: 'Money Talks!', 30 November, available: www.allanshafer.com/docs/What%20is%20the%20Value%20of%20Money.doc (accessed 25 January 2010).
Shipman, C. (2010) 'Goldman Sachs CEO Lloyd Blankfein Speaks', *ABC News* 28 April, available: http://abcnews.go.com/GMA/goldman-sachs-ceo-lloyd-blankfein-speaks/story?id=10495958, (accessed 24 August 2010).
Sievers, B. (2010) 'Beneath the Financial Crisis', in H. Brunning and M. Perini (eds) *The Psychoanalytic Perspective on the Turbulent World*, London: Karnac.
Sievers, B. (2011) 'Towards a Socioanalysis of the Current Financial Crisis', in S. Long and B. Sievers, (eds): *Towards a Socioanalysis of Money, Finance and Capitalism: Beneath the Surface of the Financial Industry*, London: Routledge.

Sievers, B. (2012) 'Towards a Socioanalysis of Capitalist Greed', *Critique: Journal of Socialist Theory* 40(1): 1–24.
Simmel, G. (1907/1989) *Philosophie des Geldes*, Frankfurt: Suhrkamp.
Sinn, H.-W. (2009) *Kasino Kapitalismus. Wie es zur Finanzkrise Kam, und Was es Jetzt zu Tun Gibt*, Berlin: Econ.
Skipper, H.D. and Kwon, W.J (2007) *Risk Management and Insurance: Perspectives in a Global Economy*, Malden MA, Oxford: Blackwell.
Sloterdijk, P. (2006) *Im Weltinnenraum des Kapitals*, Frankfurt: Suhrkamp.
Slovic, P. (1987) 'Perceptions of Risk', *Science* 236: 280–285.
Slovic, P., Finicane, M.L., Peters, E. and MacGregor, D.G. (2004) 'Risk as Analysis and Risk as Feeling: Some Thoughts about Affect, Reason, Risk, and Rationality', *Risk Analysis* 24: 311–322.
Spoelstra, S. (2005) 'Robert Cooper: Beyond Organization', in C. Jones and R. Munroe (eds) *Contemporary Organization Theory*, Oxford: Blackwell, 106–119.
Stein, M. (2003) 'Unbounded Irrationality: Risk and organisational Narcissism at Long Term Capital Management', *Human Relations* 56(5): 523–540.
Stiglitz, J.E. (2008) *Government Failure vs. Market Failure: Principles of Regulation*, paper prepared for Tobin Project's conference on 'Government and Markets: Toward a New Theory of Regulation', 1–3 February, Yulee, Florida, available: http://academic-commons.columbia.edu/catalog/ac:126997 (accessed 23 May 2011).
Stone, O. (1987) *Wall Street*, 20th Century Fox.
Strange, S. (1986) *Casino Capitalism*, Oxford: Blackwell.
Strange, S. (1998) *Mad Money*, Manchester: Manchester University Press.
Stranger, M. (1999) 'The Aesthetics of Risk. A study of Surfing', *International Review of the sociology of Sport* 34(3): 265–276.
Strati, A. (1999): *Organisation and Aesthetics*, London: Sage.
Szegö, G. (2010) 'Crash 08: a Regulatory Debacle to be Mended', special paper no 189, *LSE Financial Markets Group Paper Series*, London School of Economics and Political Science.
Taleb, N. (2007) *The Black Swan: The Impact of the Highly Improbable*, New York: Random House.
Tedlock, B. (2001) 'Divination as a Way of Knowing: Embodiment, Visualisation, Narrative, and Interpretation', *Folklore* 112: 189–197.
Thomä, D. (2009) 'Rede und Antwort Stehen. Die Finanzkrise Lässt Sich Auch als Verantwortungskrise Begreifen', *Neue Zürcher Zeitung* 24 July, available: www.nzz.ch/nachrichten/kultur/aktuell/rede_und_antwort_stehen_1.2805991.html (accessed 5 August 2010).
Thompson, H.S. (1965) *Midnight on the Coast Highway*, available: www.citizenarcane.com/index.php/archives/2005/02/22/midnight-coast-higway/ (accessed 18 June 2008).
Thompson, M. (1980) 'Aesthetics of Risk: Culture or Context?', in R.C. Schwing and W.A. Albers Jr. (eds) *Societal Risk Assessment: How Safe is Safe Enough?*, New York: Plenum Press, 273–285.
Toft, B. (2001) 'Financial Risk, Decisions and Behaviour', *Risk Management: An International Journal*, 7–15.
Turner, A. (2009) 'How to Tame Global Finance', *The Prospect Interview Panel* 162, available: www.prospectmagazine.co.uk/2009/08/how-to-tame-global-finance/ (accessed 5 August 2011).
Turner, A. (2010a) *After the Crises: Assessing the Costs and Benefits of Financial Liberalisation*, 14th Chintaman Deshmukh Memorial Lecture, Reserve Bank of India,

Mumbai 15 February 2010, available: http://rbidocs.rbi.org.in/rdocs/Speeches/PDFs/ISRT12022010.pdf (accessed 5 August 2011).

Turner, A. (2010b) 'What Do Banks Do? Why Do Credit Booms and Busts Occur and What Can Public Policy Do About It?', in A. Turner *et al.* (2010) *The Future of Finance: The LSE Report*, London School of Economics and Political Science, 5–86, available: http://harr123et.files.wordpress.com/2010/07/futureoffinance-chapter11.pdf (accessed 5 August 2011).

Vaknin, S. (2005) 'Moral Hazard and the Survival Value of Risk', *Global Politician* 20, available: www.globalpolitician.com/2801-economics (accessed 5 August 2011).

Vanderbilt, K. (1968) 'Art and Nature in "The Masque of the Red Death"', *Nineteenth-Century Fiction* 22(4): 379–389.

Vogl, J. (2010) *Das Gespenst des Kapitals*, Zürich: Diaphanes.

Walter, S. (2010) *Basel II and Financial Stability*, 5th Biennial Conference on Risk Management and Supervision, Financial Stability Institute, Bank for International Settlements, Basel, 3–4 November, available: http://bis.org/speeches/sp10109a.htm, (accessed 4 May 2011).

Walter, S. (2011) *Basel III: Stronger Banks and a More Resilient Financial System*, conference on Basel III, Financial Stability Institute, Bank for International Settlements Basel, 6 April, available: http://bis.org/speeches/sp110406.htm (accessed 4 May 2011).

Warren, S. and Rehn, A. (2006) 'Oppression, Art and Aesthetics', *Consumption, Markets, and Culture* 9(2): 81–85.

Wehling, P. (2001) 'Jenseits des Wissens? Wissenschaftliches Nichtwissen aus Soziologischer Perspektive', *Zeitschrift für Soziologie* 30(6): 465–484.

Weick, K.E. (1995) *Sensemaking in Organizations*, Thousand Oaks, CA: Sage.

Weitzner, D. and Darroch, J. (2009) 'Why Moral Failures Precede Financial Crises', *Critical Perspectives on International Business* 5(1/2): 6–13.

Wellink, N. (2010) *A New Regulatory Landscape*, 16th Conference of Banking Supervisors, Singapore, 22 September, available: http://bis.org/speeches/sp100922.htm (accessed 4 May 2011).

Wolfe, T. (1988) *The Bonfire of Vanities*, London: Pan.

Wong, L. (2009) 'The Crisis: A Return to Political Economy?', *Critical Perspectives on International Business* 5(1/2): 56–77.

Index